3638 0615

P9-DBU-001

The
Authentic
Confucius

A Life of Thought and Politics

ANNPING CHIN

SCRIBNER

New York   London   Toronto   Sydney

♦

SCRIBNER
1230 Avenue of the Americas
New York, NY 10020

First Scribner hardcover edition November 2007

SCRIBNER and design are trademarks of
Macmillan Library Reference USA, Inc., used under license
by Simon & Schuster, the publisher of this work.

For information about special discounts for bulk purchases,
please contact Simon & Schuster Special Sales at
1-800-456-6798 or business@simonandschuster.com.

Designed by Kyoko Watanabe
Text set in Adobe Caslon

Manufactured in the United States of America

1   3   5   7   9   10   8   6   4   2

Library of Congress Cataloging-in-Publication Data

Chin, Annping, [date]
The authentic Confucius : a life of thought and politics / Annping Chin.
p. cm.
Includes bibliographical references and index.
1. Confucius. 2. Philosophy, Chinese—To 221 BC. I. Title.

B128.C8C4927 2007
181'.112—dc22
[B]
2007022345

ISBN-13: 978-0-7432-4618-7
ISBN-10: 0-7432-4618-7

To Jonathan,
Meimei, and Yar

. . . and Brutus, with heaven and earth conspiring against him and Roman liberty, stealing some hour of night from his rounds to read and annotate Polybius with complete assurance.

MICHEL DE MONTAIGNE,
"OF EXPERIENCE"

Contents

Acknowledgments   xi

Chinese Dynasties   xiii

Prologue   1

Introduction   9

1. Leaving Home   23

2. Families and Politics   41

3. Companions   63

4. Wanderings   85

5. Return   119

6. Teaching   142

7. The Rites of Life and Death   172

8. Defenders   192

Epilogue   221

Notes   223

A Note on the Sources   251

Bibliography   253

Index   261

Acknowledgments

I owe the most to my parents, who created a world for us, first in Tainan, Taiwan, and then in Richmond, Virginia. From them, I acquired a love for classical texts and the strength to step out on my own.

The scholars I got to know in China and Taiwan in the last five years, like those for so many generations before them, have also been important to me. Their bearings on this book are hard to put into words. Just being in their presence gave me a charge and added urgency to my work. My own students, too, have spurred me on. Their interest in Confucius kept me absorbed. I am especially grateful to John Delury, with whom I had many discussions about the early philosophers. John was also my fellow traveler to Qufu. Our journey was fog-bound and full of perils but never short of mirth. Without John, I probably would not have found my way home.

As in the past, Andrew Wylie was supportive from start to finish. Nan Graham and Samantha Martin offered important suggestions that made the book clearer. Janet Fletcher was again shrewd and thorough in her copyediting. I benefited from the comments of Li Feng and Liang Tao. Tao Yang, Ya-hwei Hsu, and Masato Hasegawa offered crucial help toward the last stage of this book. I was also fortunate to have the assistance of Abraham Parrish, the map curator at the Yale Library, who could not have been more generous with his time and patience.

Finally, my thanks to my husband, Jonathan, and my children, Meimei and Yar. Because of them, I am richer. Also because of them, I am anxious, for fear that I have failed to measure up to their expectations. To them this book is dedicated.

Chinese Dynasties

Shang dynasty (1570–1045 BC)

Zhou dynasty (1045–221 BC)
    Western Zhou (1045–771 BC)
    Eastern Zhou (771–221 BC)
        Spring and Autumn period (771–481 BC)
        Warring States period (481–221 BC)

Qin dynasty (221–207 BC)

Han dynasty (202 BC–AD 220)
    Western Han (202 BC–AD 9)
    Eastern Han (25–220)

Six dynasties (220–589)

Sui dynasty (589–618)

Tang dynasty (618–906)

Five dynasties (907–960)

Song dynasty (960–1279)
    Northern Song (960–1126)
    Southern Song (1126–1279)

Yuan dynasty (1279–1368)

Ming dynasty (1368–1644)

Qing dynasty (1644–1912)

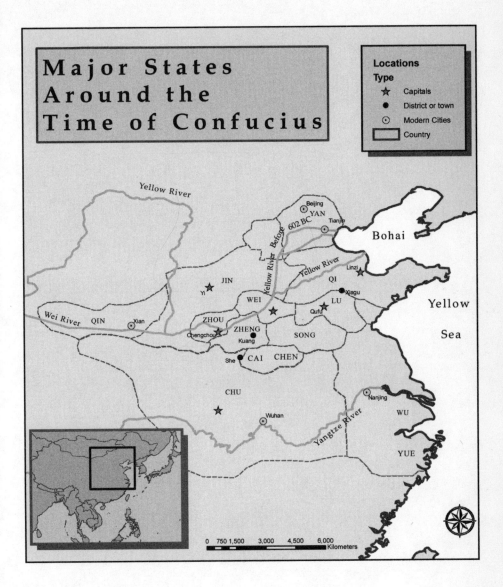

Major States Around the Time of Confucius

Locations

Type
★ Capitals
● District or town
⊙ Modern Cities
▭ Country

The
Authentic
Confucius

Prologue

CONFUCIUS CONCENTRATED ON LIVING LIFE AS WELL AS he knew how. He wished only to be granted a few more years so that, he said, "when I reach the age of fifty, I may try to understand the principles of change and I shall be able to steer clear of making serious mistakes." It was learning, therefore, and a desire to perfect himself, together with an awareness that this life was the only occasion he had to fulfill his wish and promise, that distinguished him. Perhaps there were other men, contemporaries, who wanted the same things, but none desired them as strongly as Confucius and none was as determined as he to scour all the knowledge passed down to him—history, poetry, ritual practice, and music—so that he might understand what was essential and enduring about human nature and the human lot and "steer clear of making serious mistakes."

Men like Confucius were not destined to have fame. Their concerns lacked immediate appeal. Who, after all, would want to work hard for self-knowledge and self-reform, which offered neither relief from the uncertainty of life nor solace when death seemed inevitable? Even admirers told Confucius that their strength gave out when they tried his way. Yet to have just a few listeners who were willing to mull over what was said and to suggest to the world the merits in those words would give the speaker, even after he died, a chance to demonstrate that he could matter. Such was the case with Confucius. Still, he would have been astounded by the extent of his influence over time and the height of his stock in a world he left long ago. And he would have been troubled by the overuse of his every utterance, and by the stories written about him—even those meant to enlarge his stature.

Until the mid-twentieth century, China was so inseparable from the idea of Confucius that her scheme of government and society, her concept of the self and human relationships, and her construct of culture and history all seemed to have originated from his mind alone. To outsiders like us, Confucius is evocative not only of China but also of concepts such as family, education, teacher, scholar, scholarship, refinement, humility, civility, order, obedience, the father, women oppressed, repression of impulses, conformity, timidity, weakness. We give him credit for all that has gone right and wrong in China because we do not really know him. That is the reason why I wrote this book. I wanted to know Confucius, and I wanted the book to be a discovery. Since the beginning of my teaching career, I had been drawn to his thinking, to his love of learning, and to his attempt to keep the idea of the moral within human reach. Yet, at the same time, I wanted *him* to be within *my* reach; I wanted him to take me to his teachings. And so, for two decades, I wandered through early books and their commentaries, scouting for leads that might yield a little bit more of Confucius. As I was writing this book, the drive became a tighter search for an authentic Confucius.

Confucius was born in 551 BC, toward the end of an era the Chinese referred to as "the Spring and Autumn." His family name was Kong; he was given the personal name of Qiu and the courtesy name of Zhongni. Since the seventeenth century, Master Kong, or Kongfuzi, has been known in the West by the Latinized form Confucius. The place he called home was Lu. Lu was a regional state in northeast China—one of many that were bound to the imperial court of the Zhou dynasty through history, culture, family ties, and moral obligation. There is adequate material on the state of Lu and the history of the Zhou—especially the second half of that long dynasty, the Eastern Zhou, the period pertaining to our story—but reliable sources on the life of Confucius are scarce because he had only a weak link to the powerful men of his time and a minor role in their political ventures and so was rarely mentioned in their records. Yet I decided, from early on, that the story I wanted to tell would have to come from those sources. If that meant there would be important gaps in this version, I would have to accept it.

The most conspicuous gap concerns Confucius' marriage. Early treatments of Confucius' life imply that his marriage ended in divorce, but we cannot know for sure if that is true, as these sources were written at least three hundred years after the fact. We can only present the divorce as one possibility of what might have happened. What's more, topics such as marital relationships and divorce, which are of great interest to us, need not have been so for Confucius and his contemporaries; and even if they were, we do not know in what ways and to what extent. Yet the gaps are not a terrible loss. One can even say that they are the antidote to presumption. Confucius himself felt this way. He said: "I am old enough to have seen scribes (*shi*) leaving a gap when they were unsure about a word and horse owners leaving the driving to professionals. Nowadays there are no such cases." In China, scribes would eventually take on the responsibilities of historians. From what Confucius observed about the scribes of his day, one would not be surprised to find historians three centuries later doing the same thing as those scribes—filling in the blanks when they should have left them alone.

Once we accept the fact that fragments are all we have, we are better able to concentrate on what they have to say. They might not divulge much about Confucius' personal life, but they do offer more than sufficient grounds and footing to discover him. The two sources central to this book are the *Analects* (*Lunyu*) and the *Zuo Commentary* (*Zuo zhuan*). The *Analects* is the work most closely associated with Confucius. Loosely put together in twenty sections, it is more a repository than a book. In it, many types of records about Confucius can be found: bits of a logbook of his activity and repose; parts of conversations he had with those he knew well or happened to meet; his remarks and appraisals (sometimes without a context); and what others observed about him. From this collection alone, we are able to learn what Confucius thought about the early heroes and the people of his time; what angered or irritated him; what delighted or enthralled him; how he felt about archery contests, music and musicians, poetry and speech; and what he understood about human nature and human potential. On the whole, the *Analects* resists casting Confucius as an agent of his teaching: he was not tidied up or held back from springing a surprise. As a result, we benefit from the editors' tact, but so does he.

The idea of putting these records into a collection probably took shape within the hundred years or so after Confucius' death. We do not know who the earliest compilers might have been. Just a handful of his followers make rather forceful appearances at the beginning and end of the book. We suspect, therefore, that they initiated the project—that it was these men who made the first effort to impart their knowledge of a man they did not want the world to forget.

The second source, the *Zuo Commentary*, covers most of the Spring and Autumn period of Chinese history, from 722 to 468. It is a *zhuan*, a series of illustrative elucidations and commentary, to the *Spring and Autumn Annals*, which is the official chronicle of the state of Lu. The chronicle, being a government record, notes only events with considerable political ramifications: affairs between states; the weddings and deaths of regional rulers; the ins and outs of chief counselors; the successes and failures of important missions, covenants, and expeditions; expulsions and executions; uprisings and usurpations; ancestral sacrifices and nature's portents. But the structure is schematic, and the content so concise that nearly all the human drama is left out. The *Zuo Commentary* tries to fill in the details, such as why a war took place or a counselor was driven out. And even though the organization of this work—in a choppy, entry-by-entry series of frames—complements the chronicle it serves, most of the writing in each frame possesses the attributes of a narrative. Dialogues and speeches stand out in this history. They animate the men and women in it and allow us to demarcate the strong from the weak, the genuine from the plausible; and they manage this without rhetorical contrivances. In this way the *Zuo Commentary* has a lot in common with the *Analects*, whose strength also lies in what people said to one another and in what others overheard them saying among themselves. The *Zuo Commentary* also explains where Confucius came from—not his family ancestry but his cultural descent and the spur of his moral impulses. Why, for instance, did Confucius feel that a thorough knowledge of poetry could add to one's moral capital and at the same time boost one's political advantage? Confucius did not claim to be an original. He told us so when he said, "I transmit but do not create. I am fond of antiquity because I have faith in it."

At one time, when this project was still in its infancy, I considered including many more stories of Confucius written before the first century. I thought of using them as one would primary documents, letting them help me shape Confucius' life. But a more careful reading convinced me that most of the stories were inventions, so I abandoned the idea except in cases where my instincts and my knowledge of the period convinced me that the storyteller's imagination had caught something true. Here the *Analects* served as my guide. This source is not altogether a veritable record, but it tells us the most about Confucius, having sketched out what appears to be a likeness of him. Without the *Analects* as a measure of the man, the historical Confucius would have vanished in the later creations of him, however splendid they may be.

Finally I must mention the work of Sima Qian, a historian from the Han dynasty in the first century BC. This man was the first to attempt a long and ambitious biography of Confucius, a biography that remains the standard in Chinese historiography. Because Sima Qian was situated much closer in time to Confucius than we are (five hundred years later as opposed to twenty-five hundred), if we question his accuracy at any point, we have to be well prepared to say why we are challenging him. As everyone who has read him knows, however, Sima Qian was a historian most willing to use the imagination to help him re-create the past. In his pursuit of a story and the characters in it, he did not let the logs of history weigh him down or the gaps in annals trouble him. His biography of Confucius was only one among more than a hundred biographical studies in his oeuvre. Our knowledge of how he worked allows us to consider more carefully those questions he overlooked because, for him, to invent a few facts or to supply a few transitions was a better use of time than to be consumed by a search for veracity. A significant part of my version of Confucius' life is, therefore, a response to Sima Qian's. Mine is not a continuous narrative like his; the gaps reflect the gaps in the sources.

I come into the story around 500 BC, at the point where Confucius enters the records of history. China was in a glum period. She felt old and dispirited, and was so impatient for change that she was ready to renounce all that was good about her and all that had worked for her and to let anyone have a go. Confucius was now in his fifties. He had given a lot of thought to what constituted virtue and what might be fair and effective practices in government, and had just begun to involve himself in serious politics. When he miscalculated the strength of his opponents in a showdown at the court of Lu, he took flight. The first half of this book is about his years of wandering and the three or four men who followed him into the unknown. Though these men referred to themselves as his disciples, they were more like apprentices; they believed that by learning from Confucius and staying close to him, they, too, could acquire his skills and his disposition. On this journey, Confucius would have been lost without his companions, and his attributes would have been less distinct if his fellow voyagers had not been there to bring them out.

Toward the beginning of this book, in the chapter "Families and Politics," I also try to place Confucius in the Spring and Autumn history of his home state. Confucius was a counselor. He also possessed a historian's awareness of the past. Only the history of the early counselors, especially of those from his own state, can help us understand why he pursued such a calling and what relation it had to his teachings.

The second half of the book begins with Confucius' homecoming after fourteen years of self-exile. It takes him to his retirement from politics and his late years, at which point I follow with my own description of what I understand to be his teachings. The book closes with his death and then a final chapter on two thinkers from the fourth and third centuries BC, Mencius and Xunzi, who created out of Confucius' original vision more clearly marked paths for those intent on living a moral life. The two philosophers did not agree on many things, but their differences would receive full amplification in China's intellectual and political worlds in the twenty-three hundred years to come and so are worthy of our consideration.

While I was working on this book, extraordinary things happened in China in the fields of archaeology and textual scholarship. Two batches of manuscripts on moral cultivation and political thought, written on bamboo slips, came to light: one batch dug up by archaeologists, the other pilfered by grave robbers and then sold on the Hong Kong antiques market before the manuscripts were bought, a few bundles at a time, by the Shanghai Museum. The texts were written around Mencius and Xunzi's time, 300 BC or earlier, before China was unified, in the period known as "the Warring States." Ever since the texts' discovery in 1993, paleographers have been poring over them, debating the meaning of the unfamiliar scripts and the sequence of the sentences, especially when a text is incomplete or has obvious gaps or when a bamboo slip is only a fragment of what it was. Meanwhile, historians of early China and scholars of its philosophy have been following the published studies of the materials with great interest, for they know that these excavated texts can tell us a lot about the Chinese mind prior to the emergence of the imperial age. They also believe that these texts will change the way we read the literature in the received tradition, including Confucius' *Analects,* the *Zuo Commentary,* the Confucian classics, and writings attributed to many Warring States philosophers. In the last six years, I, too, have been involved, in small ways, with this collective enterprise. Confucius, often with a disciple, appears in eight of the forty-five published texts (eighteen of which were in the first batch and twenty-seven in the second). I was naturally drawn to these, but all in the two collections had an influence on this book.

One Chinese paleographer I got to know told me about the risks of removing the ancient mud from the bamboo. As the strips lie in their cleaning solution, he said, and the words begin to emerge, some of the words literally rise from their bamboo surfaces, seeking flight or freedom in their demise. This is the closest I have come to thinking of words as alive. Sometime after, I made a wish. Even as I accept the impermanence of life, I said, I want words to be the exception—not all words, but surely words in the classics and histories, words of the early poems, philosophers' words, and the words of Confucius. I want them to stick around so that we can taste them again and again and play with their flavors in our head.

Introduction

On a recent visit to China, I had a chance to talk to a group of high school students from Zoucheng, a town in Shandong province, just twenty kilometers south of Confucius' birthplace, Qufu. Zoucheng was the home of Confucius' follower Mencius. The students wanted to know what I thought of their government's latest push to create "a harmonious society" with "harmonious ties" to the outside world: whether it had any relation to Confucius' teachings and whether the incantation of Confucius' name in this campaign had anything to do with the historical Confucius. And since they spent nearly every waking hour of their lives preparing for the fiercely competitive college entrance examination, they also asked whether what they were doing had any bearing on pursuing harmony in a Communist state and finding Confucius in it.

These students wanted my views though they knew the answer better than I. For they were keenly aware of the disjunction between the lives they lived and the lives their leaders claimed to envision for them. They knew that no collective goal of the state, no matter how lovely its promise, could bring consolation to them and to their parents should the outcome of their entrance examination turn out to be disappointing. This is a new China, and these students have moved beyond Marxism. If Confucius were alive, he would have understood their anxiety and their fear of failure.

The students from this part of Shandong province have given more thought to Confucius than students from anywhere else in China. They are more conscious of him because Confucius was from this region—he is one of theirs. In fact, for more than two thousand years, the pride of Shandong was linked to his name, to his moral acumen and political sagacity. In the last century, however, the association has become ambiguous. In the 1910s and 1920s, under mounting pressure to transform their country into a modern nation-state, Chinese intellectuals and reformers openly debated the question of Confucius: whether his teachings were still suitable for a China that had been fatigued and made vulnerable by foreign exploitation; more important, whether Confucian ethics were prone to being misused by the state and rulers and by anyone who was politically or socially superior; and whether those with power forged precepts like filial duty and brotherly respect so that they could brandish them like weapons to insure inequality. During that period, strong words were exchanged between the right and the left, but the disagreement did not lead to all-out violence. Students could be expelled for desecrating the altar of Confucius in their school, but acts of open defiance were, on the whole, isolated cases. The differences were fought mainly on paper and within the limits of civility. The reappraisal of Confucius took many forms, on the stage and in fiction, in studies of history and through critical scholarship. It was in part China's own self-examination.

The attack on Confucius continued into the post-1949 Communist years. But by this time, the drive was no longer correction but destruction, and it went completely out of control by the fall of 1966. This was at the beginning of the Cultural Revolution. The campaign called for the wiping out of "old thought, old culture, old customs, and old habits." The radicals and the zealots, without thought or imagination, understood the bidding as unlimited license to abuse and brutalize men and women of learning; to burn books, smash cultural relics, and raze sacred sites. They were masters of their own destiny yet were enslaved to an inhuman idea, and so when they set to work, these youths showed no reserve. They pillaged the mosques in Xinjiang, vandalized the temples in Shanxi and Shaanxi, set ablaze statues of the Buddha in Hefei and Loyang, and were not going to spare the Confucius Temple, the Confucius Mansion, and the Confucius Tomb, the three hallowed sites in Confucius' home county, Qufu. When the outsiders arrived, Qufu officials and the older residents offered whatever defense they could muster. But the students from the local schools wavered: they were not sure where they should stand in the conflict. In the end many succumbed to the sheer weight of the revolution. The students did not torch the Confucius Temple, but they dug up Confucius' grave "to declare him safely dead."

Eight years later, Confucius was dragged out again to be paired with Lin Biao in the "anti–Lin Biao, anti-Confucius" campaign. Lin was Mao's closest comrade and designated successor in the early years of the Cultural Revolution. In 1971, he died in a plane crash. According to official reports, he had betrayed Mao, and when his plan to assassinate Mao did not materialize, he and his family tried to flee to the Soviet Union in a military plane, but the plane went down in Mongolia. Lin was charged posthumously with treason. Three years later, in the midst of yet another mass movement aimed pointedly at Confucius, Lin Biao was declared to be a "Confucius of contemporary China" because according to some investigators he had hung a scroll in his study with four characters taken from Confucius' *Analects*. There were also other allegations intended to justify putting Lin Biao and Confucius on the same banner and in the same criticism sessions.

In the 1980s, after the Cultural Revolution had formally come to a close, scholarship and classical learning slowly found their way back to the universities and the research institutions funded by the state. Confucius' *Analects* was introduced again in the classrooms, together with the Confucian classics. From the mid-1990s until now, the discovery of the bamboo-slip texts from 300 BC has been fueling Confucian studies, but much of the work and discussion has taken place within the confines of the academy. Places like Qufu have received more visitors in the last two decades, but, for the Chinese, having a livelier tourist industry in these Confucian sites is not the same as reading in the papers that their party leaders are touting the virtues of a Confucian society and that their government is in the process of establishing Confucius Institutes to teach the Chinese language in Africa, Europe, Southeast Asia, and South and North America.

The latest development is a mixed blessing for the people of Qufu. Many of them still remember what happened in the fall of 1966. Some took part in the desecration of the Confucius burial grounds. A few are still living with the ghosts they once thought they had to exhume because of the disgrace into which the ghosts had fallen. Now they must welcome them back as benign spirits— and a calming presence—in this new round of virtual politics. But at least the politics is not another ideological onslaught. The Confucius Institutes teach the Chinese language to people around the world. They are conceived as agents of China's peaceful expansion— harbingers of good news.

Confucius probably never expected to be associated with language learning. Even though the *Analects* says that Confucius "always used correct pronunciations" when reciting from the *Classic of Poetry* or from the *Classic of Documents,* his interest in language was on a deeper level. "Correct pronunciations," in this case, refer to how words should sound, say, as they were first sung in a poem presented in the royal court of Zhou. Like an exegete, Confucius believed that he could edge closer to the meaning of old poems and ancient writings when he had restored the correct pronunciations. He did not think that it was right to recite the classic odes in contemporary pronunciation or in his native Lu dialect: some gist or nuance was bound to be lost. Confucius would not have wished China to widen her influence by making her language more accessible. It was simply not in his political thinking, and it would contradict how he felt about words and speech. One can never be too careful when teaching others to speak, he says: words are an extension of thought, and when voiced, they must be appropriate. Yet his latest comeback through the international language institutes is not completely absurd. It is, after all, his reputation as a teacher that lends some respect to these learning centers.

In China, Confucius is known as *xianshi*, "first teacher," "the teacher before all teachers." Yet in real life he did not become so until he was in his mid-sixties, just a few years before he died. His ambition up to that point was to save the world from decline through political purchase. His family gave him no assistance. He was the son of a common gentleman, a *shi*, which meant that his position in society depended entirely on what he did with his life, how he spent his time and applied his skills and knowledge.* He inherited no privileges or entitlements except for a chance to have an education and a status that was above a commoner. Even so, Confucius was lucky because he came into the world at the right time.

That world was in upheaval, but it was ready to consider how to reorganize and recast itself. An aged enfeoffment system, which had been the framework and the adhesive of the Zhou political universe since the founding of the dynasty in the mid-eleventh century BC, was barely functioning after centuries of abuse. Regional rulers, who were responsible for holding the dynasty together through their loyalty to the Zhou king, had, for three centuries, been preoccupied with aggrandizing themselves. Meanwhile, the hereditary families in each state had been preying on their ruler's wealth and power. By Confucius' time, the hereditary families themselves were tearing one another apart through such petty scuffles as cockfights and jealous feuds. (Cockfights and sexual exploits were fiercely competitive in the sixth century BC.) The decline of the aristocratic class allowed the *shi*, the common gentlemen, who had been in the service of the noble households as stewards or warriors, to move into administrative positions in the state government and to take part in state politics. This was the path Confucius followed.

The most talented of the common gentlemen, Confucius being the most notable, also set out to redefine ideas such as worth (*xian*),

---

Shì is a different word from "shĭ," meaning "scribe," or "shī," meaning "teacher."

nobleness (*shang*), and virtue (*de*). It is a person's ability and character, not his heredity, they said, that should grant him a place at the
top. They brought to their argument their own achievements. They
also turned to the old documents for validation. Thus a statement
made by a venerated man five hundred years earlier, explaining why
a depraved king should be deposed, could be read to mean that anyone in office who was incompetent or unscrupulous should be
demoted to the rank of a commoner. And these common gentlemen
would add that a man who had lost his noble rank could no longer
be called a *junzi*, "son of the lord," regardless of his pedigree. The
name *junzi*, which had once signified only social position and provenance, by the time of Confucius had acquired a moral tone. More
and more, it applied only to men with noble character.

Men like Confucius talked about their work in this regard with
exaggerated modesty, describing it as "transmission" of truthful ideas
or "rectifying names." Their task may sound straightforward, but
there were many risks. The more responsible of the gentlemen realized this. They were cautious about what they were doing because
they knew that they were handling hefty ideas and big names, and
that distortion was easy. At the same time, these men recognized the
potentials of their historical situation, which had given them a reasonable chance to compete in the political world and even room to
rewrite the rules so that the outcome would favor the virtuous and
the competent. This may in part explain Confucius: he was so bold
as to attempt a coherent teaching about what was virtue, who had
worth, and what might be an ideal government, yet he was also wary
lest his handling of ideas and names might cause them to lose their
vigor and veracity. Thus he relied on history and his knowledge of
cultural practice—not just his intellectual gifts—to help him compose his vision of a moral political order, and the man he looked back
to for guidance was the Duke of Zhou, brother of the founder of the
Zhou dynasty, King Wu.

The Duke of Zhou had accomplished for the early Zhou what
Confucius set out to do for his own age. The Duke of Zhou was a
counselor to his brother King Wu, and a regent in a period when

King Wu's heir was too young to rule. He carried out the work of a ruler without ever having been one, and his accomplishments were veritable. These facts encouraged Confucius in his own ambitions, but the Duke of Zhou was five hundred years removed from him. Thus it was the Duke of Zhou's spirit and the ethos of the early Zhou that Confucius called upon to give him direction.

Besides the Duke of Zhou, there were other counselors Confucius admired—Zichan and Guan Zhong, for instance—men closer to his own time and faced with problems akin to his. Yet records of these men showed that not all of their political labor turned out to be honest; circumstances could force them to be expedient. Confucius thought that these counselors were praiseworthy, but his judgments were measured—in fact, so finely calibrated that they are informative about the political history of the Spring and Autumn period and instructive about him. They tell us, for instance, how he reacted to extreme loyalty and extreme scrupulosity, whether he could overlook an irregularity in a man's political career if what happened on that one occasion allowed the man to achieve a greater good, and how he felt regarding those brief and violent episodes that could speed up a change for the better.

Confucius thought aloud about these questions with a group of young men who addressed him as "Master," *zi,* and called themselves his "disciples," *tu.* Some of the men were sons of aristocrats or children of common gentlemen. Others were merchants, farmers, artisans, soldiers, criminals, or sons of criminals. Some were from the capital city, others from fortified towns and the villages in the surrounding countryside. Some were refined and others were rough-hewn. Three stood out: Zigong, Yan Hui, and Zilu.

Zigong was a merchant who aspired to a career in politics. Around this time, it was possible for merchants to pursue such an ambition. A hundred years earlier, they could not even work for themselves. Like artisans, merchants were dependents of the aristocratic families. They earned their keep by helping their lords procure goods that could not be found locally, and their sons would inherit their jobs after they died. The decline of the large elite families and an overall sense that changes in the social structure were imminent encouraged the merchants to break free and to have a go on their own. By the middle of the Spring and Autumn period, peasants, too, were acquiring more independence from the families on whose land they worked and lived. Up until the sixth century BC, their relationship with their lords had been one of mutual obligation—productive labor in exchange for protection and bare livelihood—but that relationship was coming to an end, to be replaced by a more efficient system of tax payment in kind. The new relationship was less personal, but it let the peasants feel that they owned the land they plowed; thus they were prodded to work harder, improve their farming technique, and increase their productivity. Along with agriculture, other industries—such as the manufacture of bronze, iron, and pottery—were advancing rapidly. By the end of the fifth century BC, industries and craftsmanship began to become more specialized, so that a warrior from Qi might want to have his sword forged in Yue, and a palace lady from Qin might fancy to have her skirt dyed in Qi and her precious stones carved in Chu.

The demand for fine goods and raw materials found only in certain regions kept the merchants on the road. The Chinese had had a road system since the beginning of the Zhou dynasty. Road construction continued on an even larger scale during the Spring and Autumn period. At this time, wars and diplomacy and other kinds of interstate activities provided the push for making the roads wider and sturdier than before so that they could hold up the weight of an army on the march and gift-laden chariots with hundreds of escorts in tow. Along these roads, merchants could also be seen hauling their goods. And as their numbers swelled, some began to take on roles as informants for their rulers, reporting on troop movements and other useful news, such as who was sending what to whom, and whether twenty chariots of furs and rawhides could seal an alliance for the state of Chu with the state of Wei. Before long, some of the merchants began to groom themselves for political roles. This was not hubris, for toward the end of the Spring and Autumn period, merchants could become high ministers, and high ministers might leave their posts and become merchants. Zigong was such a man, ever-shifting and mobile, which the world then found quite acceptable.

Confucius' follower Yan Hui was another kind of common gentleman. He was as smart and imaginative as Zigong and just as ambitious, but he would not have chosen to become a merchant. And even if he had, he could never have been good at buying and selling. Yan Hui was poor because his family was poor. But he had a lofty mind and was content to live in "a shabby neighborhood." Yan Hui was not someone prosperity left behind. But that could not be said of most people during the Spring and Autumn period.

The most destitute at this time were farmers who had fallen victim to heavy taxes. When farmers let go the attachments that bound them to the powerful families, the families no longer felt morally obliged to offer them support. Thus when they plunged, the farmers could expect to hit bottom. Such was the price of the slight independence these farmers gained in the political shift from an enfeoffment structure to a joint concern of sovereign states. Commoners were becoming subjects of the state, including those living outside of the capital, on the periphery or "in the field," men like Confucius' follower Zilu, whose ancestors could never take part in matters of the state. Yet throughout this period of change, no one in China, no Socrates in Lu or Wei, tried to articulate what this new relationship might mean in terms of the moral and legal obligations the state and the subject each had for the other. This was probably because men with learning were still yearning for a time when moral duties were not pronounced in rules and ordinances. If the impulse to act correctly did not come from yourself, Confucius said to a follower, what good could it do for you? In his mind, the moral was beautiful, and it should not succumb to rules. Rules diminish its beauty and subtlety, and adherence to them is an admission of one's own moral failure.

Nonetheless, Confucius could not deny the plus side of the political change that was unfolding before him. A topic like "worth," for instance, had entered the public debate and would now have some import in the selection of government officials, which could only benefit men like him. Yet despite his personal gains, Confucius was still searching for certain constants in history and poetry, in habits and sentiments, in rites and music, that could help him compose his thoughts and build something stable and vast. He liked conversations. They helped him think, but he never expected anyone to write them down. Confucius did not wish to have his words end up as rules, or to be immortalized himself. For he loved the idea of being human. He loved the entirely private journey of finding what was right and feasible among life's many variables.

On that journey, which included fourteen years of travels, Confucius talked to scores of people, from rulers to rustics, counselors to recluses, but also thugs, musicians, and madmen. With rulers, the subject was the fundamentals of government: where to begin if the ruler wished to see his state prosper; how the ruler should prepare himself; what he should expect from his ministers; and what mistakes could lead his country to ruin. With court counselors, the subject was human character: what Confucius would look for in a man; whom he would recommend for high office; why one person was suitable to be an advisor to a king and another merely a steward on a large estate. In his conversations with simple folk, Confucius never seemed arrogant or aloof. He could never feel superior because, he explained, no matter who put a question to him, "my mind was a complete blank. I kept hammering at the two sides of the question until I got everything out." Confucius was evasive when talking to political thugs and ebullient when speaking about musicians. Throughout his long journey, he also sought out recluses in the wild, men who were in such despair with the political machinators of the world and so tired of earthly concerns that they preferred finding their own peace among the mountain cassia and forest pines, in grass huts and alone, far away from the human hullabaloo. From them, Confucius learned a different point of view, against which he could gauge his own.

But it was with Zigong, Yan Hui, Zilu, and a few other followers that Confucius felt most comfortable talking about any subject, and if the subject was abstruse or a tangle, he would use the occasion to try sorting it out and to hear what others had to say. Sometimes he was able to gain something for himself. These conversations covered a wide range of topics: mourning rites and sacrificial rites; how to serve one's parents when they are alive; how to serve them when they are dead; how to serve them when they are horrid; how to decide who has benevolence and who has acumen, and whether a benevolent man can be hoodwinked; how to learn and what knowledge to retain; how to listen to poetry and what to cherish in music; what to do if one could have one's way in the world. These dialogues make up a large part of his teachings, and they illustrate his techniques and tact as a teacher. They are not, however, philosophers' conversations. They do not resemble Socrates' dialogues with, say, Gorgias or Callicles, though the topics are similar. Confucius, too, sought to distinguish genuine art from fake art, moral persuasion from sweet talk, the noble statesman from the political pander. But his moral thought was not Plato's dialectical ethics. Opponents were rarely present in these conversations, and when they did appear, Confucius did not feel that he had to defeat them on their grounds and with their rules before he was ready to speak about who had knowledge and what was true. He did not get involved with rhetoricians, and he was not speaking just to students of philosophy or those with an analytical bent. Any listener could have joined in the conversation and recognized something relevant to his own life.

Accessibility, however, presented its own difficulties. When there were also the problems of gaps in the records and insufficient context, it allowed the teachings of Confucius to take on all kinds of interpretations: some were strong and morally compelling, some were banal, and others were merely convenient. Yet in the right hands or an imaginative mind, these ideas could assume lives of their own and become the source of fresh concepts, brand-new teachings, and materials for further disquisition. An example would be the notion of *ren,* or benevolence. Confucius identified it as a distinct human character. It is warm and beautiful, he says: one gravitates to it "like home." Two followers of Confucius from the eleventh and twelfth centuries, Cheng Yi and Zhu Xi, placed *ren* in the metaphysical category, calling it "the principle of love." The principle of love is not the same as love, they said. The love a person has for his parents and the respect he has for his older brother are only expressions of *ren*, which is not the same as *ren*. *Ren* is the principle or the reason that love exists, they continued; its productive and generative character is what humans have in common with heaven and earth. In this upgraded version, *ren* had acquired cosmological importance. It would be in a much stronger position if it were to find itself in a competition against a subtle aspect of Buddhist philosophy. Of this Cheng and Zhu were keenly aware.

By the end of the nineteenth century, China was in a different kind of contest. She had had a string of disasters in her confrontations with Britain, France, and Japan, and could not afford to lose another round. Metaphysics and cosmology could not have helped her in this competition. She needed, among other things, gunboats and warships, a modern army and prudent governance. And her people would have to put away their differences and stand together as one. The call for unity was in the air. Two reformers from this period, Kang Youwei and Tan Sitong, both turned to *ren*—to Confucius' original idea of finding a home in *ren*—to help them lay the emotional ground of a harmonious society. And to insure that this community would be inclusive and sturdy, they relied on the works of the two Song dynasty thinkers, Cheng Yi and Zhu Xi, who gave *ren* its cosmological largeness and metaphysical certainty.

It is still too early to tell whether the present Chinese government is trying to do the same in its call for a "harmonious society" and "China's peaceful rise" in the global community. Scholars in China are encouraged to pursue their research in Confucian studies and to inspire their students to do the same. Government money is available if they wish to organize academic conferences around topics in Confucianism. But officials also want their presence to be felt. Several could be seen at such an event recently, along with the ritualists from Hong Kong and South Korea, and the local troops. The officials were there because they liked the publicity and they liked to give the semblance that they were capable of thought. The ritualists were there because they had no one else to talk to about their stale knowledge. The troops were there for the free food and white spirits. But the occasion belonged to the scholars and their students. Several wrote on the idea of *ren*: Why did Confucius pair *ren* (benevolence) with *li* (the rites), a moral concept with secular practice? How did *ren* evolve in the three hundred years after Confucius died. The scholars also discussed whether there was metaphysics in Confucius' thought and why the recently excavated texts might support such an argument; whether at one time there were "hundreds of chapters" of the *Analects,* from which the editors selected only twenty; and if there were "hundreds of chapters," what happened to them and whether the extant version accurately reflects Confucius' teachings.

If Confucius were present at this affair, he would recognize the politics. He would listen to the officials talk their talk. He would look at them with sideways glances. He would have a drink with the soldiers in uniform and avoid the ritualists altogether. He would sit next to a scholar and chat with the students, and he would feel assuaged.

Chapter One

Leaving Home

Aт the height of his political career, Confucius suddenly resigned from office and took to the road with no prospects and very little cash. The year was 497 BC. He was fifty-four, holding the position of minister of crime in his home state of Lu when this happened. The move essentially ended his public career, but he could not have known it then.

Confucius had always wanted a place near the top, though not for the usual reasons. He was not seeking fresh emolument or an extra charge of power. His ambitions were for a noble end, but to achieve them he needed more political leverage. The minister of crime was only a middle-level official. The position allowed him an occasional audience with the feudal lord, and he would go to him when called upon. His immediate supervisor, however, was the chief counselor. He saw this man more often, and it was through his relationship with the chief counselor that he would gauge where he stood in the eyes of his ruler and whether he mattered in the affairs of the state. In 497 BC, Duke Ding was the ruler of Lu, Jihuanzi was his chief counselor, and Confucius reported directly to Jihuanzi.

No one can say for sure why Confucius gave up his job that year. It had taken him a long time to get where he was, working his way up from keeper of granaries and livestock in Jihuanzi's clan to district officer, then to minister of works, and finally to minister of crime. Salaried positions were not uncommon during this period of Chinese history, but the more coveted offices were given to aristocrats living on hereditary emoluments. Confucius himself was on the edge of being aristocratic, but his provenance could not quite admit him to this privileged group. According to some reports, his early ancestors were the Kongs from the state of Song, a titled family that produced several eminent counselors for Song. But in the mid-seventh century BC, political rivals dealt the family a hard blow, after which the Kongs could no longer hold their heads high. Consequently, several members of the family moved to Lu. Among them was Confucius' great-grandfather. By the time Confucius was born, the Kongs had long adopted Lu as their home, but they had lost altogether their hereditary titles and the privileges their ancestors had enjoyed in Song. They were now common gentlemen (*shi*), just a grade above the common folk.

There were many such men in the Spring and Autumn period—marginal people with the pride of the elite and an education in the six arts of ritual, music, archery, charioteering, writing, and mathematics. These men knew that they were from superior stock, but with the decline of their family fortune, all they were allowed was an education, and all they could rely on for employment and an income was the knowledge and skills they had acquired; and so they lived with an uneasy feeling that if they did not apply themselves fully in any or all of the six arts, they could fall below the margin. The common gentlemen from Confucius' time were diligent and flexible; they could be warriors or bureaucrats. Confucius' own father, Shu-liang He, was a soldier and a district steward in Lu.

When Confucius was conceived in 552 or 551 BC, Shu-liang He was already an old man, with nine daughters by a principal wife and a clubfooted son by a concubine. Still, he managed to persuade the head of the Yan family to let his daughter—a girl in her teens—have a child with him. The early Chinese historian Sima Qian writes, "[Shu-liang] He and the girl from the Yan family made love in the fields and conceived Confucius." No early accounts explained why the couple "made love in the fields (*yehe*)." One would assume that before approaching the Yan family, Shu-liang He had ended his first marriage because that wife failed to produce a male heir, and that he had driven away his concubine because she gave him an imperfect son. If the Yan girl was indeed his legitimate wife, why did the nuptials take place under such unnatural circumstances? Was their relationship perceived as being in some way illicit? After their union in the wilds, adds Sima Qian:

> The couple prayed at Mount Ni, and she gave birth to Confucius. Confucius was born in the twenty-second year of Duke Xiang of Lu with a concavity in the top of his head, like a roof with turned-up eaves. [And since his parents prayed at Mount Ni (Ni Qiu),] he was given the personal name of Qiu and the courtesy name of Zhongni. His family name was Kong.

Confucius was only three when his father died. Mother and son had a hard time scraping by, and she died when he was still a young man. He married a woman from the Binguan family when he was eighteen. His wife soon bore him a son, and sometime later a daughter.

Confucius was unusually tall. Some claimed that he "grew to a height of well over six feet." The pumped-up figure could mean that he was seen as bigger than life. Confucius himself, however, never tried to inflate his image or his abilities. He readily told others that he "was skilled in many menial things." He did not think that a gentleman need be so proficient in menial tasks, but he had no choice, he said, for he "was poor and from a lowly station" and could not enter government service as easily as young men of prominent families could, and so "could not prove himself in office" just because he felt he was ready. Thus he went forth unto his work and labor with patience, and he moved upward gradually from keeping accounts and looking after livestock to positions of relative importance in the state bureaucracy.

By the time he became the minister of crime, Confucius also had a following that included men like Zigong, Yan Hui, and Zilu. Most of these men had few resources to begin with. Even when they were from well-to-do families, if they were not the eldest sons they would have received only a trifle of the inheritance after their fathers died, certainly not enough to live on. Thus by becoming apprentices to a gentleman and by pursuing the learning of a gentleman, they hoped to stand on their own one day, with a gentleman's disposition and profession. In the meantime, they relied on their teacher for material support and contacts to help them get started on a political career. Disciples of Confucius believed that he could make them into what he had become. And like apprentices in a trade, they would spend years at their master's side, emulating him and caring for him as if he were their own father. They chose to be attached to him, and he, the teacher, was, in small ways, a lord unto himself. Thus when Confucius decided to leave Lu in 497, he was not only giving up his job, he was running the risk of losing all his followers.

The *Analects*, which is the oldest record we have about Confucius, mentions only once the matter of his surprise departure:

The men of Qi made a present of singing and dancing girls. Jihuanzi accepted the girls and did not go to court for the next three days. Confucius left.

Confucius' fourth-generation disciple, Mencius, offers another explanation:

Confucius was the minister of crime in the state of Lu, but [the ruler] did not adopt his measures or make use of his talents. Still, Confucius took part in an official sacrifice. Afterwards, he was not given a portion of the meat from the sacrificial animal. So he left right away and did not even have time to take off his ceremonial cap.

Mencius then adds:

Those who did not understand him thought that Confucius was begrudging about not getting a share of the meat. But those who understood him knew that he had to go because [the ruling elite of] Lu had acted contrary to the rites.

Four centuries later, the Han dynasty historian Sima Qian put the two accounts together, filled in a few titillating details, tidied up the inconsistencies, and produced a more complete story. According to this version, Confucius in 497 was so successful in his administration that "vendors of lamb and pork stopped charging inflated prices, men and women walked on different sides of the street, no one picked up things left on the road, and outsiders coming to the city did not have to look for officers to help them get settled because everyone made them feel at home." The counselors from the neighboring state of Qi watched this development with growing concern. They feared that with Confucius in charge of government, the ruler of Lu might very well "become the next hegemon," which meant that their country would be swallowed up first, since it was nearest to Lu. To stop that from happening, the men of Qi decided to thwart Confucius' effort:

> They chose eighty pretty girls in Qi, dressed them in gorgeous clothes, had them instructed in the dance to the Kanglo music, and sent them with sixty pairs of dappled horses as a gift to the Duke of Lu. The dancers were in plain sight with the horses outside of Gao Gate in the south city. Jihuanzi, who went in disguise several times to have a look, was tempted to accept the presents. He persuaded Duke Ding to have a stroll with him on the high road so that they could take a peek at the dancers. They lingered all day, watching the girls, and so neglected state affairs.

At this point, Sima Qian tells us, Confucius' follower Zilu urged his teacher to quit his job and go elsewhere. Confucius, however, was reluctant, wanting to give the ruler and his chief counselor another chance. He said to Zilu: "There will be a sacrifice today in the outskirts of the city. If our ruler shares portions of the sacrificial meat with the court officers, then I will stay." The episode concludes with "no meat being offered to the officers" and Confucius leaving Lu a disappointed man.

Despite the unhappy ending, this is an optimistic story; in fact, it is too upbeat to be credible. The author wants us to believe that when given the authority to fulfill his position, Confucius was able to accomplish impressive feats. Thus, he says, when the office of the minister of crime was at his disposal, within three months Confucius was able to create civil orderliness and social harmony in a world where transgressions had been rampant for so long that people were beginning to accept dishonesty and discordance as the norm. Sima Qian must have exaggerated or made things up, which is understandable because he was writing at a time when China was unified after many centuries of political division and Confucius' teachings had proved to be particularly useful to the theorists and stewards of the new order. Though fiercely independent, Sima Qian could not be completely free from the influence of a Confucian point of view. So, like most of his contemporaries, he rooted for Confucius and projected his expectations onto the biography he wrote of this man.

Mencius was less sanguine. He was Confucius' most important heir, yet he writes that when Confucius was the minister of crime, the ruler did not make use of his talents. Since Mencius was also a second-generation disciple of Confucius' grandson, he must have been better informed than Sima Qian. He also tells us that Confucius was waiting for an excuse to leave Lu, so when there was "a minor breech" of the rites, he made himself scarce. This explanation seems to edge closer to the truth regarding Confucius' behavior in 497, yet Mencius is still hiding something. Why, for instance, did Confucius leave in such a hurry? If all along he knew that he had to go because his ruler never thought of him or his plans as significant, why did he not prepare himself for the impending moment? As for the dancers from Qi, they may be part of another story.

The interplay among these three early sources and their apparent contradictions perfectly introduce the conundrum of how to bring

order and meaning to our understanding of Confu
might start with the *Spring and Autumn Annals,* the
Confucius' home state of Lu. But since the structure
skeletal and the entries are minimal, one has to
together with the *Zuo Commentary* to comprehend anything about
the goings-on during the Spring and Autumn period. And this commentary says that in 498 BC, the year before Confucius' departure,
an internal uprising nearly brought Lu to destruction. For a while it
appeared that the rebels were about to eliminate their ruler along
with the men who headed the three hereditary families, men who
were not only the chief ministers of the governing council but also
the ruler's closest relatives. Had the rebels been successful in the confrontation and had they gone on to crown themselves, this would
have formally terminated Lu's feudal tie with the Zhou king. In
other words, Lu would no longer have been a feudal state of the
Zhou kingdom, and the history of Lu would have had to begin a
new chapter. However, things did not end up that way. According to
the *Zuo Commentary,* Confucius played a crucial role in these events,
and he did so, in fact, long before the rebellion had materialized. We
find that the *Analects* is able to corroborate much of this story.

The very schematic *Spring and Autumn Annals,* to which the *Zuo
Commentary* is attached, has eleven entries for the year 498. Three
out of the eleven deal with affairs in other states—the death and
funeral of a feudal lord; the military exploits of one state against
another. One mentions a rain-praying ceremony in the fall; another,
a solar eclipse in the eleventh month. The remaining entries allude
to the malignity and the violence in Lu that year: first, the head of
the Shusun family led an army and demolished a city that for generations had been the family's stronghold; then, shortly afterwards,
the head of the Jisun family—the chief counselor Jihuanzi—tried to
do the same to his city.

The *Zuo Commentary* explains that Confucius' disciple Zilu was
a retainer in the Jisun clan, and that it was Zilu who encouraged the
hereditary families to destroy their cities, telling them that it would
be better to make a fresh start than to let the rebels gain control of

eir bases. Following Zilu's advice, the Shusuns razed their original home city, and the Jisuns were just about to do the same to their home city in Bi when one of their retainers, Gongshan Buniu, "took command of the men of Bi and sprang a surprise attack on the capital of Lu." In desperation, the commentary continues, "the duke and the heads of the three families entered the Jisun palace grounds and climbed the Wuzi Terrace." The rebels tried "but could not take them." "Arrows grazed past the ruler" while he waited for his fate. At this point, Confucius, in his capacity as the minister of crime, ordered two state officers to lead an assault against the insurgent band. "The men of Bi fled north. The government troops pursued them and crushed them in Gu. The two rebel leaders ran for the state of Qi. Immediately after, the Jisun clan destroyed their stronghold at Bi." The third family, the Mengsuns, however, had a change of heart. When it was their turn to dismantle their base, the chief retainer persuaded the head of the family not to do it. "The city of Cheng is the Mengsuns' security," the man said. "Without it, there won't be any Mengsuns." At the end of 498, the ruler sent an army to finish up what the Mengsun family could not carry out themselves, but the expedition failed.

Sources a century or two later than the *Zuo Commentary* contend that it was Confucius, not his follower Zilu, who was behind the plan to uproot the Three Families. One says:

When Confucius was in the service of the Jisun clan, after he had been compliant for three months, he told them that a private home should not have a stockpile of weapons; that a district city should not have walls one hundred *zhi* in length. Thereupon he led a military division and destroyed, first, the city of Hou and then the city of Bi.

Another story went so far as to give Confucius the credit for "restoring the office of the duke and dealing a serious blow to the private families." But records in the *Zuo Commentary*, which is the more reliable source, imply that the disruption of 498 neither strengthened the ruler of Lu nor significantly weakened the Three Families. The commentary makes no grand claim for Confucius. Yet by stating that Zilu was the one who instigated the destruction of the cities, it implicates Zilu's teacher. In the *Analects,* Confucius had more than once indicated that Zilu was the disciple who would do anything for him and also the disciple who most needed his approval. This, however, did not endear Zilu to him. One time, in a moment of moral anguish, Confucius declaimed: "If I cannot practice a proper way here, in this world, then I shall take to the open sea and drift around on a bamboo raft. The person who will follow me would be Zilu." We are told that Zilu was overjoyed when he heard these words, ready to have his loyalty and fortitude put to the test, not realizing that his teacher made the remark for rhetorical effect. Confucius was cool and sarcastic in response. He said, "Zilu loves courage more than I but is too blunt to understand anything subtle."

Confucius was the minister of crime when Zilu skillfully guided the Three Families to the first stage of their self-destruction, letting them believe that the drastic action they were about to take was their only option for saving themselves. Since Zilu was short on tact and judgment, one suspects that he must have consulted Confucius about how to proceed. Or was this Confucius' idea? Moreover, given the fact that Confucius was the chief law officer, they would have had to weigh the risks. They must have realized that their plan could lead to an insurrection.

The *Analects* is forthcoming about Confucius' knowledge of the insurgent activities in Lu and his relationship with the rebel leaders. One of the leaders, Gongshan Furao, had invited Confucius to work with him just before Confucius received his appointment in the duke's government. (This Gongshan was the same Gongshan Buniu whose foray into politics triggered the crisis of 498.) At the time, Confucius was aware of this man's ambitions: Gongshan was the chief retainer in the Jisun family, and he probably had enough support from the family's private army and from the people living in the family's citadel to stage a takeover. To accept Gongshan's offer would have meant that Confucius was ready to topple an old political establishment and entrust the fate of his country to the younger, tougher outsider. When Zilu learned that his teacher was willing to consider the offer, he became anxious, begging Confucius to think again. He said, "We may be at the end of our road, but why must we go to Gongshan?" Confucius' reply reveals his big ambition: "This man must have had some purpose in mind when he summoned me. If he can put me to use, can I not, perhaps, realize a Zhou dynasty in the east?"

Even when he had nowhere to go, the open sea was never an option for Confucius. Instead, he considered the bandits' lair. He did not contemplate becoming one of the bandits, only how to take advantage of the opportunity offered so that he could have a go at what he hoped to achieve. Confucius also liked to be "put to use." Among his followers, probably only Zilu mistook his earlier declamation about leaving the world to be sincere; so it was also Zilu who was most troubled by Confucius' willingness to work with or even to meet with the disreputable and the indecorous. When, on yet another occasion, Zilu confronted Confucius about his judgment in a similar matter, quoting his teacher's own words as support, Confucius replied that it was true that he had indeed said, "A true gentleman does not enter the domain of someone who, in his person, has acted in an unvirtuous way." But he continued:

> Has it not also been said, "Hard indeed is that which can withstand grinding" and "White indeed is that which can withstand black dye"? Moreover, how can I be like a gourd that hangs from the end of a string, not being eaten?

Few men were as hard-edged or as dark and dangerous as Yang Hu, another retainer in the Jisun family. Not long before Gongshan approached Confucius, Yang Hu had tried to do the same. On that earlier occasion, even Confucius was cautious, trying his best to avoid a face-to-face meeting with this man. So when Yang Hu sent him a present of a piglet, Confucius waited until Yang Hu was out of his house before going there to pay his respects. But on the way back, they bumped into each other. Yang Hu spoke first. "Come here!" he called to Confucius. "I want to talk to you." He then proceeded to give Confucius a lecture:

> Would you call a man benevolent if he clutches a cherished jewel in his bosom while letting his state be in a muddle? I should say not. Would you call a man wise if he is eager to take part in government while letting opportunities slip by again and again? I should say not. Days and months are rushing forward. Time is not on our side.

When Yang Hu finished, Confucius said, "Right. I shall take up office."

Confucius' response to Yang Hu is elusive. He does not let us know whether he was merely going along with what Yang Hu had said so as to avoid a confrontation, or whether he was seriously ready to accept Yang Hu's offer of employment. However, what is clear from the brief account is Confucius' relationship to Yang Hu. Confucius dreaded a meeting with him and was not strong enough, not even with his knowledge and his good character, to rise above his unease and his fear of Yang Hu. So he dodged around and played games with him, and when caught, Confucius had to listen quietly to Yang Hu's disquisition on morality and wisdom.

The old chronicle—the *Spring and Autumn Annals*—does not dignify Yang Hu with a name, referring to him merely as "the bandit." Yet this man was not a simple brigand. He dominated Lu politics for at least five years, from 507 to 502, riding roughshod over all three families. Yang Hu had a precursor in Nan Kuai, another retainer in the Jisun family, twenty-five years earlier. This man had had plans to reorganize the clan, to drive out the principal members of the family, and to strengthen the position of the Duke of Lu. His intentions might have been noble, but he was a bungler and so obviously incompetent that even the people from his home village were skeptical. They mocked his "simple-minded scheme" and his "grand conceit" that a family retainer could dream of "helping a ruler plan his future." On the eve of the revolt, two of his top lieutenants quit on him. The plot was, therefore, abandoned without being given a chance.

Yang Hu was bolder and smarter than Nan Kuai. Also, the world was ready for a man like him. He had key supporters placed in all three families and the run of the government for some time before he contemplated usurpation. And he nearly accomplished the work Nan Kuai had begun. But unlike Nan Kuai, Yang Hu always acted to further his own interests, never pretending that he was undermining the hereditary families in order to boost the ruler. Yang Hu probably would have liked to be the ruler. Questions of propriety would not have held him back. When Confucius bumped into him, Yang Hu was still a retainer but already behaving like a king. He called Confucius to him and demanded to know why Confucius was reluctant to serve the state, which the latter must have understood to mean why he had not served Yang Hu.

Of Yang Hu's political demise in 502, the *Zuo Commentary* offers a lively account:

> In the tenth month, winter, on the first day, sacrifices and prayers were conducted in sequential order for the deceased feudal lords in the state of Lu. On the second day, the *di* sacrifice was performed collectively for all the deceased feudal lords in the temple of Duke Xi. On the third day, Yang Hu prepared a feast for the Jisun family in Fu Garden. He ordered troops and chariots in the capital to be in war-readiness, saying, "The fourth day is just around the corner."

Yang Hu's plan was to have the chief counselor, Jihuanzi, killed while he was on his way to the banquet and then to launch an assault on the other members of the Jisun and Shusun families, using the state army. On the third day, Yang Hu had gone ahead to the site of the party; some distance away, Jihuanzi traveled in a carriage surrounded by military escorts loyal to Yang Hu, "carrying broadswords and shields." Yang Hu's brother guarded the rear of the procession with his men. Jihuanzi knew that he was approaching the end of his road. Suddenly he turned to his driver and said, "Your ancestors have been good retainers in my family. Can you not carry on their tradition?" The driver replied that it was too late for Jihuanzi to be making such a request: "Yang Hu is in charge of government. Everyone in Lu obeys him. To oppose him is to ask to be killed. What good would I be to you if I am dead?" Jihuanzi persisted until finally he convinced the driver to make a dash for the city still under the control of the third family, the Mengsuns.

The story ends with the Mengsuns defeating Yang Hu's troops in the capital city and the death of Yang Hu's brother. When the battle was over, Yang Hu "took off his armor, walked over to the duke's palace, rifled the precious jades and the great bow," and went home "to have a meal and a nap." When his followers announced that the rival troops "were about to arrive," Yang Hu said: "Hearing the news that I have been driven out, the people of Lu are only too glad that their lives have been spared. So why would they want to waste their time to come after me?" In the words of a later scholar, "With a swaggerer's disposition and an unkind nature, Yang Hu [for a while] took center stage in the state of Lu and had complete control of its political affairs." The scholar continues:

> The people of Lu feared him as much as they feared thunder and lightning. Even ghosts and spirits dared not offend him. Yet when he lost out, he went straight to the ruler's palace, carried off his precious jades and great bow, and came home to Wufu Road to stay, cool and unruffled. He was the sort of man that no one could put in a tight spot.

It is not clear whether Confucius considered working with Yang Hu, but he was tempted by Gongshan's offer. Gongshan was Yang Hu's protégé, and he had managed to secure his boss's position following Yang Hu's escape to the state of Jin. It is curious that the Jisun family, knowing that Gongshan was a leader in Yang Hu's conspiracy, not only did not try to get rid of Gongshan but gave him Yang

Hu's old job. Possibly the Yang Hu debacle was just a temporary set-back for the retainers, or perhaps these men were so entrenched in Lu politics that the hereditary families were resigned to the fact that it was just a matter of time before they would have to yield their power formally to the upstarts. That could explain why even Confucius dreamt of "realizing a Zhou dynasty in the east" with the muscle of the retainers.

It was the Lu government's decision to appoint Confucius minister of crime that changed his plan. The job took him to a remote valley called Xiagu in the year 500, on a mission with Duke Ding, the ruler of Lu, to officiate a temporary alliance with Qi. The two states had been going at each other since the beginning of Duke Ding's reign in 509. First, there was a protracted dispute over the district of Yun. Then, in 503, Qi became a formal adversary when it decided to turn against a close ally of Lu. In 502, the year Yang Hu revolted, Duke Ding personally led three separate expeditions against Qi. However, when Qi refused to give Yang Hu assistance after he had lost his bid to become the overlord of Lu, the rulers of these two states saw a chance to reconcile. This was what brought Duke Ding and Confucius to Xiagu. But Qi did not come to the meeting in good faith. One of their counselors told his ruler that Confucius "knows the rites but lacks courage." This counselor urged his ruler to "send the people of Lai to apprehend the Duke of Lu by force," adding, "This can only be to our advantage."

These "people of Lai" were non-Chinese living to the north of Qi. In 567 BC, the Qi army demolished their only city, murdered their ruler, and dispersed the people of Lai in the valley of Xiagu. To use the Lai in this act of subversion seemed a smart move for Qi because it would allow them to shift responsibility to a people that most Chinese regarded as violent and subaltern. Moreover, since the Lai inhabited Xiagu, it would not appear as if the Qi brought them from outside as their hired thugs. However, as soon as Confucius realized the danger his ruler was in, he ordered the military escorts he had brought with him to step forward. He addressed the ruler of Qi and said:

Two rulers intend to be on good terms, yet one of them arms the men that his people once subjugated and encourages them to create disorder. This is not how a ruler of Qi should be conducting business with other feudal lords.

Confucius then emphasized that it was not right for "barbarians to cause unrest among Chinese states," "for captive people to interfere with a covenant," and for "soldiers to threaten a peace negotiation." He asked the Qi ruler to desist. "To continue," he added, "would be inauspicious from the perspective of the spirits," "inappropriate from the perspective of men," and "a serious transgression by the measure of integrity." When Confucius finished his argument, the ruler of Qi withdrew the armed men of Lai, at which point Confucius laid down the terms of the treaty. Through the chief negotiator, he told the other side that his ruler would honor the alliance only after the Qi returned the three districts they had seized from Lu in recent skirmishes.

After both sides signed the agreement, the ruler of Qi wanted to celebrate the occasion with a feast. Again Confucius spoke. He pointed out that it was against the rules of propriety for the rulers of two Chinese states to have a banquet in no-man's-land. "With the task already completed," he said, "to have a feast is doing more than what is necessary." He continued:

> Moreover, the *xi* and the *xiang* wine containers should not leave the ancestral temples of our countries. The music of bells and stone chimes should not be performed in the wild. To have a feast in a place like Xiagu, [which is neither yours nor ours,] replete with sacred vessels and music, is to forsake the rites. Yet to do it without refinement implies that we have to use chaff and weeds, which is an insult to our sovereigns.

"A feast is meant to illumine and celebrate virtue," he told the Qi ruler. "If it cannot, then it is better not to do it."

The banquet "did not take place," we are told, and soon after the ruler of Lu returned home "the people of Qi gave back the three districts of Yun, Huan, and Guiyin."

There is another version of this account, less reliable yet more popular because it is pungent and also because the historian Sima Qian adapted it in his biography of Confucius. The author of this version extracted certain elements from the earlier record in the *Zuo Commentary*—the Lai people, the valley of Xiagu, an imagined celebration, Confucius' presence—to create an ambiguous and lurid tale. First, the soldiers from the opposing side together with the Lai people advance toward the Duke of Lu "to the rolling of drums." Confucius commands his military officers to push them back, and he tells the Duke of Qi that non-Chinese have no business in a place where the Chinese are trying "to be civil to each other." The ruler of Qi apologizes and berates his own advisors for "leading him toward the vulgar practices of the barbarians." Later that day, the Qi officers order singers and dancers to perform in front of the tent where the Duke of Lu is staying. Confucius orders that the entertainers be executed because "they have made a mockery of their own ruler." This source says, "Their heads and feet went out of separate gates." In other words, the singers and dancers were decapitated.

Sima Qian in his turn added more details to this version. His account is racier but also clearer. According to him, the entertainers wore feathers, and they carried "long and short swords" and "spears and shields." They raised a ruckus, and they were not Chinese. They also performed a second time, repeating their first show after the ruler of Qi had directed them to stop—which Confucius interpreted as an act of defiance and proof that they were troublemakers.

Probably neither this version nor the earlier one that Sima Qian chose to elaborate on is authentic. Unlike the account in the *Zuo Commentary*, which is essentially a record of the speeches Confucius made in Xiagu, these two stories make use of too many narrative devices. The *Zuo Commentary* reflects the history writing of 400 BC, while the two later accounts reflect that of 100 BC. Still, all three agree that in 500 BC Confucius was tough and decisive—a self-assured man who did most of the thinking and talking at the negotiation in Xiagu. The *Zuo Commentary* says that Confucius went to the meeting as the ruler's "chief counselor (*xiang*)." Only heads of the hereditary families could hold such a position; therefore, it must have been that, in the aftermath of Yang Hu's tenure, the Three Families were still in a debilitated state, and so Confucius stood in as their temporary replacement.

Confucius must have felt satisfied with his performance at Xiagu. The Qi were boorish at first but soon acceded to his demands. Their ruler showed respect for Confucius' knowledge of the rites and of correct conduct. These things must have emboldened Confucius to think that he could strike a mortal blow at the Three Families before they had a chance to collect themselves. In fact, in the summer of 500, soon after the Qi fulfilled their promise to return three districts to Lu, another retainer, this time in the Shusun family, revolted. He was also driven out at the end, not by force but by trickery. The man who masterminded the ruse was an official in charge of artisans. Some scholars believed that he was a disciple of Confucius.

This takes us to 498 BC. By then, Confucius seems to have given up altogether the idea of using the retainers to get rid of the hereditary families. Instead, he and his disciples were steering the families toward self-ruin. When things got out of control that year—after the men of Bi rose up and took their arms to the streets of the capital—Confucius reversed course because he could see that Lu was heading toward chaos. However, his rescue effort neither won him any merit nor helped to dispel the suspicion the Three Families must have had about him. This is obvious from Jihuanzi's behavior toward Confucius in 497: by not giving him a share of the sacrificial meat, the head of the Jisun family—and chief counselor of the state—either was signaling Confucius that he was ready to push him out because he did not trust him, or, worse, that he already considered Confucius inconsequential. As for the singing girls from Qi, it could be a coincidence that they showed up in Lu in the same year Confucius left home. Qi and Lu had had a history of goading each other into war or folly, and so the two events need not have been related.

The people of Qi might have harbored a grudge against Confucius because he managed to embarrass their ruler and help his own to collect what he wanted from them in 500 BC. But if, by 497, Confucius was already irrelevant in Lu politics, why should they send girls on horseback to taunt him? Or did Confucius use the "minor transgression" the girls occasioned as one more reason for him to get out?

When Confucius left for his travels in 497, he was relatively free from family obligations and entanglements. His parents had been in their graves for decades. His marriage had ended. His son was already thirty-five years old, and his daughter could not have been much younger. Had his children been at a tenderer age or either of his parents still living, Confucius might have considered staying where he was. Some later sources tell us that the chief counselor, Jihuanzi, expressed regret that Confucius was leaving. If he did, he must have lied.

CHAPTER TWO

Families and Politics

IF JIHUANZI CONSIDERED CONFUCIUS EXPENDABLE, CONFUCIUS thought of Jihuanzi as the one who would prove to be the last of the hereditary counselors in Lu. Others remembered him as having said, "If it is the hereditary counselors who are in charge, it will be unlikely for them to hold on to their authority for more than five generations." Since Jihuanzi was fifth in the line of hereditary counselors in Lu, it seemed that Confucius was divulging a secret known only to those who were attuned to the fates. Yet Confucius never considered himself a prophet, because he believed that he was not born with knowledge. Those who were born with knowledge were few and far between—"at the top of the heap," according to him and almost everyone else who lived in early China. They could "make a shrewd guess about how much is stashed away in a storehouse" and foretell with accuracy future events and tomorrow's weather, and Confucius was not one of them.

The way Confucius talked about the hereditary counselors was, therefore, not a prediction but part of a large observation he made about kings, regional rulers, and pretenders to power. It was not foreknowledge but knowledge he deduced from what he had learned about the history of the Zhou dynasty and particularly the history of Lu. He said in the *Analects:*

> When the moral way prevails in the world, it is the emperor who orchestrates rites and music, and punitive expeditions. When the moral way does not prevail in the world, it is the regional rulers who orchestrate rites and music, and punitive expeditions.

It is in this context that he maintained:

> If, indeed, the regional rulers are in charge, it would be unlikely for them to hold on to their authority for ten generations. If it is the hereditary counselors who are in charge, it would be unlikely for them to hold on to their authority for more than five generations. If it is the family retainers who are in charge, it would be unlikely for them to hold on to their authority for more than three generations.

Early Zhou history can attest to the accuracy of Confucius' first statement. It was King Wen who initiated the overthrow of the Shang dynasty and King Wu who finished his father's work in 1045 BC, when he defeated the Shang army in the east and the last Shang king set himself on fire in a ritual suicide. But a sudden illness took King Wu's life, just two years after he returned home in the west and established his capital by the River Wei. The reigns of King Wu's son and grandson have been described as a time of "peace and stability." "For more than forty years," the early history says, "there was no need to carry out punishments."

This "peace and stability" was not incidental but hard-earned, as the records show, for these early rulers also had their share of trouble. When King Wu died, his heir apparent, King Cheng, was only a child, too tender and inexperienced to consolidate an empire that was won swiftly and unexpectedly—in fact, on the basis of a single victory. Even the attribution to divine agency—that "Heaven sent down destruction on the Shang" and "gave the Zhou authority to rule"—did not offer hard assurance that the Zhou could hold on to Heaven's mandate. At this critical moment, the Duke of Zhou, a brother of the deceased king, stepped in, appointing himself the court regent and a "screen" for his young nephew. Two siblings of the Duke of Zhou resented what he had done, and so they staged a revolt in the east that led to a protracted war which nearly ended the dynasty before it had a chance. When the war was over, the Duke of Zhou had one brother executed and the other banished. And to defend the dynasty against further insurrections in the east, he mapped out a strategy. He dispatched relatives of the king to tactical locations in that region, asking them to establish permanent settlements there with people they would bring from their home areas in the west. He then used the regional settlements to outline a relationship between the regional rulers and the Zhou king. The plan the Duke of Zhou designed for the prince, the *fengjian* enfeoffment system, would become the foundation of Zhou rule and the dynasty's crowning achievement.

The *fengjian* enfeoffment system was in full swing in the early years of the Zhou. Through the agency of the regional governors, King Cheng and his heir were able to oversee the consolidation of the Zhou from their western capital and to further expand the size and influence of their empire without overspending the energy of a still-youthful dynasty. These two kings always coordinated their commands with the rituals at court. Whenever they appointed a member of the imperial family to create a colony elsewhere, they would hold an audience in the capital, and the ceremony that followed would include a feast and libation, and a display of archery. Court scribes would be present on such occasions. They would prepare a record of the royal command and of the words exchanged, and they would include a description of the rituals. At the conclusion of the investiture, the conferee would depart with a copy of the record, and often he would have it inscribed on a bronze vessel to commemorate this important moment in his life. Bronze inscriptions from the first sixty years of the Zhou dynasty seem to corroborate the traditional view that this period was one of "peace and tranquility"; they also show the kings to be in full command of court rituals and military decisions. It made sense, therefore, that Confucius should put the two together. He tells us: When there is just rule, it is the king who is in charge of rites, music, and war.

Things began to fall apart by the early tenth century BC. One king let his ambition overreach the potential of the Zhou army, and so in one devastating campaign against a non-Chinese group in the the south, the entire division of his western army was wiped out. His successors managed to rebuild the royal army, but the confidence and pluck that characterized the early Zhou were greatly reduced. This meant also that the non-Chinese tribes were no longer afraid to test the strength of the Zhou whenever they saw fit.

Just as the threat of foreign aggression intensified, the regional rulers in the eastern territories began to have ideas of their own about how much autonomy they should insist on and how much they should give up. Most of these rulers were related to the Zhou king by blood or through marriage, but time and physical distance had stretched the tie too thin. Realizing that feudal allegiance was rapidly becoming tenuous, King Mu, from the latter part of the tenth century BC, introduced institutional reforms that were meant to transform the nature of government, from one that relied solely on family by way of hereditary succession to one that was willing to make appointments outside of the hereditary system and to employ men and women with knowledge and administrative skills. The reforms had lasting effects on the Zhou court in the west and the feudal kingdoms in the east. Centuries later, the Duke of Lu would offer Confucius the position of minister of crime in his government because Confucius had demonstrated through his performance in a string of lower-level posts that he would be able to handle the job well. Confucius did not inherit the office from his father.

Chinese institutional history took a different turn under King Mu, but the king's initiatives did not help the dynasty to find relief from domestic discord or foreign pressures; nor did they help the Zhou kings to regain their former prestige. Even the aristocratic families living in the vicinity of the capital seemed reluctant to lend the king their support, so the king would entice them with gifts of land for their services and for their lukewarm show of loyalty. Since the rulers of that time did not exact taxes from their subjects, the royal domain was their only source of income. And as the king's property shrank, his financial problems also became more acute.

Traditional sources and bronze inscriptions tell us that by the ninth century BC "some of the many lords"—the ruler from Confucius' neighboring state of Qi, for instance—were ready to challenge the authority of their sovereign in war, especially when he tried to interfere with their internal affairs. But to settle questions of succession or any crisis within a feudal kingdom would have been the prerogative of the Zhou king if he had possessed the respect and dignity inherent in the idea of kingship. From the writings of the early historians, it appears that none of the kings of this period had any authority or moral sway and that none could even manage the perception that he did. They all had stooped to the level of the feudal lords; and by behaving like their vassals, they had become human and, therefore, disposable.

The execution of a king did take place in 771 BC. This man was hunted down and slaughtered like an animal at the foot of a mountain after his enemies at court had invited "a hostile people" from the northwest to march into his capital and plunder his palace. Almost as soon as this king died, the regional rulers helped the heir apparent to relocate his court to the eastern capital in the Central Plain. The new monarch was a diminished figure—he was far away from home, without an army or a domain. The regional rulers would eventually give him what he needed to be a king, but his army and domain and his political purchase were minuscule compared with those of his predecessors. The regional rulers would also tell him that he should give more attention to his ritual duties and play the symbolic role of a king. The reign of King Ping began the Eastern Zhou, the second half of the Zhou dynasty.

In his history of this period, Sima Qian writes about the shift in power:

During the time of King Ping, the imperial house grew frail. With the regional rulers acting on the principle that the strong could swallow up the weak, the states of Qi, Chu, Qin, and Jin emerged as the new powers. The political authority of the empire also fell into the hands of the most senior amongst them.

Confucius would characterize this period as a time when the moral way did not prevail because it was the regional rulers who orchestrated rites and music, and military campaigns. Under such circumstances, he said, "it would be unlikely for them to hold on to their power for ten generations." Why ten generations? Because their tenure was not good enough to last. And why not? Because, in their conduct, they tried to elevate themselves above the Zhou king, thus giving no heed to the underlying principles of the enfeoffment system. Confucius stood by his assertion against all regional rulers who attempted such a transgression, including those from his own state of Lu.

Confucius had always been proud of the origin of Lu: that the Duke of Zhou, son of King Wen and half brother of King Wu, sent his own son to the northeast to establish a settlement which would become the state of Lu; and that the people of Lu could claim this man as their common ancestor. The *Analects* quotes Confucius as having said, "I must be slipping! It has been so long since I dreamt of the Duke of Zhou." For centuries scholars tried to understand why Confucius had told this about himself. Was he becoming more aware of the onset of old age? Was he worried about losing his mental acuity, even his ability to dream, or just the presence of the Duke of Zhou in his dreams? Or was he referring to his moral condition? And if so, why would the absence of the Duke of Zhou from his dreams signal a moral decline? What could be the nature of their affinity?

Though they were separated by nearly five hundred and fifty years, both men were counselors. But the Duke of Zhou was a relation of kings, whereas Confucius was a salaried official with no family history about which to boast. Nevertheless, the two men shared a similar vision of government. We have no hard evidence of how Confucius felt about the political framework the Duke of Zhou had sketched out for his prince and for the generations to come, but he said: "The Zhou represents the apogee of cultural achievements, having had before it the examples of the two previous dynasties. I am for the Zhou." This statement had to be an endorsement, if not clearly of the enfeoffment system then certainly of the moral assumptions and the cultural support of rites and music, which were the working and living parts of this political vision.

Both men also lived with an anxiety that was constant but energizing—anxiety about not having done enough because so much of life and life's future could not be known. They believed that this worry, combined with hard work, was what separated the superior from the ordinary, the true from the mediocre. When speaking of the superior and the true, the Duke of Zhou had in mind the counselors who made kings great—advisors who helped his father and brother "to subdue and put in order the empire that had once belonged to the Shang kings." These men distinguished themselves by "never ceasing to worry" that the Zhou kings and the Zhou people could lose Heaven's grace if they flagged or strayed.

But from the Duke of Zhou, Heaven demanded even more, forcing him to confront the question of what to do with his two brothers, who, out of sibling jealousy, dragged the whole country into a divisive war. The decision to have both brothers severely punished could not have been easy for the Duke of Zhou, yet he pronounced the sentences swiftly and firmly. Historians and philosophers over the ages tried to give his action an explanation. They said that the Duke of Zhou did what he had to do in order to save the empire from destruction; that his action was of a practical kind.

But what about the Duke of Zhou? What was he thinking at the time? How did he weigh his love for his family against the interests of the empire? Were his actions always of a practical kind? The advice he gave his son just before the latter set off for his colony in the east offers some clues:

A person in a ruling position does not forget his nearest and dearest. He also does not give his officials occasion to complain because he has failed to employ their skills. Unless there are good reasons, he does not abandon old friends and relations. He does not ask for perfection in anyone.

Here, the Duke of Zhou appears to be fully aware of the delicate nature of human relationships. He tells his son to be considerate of those who are "nearest and dearest" to him and those who work with him in politics; and he asks his son to be mindful of matters of greater importance so as not to let things of lesser importance spoil those relationships that should have constancy. The Duke of Zhou offered guidelines but no theory, not here and not in any of his official speeches and proclamations. He had no time to formulate a stance— his worries were those of a person facing a crisis or a problem that needed immediate attention, not of someone who had time to brood. Yet the words that were attributed to him in the early records could easily add up to a vision of political relationships and social arrange- ment that, for the sensitive mind, carried a deep moral resonance.

The Duke of Zhou retired to the east after King Cheng came of age. Sources from the early Zhou were quiet about his life after he withdrew from politics. They were also reluctant about invoking his name with the other heroes from the same time until Confucius came along and created a Duke of Zhou more powerful than he appeared in the official records. The Duke of Zhou was the coun- selor Confucius hoped to emulate and the good specter that visited him in his dreams. He embodied strengths that suited Confucius' vision of the moral. Other counselors also contributed to this vision, but the Duke of Zhou was the First Counselor.

Compared with the Duke of Zhou, most of the hereditary coun- selors from the Spring and Autumn period seemed selfish and slight. The very creation of the Three Families—the pool of hereditary counselors in Lu—was fraught with ill feeling and bad conscience. About a hundred years before Confucius' birth, three brothers of the dying ruler consented to an arrangement only after a series of violent measures had failed to settle the question of whether a son or a brother should succeed the duke. The youngest brother wanted the position for himself and had the support of the middle brother. The eldest and most imposing of the three insisted that only a son of the ruler could be the legitimate heir. He had his middle brother seized and offered him a deal: if his brother was willing to commit suicide, then he would make sure that this man "would always have descendents in Lu." The middle brother had no choice but to accept, and this was how the first of the three hereditary families, the Shusuns, came into being.

The youngest brother was more tenacious. He swiftly eliminated the two rulers his eldest brother had helped to install, and when he realized that he had gone too far—that the extent of his crime had made it impossible for him to escape legal judgment—he hanged himself. After he died, the state of Lu created a second family, the Mengsuns, guaranteeing his descendents hereditary status and emolument. The eldest brother, after he had won this power struggle, also instituted a hereditary slot for his family, the Jisuns.

Descendents of the three brothers did not show much improvement in their behavior. They also let their indiscretions play out in public and in politics. For example, a serious transgression happened in 562, eleven years before Confucius was born, when the head of the Jisuns decided to appropriate the state army for the private use of the Three Families. Each took a third of the troops, which before this time had always been at the disposal of the regional ruler, and reconfigured them in combination with the soldiers already in their service, men they had conscripted from their land. The families also divided the weapons and the chariots, leaving the ruler of Lu completely dependent on his hereditary counselors for any kind of military support. The reorganization of the army had other ramifications. For instance, the heads of the families could decide for themselves the size of their troops, whether to enforce compulsory service, and, if there was no obligatory service, what incentives to introduce in order to entice the men to enlist. At least half of the soldiers in the armies of the Shusuns and Mengsuns were conscripts. But men living within the domain of the Jisuns had a choice: they could contribute weapons and military service or they could pay a hefty levy instead.

These developments suggest that the enfeoffment system around

Confucius' time was coming apart and that Zhou society was edging toward a different political arrangement. Confucius knew the details well. He said of the Jisuns, who were an instrument of change during his time: "Their wealth is greater than that of [the descendents of] the Duke of Zhou"; "They have eight rows of eight dancers, [sixty-four in all,] to perform in their courtyard. If this can be tolerated, what cannot be tolerated?" The descendents of the Duke of Zhou were rulers of Lu. They had the rank of a duke, and when the son of the Duke of Zhou was first enfeoffed, he instituted the state income at a tax rate of one-tenth of the annual land production in Lu. The Jisuns were in the service of the duke, but by Confucius' time they had already forced their way into his office, letting themselves have a free hand in those powers and privileges that belonged to the duke, the levying of taxes being one example. Confucius' remark in the *Analects* suggests that the Jisuns were collecting more taxes than the rulers of Lu in the past had done and were keeping most of what was collected for themselves. Yet what worried Confucius was not so much the amount the Jisuns had accumulated as the principles they had violated for want of restraint. The same can be said regarding the size of the troupe that performed in their courtyard. He might have tolerated the idea of an extravagant display, but not if the display bore "no relation to the Three Families"—not if it did not fit the families' rank and did not reflect the families' worth.

Appropriating the state army was even a greater offence. No precedent could have supported such an action. The Duke of Lu certainly did not want it, and the hereditary families did not go to any higher authority to ask for permission. According to the *Zuo Commentary,* the head of the Jisuns, a brash youth called Jiwuzi, "cooked up" the idea and then broached it to Shusun Bao, who was the head of the Shusuns and also the chief counselor at court. Shusun Bao was reluctant at first, but since Jiwuzi "would not relent," he finally gave his consent so long as the Three Families were willing to swear "a terrible oath" together to discourage one another from breaking it.

Twenty-five years later, the same Jiwuzi would defy the oath and reorganize the armies once more so that the Jisuns could have a larger share. No domestic crisis or drastic shift in foreign relations could have warranted this move. Jiwuzi simply wanted more and took steps to get what he wanted. This time he asked all three families to pool together their armies and then divide the sum in half. The Jisuns wanted to take one of the halves and let the Shusuns and the Mengsuns share the remaining half. Now all the families adopted the policy the Jisuns had introduced earlier, allowing the people on their land to choose between military corvée and payment in kind. They then presented a portion of the grain tax they had collected to their ruler "as tributes."

Jiwuzi might have instituted changes along the way when he simplified the relationship his family had with the men they governed, and we know that similar developments were taking place in other feudal states at the time. But whatever new ideas he introduced, they occurred by chance. Jiwuzi did not have a vision, and he did not have the interests of his state in mind. He looked after himself and his family, and he was arbitrary. Some people might have taken a generous view of a counselor like Jiwuzi because his measures mattered in the development of state institutions. Not Confucius, though, not if he thought the counselor fraudulent and his ambitions lacking in grandeur.

Jiwuzi's older counterpart, Shusun Bao, was another kind of counselor. This man was perceptive and shrewd, and responsible in his job. At the same time, however, he was inclined to accept what he thought was inevitable even when he knew that it would be unwise to do so. Thus while he was contemptuous of Jiwuzi when Jiwuzi was still a youth and was deeply suspicious of this man's motives, he did not do much to dissuade him from his underhanded pursuits even though he was Jiwuzi's senior and was more powerful at the time. Shusun Bao simply bowed to the fact that this swaggerer one day would "dominate the politics of Lu" but would be "hopeless" at helping Lu to pull itself together.

In the *Analects,* Confucius never mentions Shusun Bao, yet one can well imagine that it was men like him who gave Confucius the most to brood about when he was formulating his own ideas regarding virtue, integrity, and the human character. Unlike Jiwuzi, who was boorish and obvious, Shusun Bao had gravity and foresight but was either not strong enough to confront the bigger forces—of history and of the irrational—or was unwilling to do so. He knowingly gave in to these forces. The *Zuo* writers were fascinated by Shusun Bao; they tell us several stories about him, the longest of which is both horrible and hypnotic, with a coda—written years after the fact and attributed to Confucius—on what should be considered proper political conduct.

It is rare to find remarks by Confucius in the *Zuo Commentary*, and when they do appear, the messages are often anomalous—always fresh, not what one would expect. So even though someone else might have inserted this commentary in Confucius' name, it remains telling that a writer of the fifth or fourth century BC should believe that aspects of Shusun Bao's life must have been of interest to Confucius even though when Shusun Bao died Confucius was only thirteen.

The story of Shusun Bao begins sometime around 575, before he became a chief counselor in Lu and the head of his clan. His elder brother was a miscreant who got involved with the ruler's mother and through her influence tried to overthrow the Jisuns and the Mengsuns. He failed, so he fled to the state of Qi. Shusun Bao followed him, in order to stay clear of the two families who might want to take revenge on him on account of the troubles the brother had caused. On his way to Qi, he spent a night with a woman in a border town. The child from this tryst would become the object of his obsession, which would send Shusun Bao to his own hell. But this would take time to unravel.

Soon after Shusun Bao arrived in Qi, he had a dream. In it, "Heaven was pressing down on him," and just as he was struggling to get out from underneath, he saw a man "dark in countenance with stooped shoulders, deep-set eyes, and mouth like a pig snout." Then: "He called out, 'Niu! Help me!' And this man saved him from his death." Shusun Bao would remember this dream. In Qi, he married a woman and had two children by her. A few years would go by. One day, the Duke of Lu summoned him home. The duke offered Shusun Bao the position of chief counselor, making him also the head of his lineage. Not long after, a woman showed up at his residence and presented him with a son who, though still a child, looked "just like the man in his dream" and answered to the name Niu.

Shusun Bao made Niu first his personal attendant and then manager of his household. He indulged this child, and as his own health declined, Niu began to manipulate Shusun's relationship with his two legitimate sons. He fabricated the perception that these two sons had betrayed their father, and so Shusun had one killed and the other exiled. By the time he became aware of Niu's deception, it was already too late. He was too ill to leave the room in which he was now confined by Niu, and Niu would send back the food and water that were brought to him. After three days of deprivation, the counselor of Lu died alone in his mansion. Before he died, he summoned his closest advisor, Du Xie, begging him to have Niu "put to the sword." Du replied: "You bade Niu to come and he did. So why get rid of him now?"

With Shusun Bao gone, Niu had the run of his clan. To deter outsiders—especially the other two families—from interfering in his affairs, he bribed some and played upon the anxieties of others and was so skillful at what he did that when Shusun Bao's legitimate son came home from exile to assume the position of clan chief, Niu persuaded "the people living in the capital city" of Lu "to hem him in" while an assassin "shot him with an arrow through the eye and killed him." A son by a concubine was put in his place. Niu thought that this young man, called Zhaozi, would be easy to manipulate. But the *Zuo* writers say:

> As soon as Zhaozi took on his duties, he assembled the members of his family and said to them, "Niu has brought disaster to the Shusuns, creating a rupture in the normal order of things by having the son of a principal wife murdered and establishing the son of a concubine in his place. He has further carved up our estate [to buy the influence of those who could be of use to him]. Now he thinks that he can wriggle out of his responsibilities, but no crime could be more heinous than his. We must kill him right away!"

Niu, we are told, "fearing for his life, fled for Qi." The grandsons of Shusun Bao caught up with him just beyond the border of Lu. They cut him down and "tossed his head into the brambles covering the Ningfeng Plain." Of this conclusion, Confucius remarked:

> It was terribly difficult for Zhaozi of Shusun not to repay [what Niu had done for him]. [The ancient counselor] Zhou Ren once said, "Men in government should not reward on account of private favors or punish on account of personal grudges."

It is significant that the final chapter of the life and death of Shusun Bao should end with Zhaozi—his son by a concubine, and an unlawful heir whose rise to power was the culmination of a series of wrongful deeds others had committed before him. More remarkable is Confucius' judgment of this man. Zhaozi was extraordinary, Confucius thought: he exercised his political purchase with only the public good in mind, which was nearly impossible to do because he owed everything—his position and his power—to private grants of favor and to men with only selfish interests. By praising Zhaozi, Confucius was not trying to overlook the impropriety of those practices that brought this man to prominence. Rather, he found something admirable in Zhaozi's character amid the hurly-burly of Spring and Autumn politics.

In Confucius' view, what Zhaozi did was in accord with *li*, or dictates of decorum—rules that are not fixed like laws but expressed as a rightness whose authority lies in the integrity of one's action. Shusun Bao's advisor Du Xie was another person who stood out in the history of this period because of his knowledge and practice of *li*. After Shusun's death, he insisted that his lord be given the burial of a chief counselor and his casket be carried in the "grand carriage" the Zhou king had once given to him. His proposal ran into opposition from the chief counselor, Jiwuzi, the restive youth who had finally grown up to take charge of the government of Lu as Shusun Bao had long ago predicted he would. Jiwuzi had never received a "grand carriage" from the king, so he worried that such a funeral arrangement might elevate Shusun Bao above him even though Shusun Bao was dead. He said that since the old counselor never rode in the grand carriage when he was alive, there was no reason that he should be carried in one to his grave. To this Du Xie replied:

> My lord, on behalf of our ruler, went to the Zhou court to pay respect to the king. The king, having been impressed with his conduct, rewarded him with a grand carriage to honor his ancestors. As soon as my lord came home, he handed over the gift to our ruler, who, of course, did not dare to disobey the command of the king and so returned it to my lord. At the time, our ruler asked his three principal counselors to write down everything that had transpired: You, sir, being in charge of household and land registration, recorded the names and titles of all those involved; my lord, being in charge of military affairs, recorded a detailed description of the carriage; Mengsun, being in charge of public works, recorded the achievements that merited this award. Now that my lord is dead, not to use this carriage for his burial is to disregard what the king has decreed. The documents of these transactions are kept in the state archives. Not to respect the documents is to abrogate the offices of the three counselors. We all assume that we have to obey the orders of our sovereign. But [in deference to the ruler of Lu] my lord dared not do so when he was alive, and if he is not allowed to use the carriage when he is dead, what other chance will he have?

Du Xie's argument was unbeatable. He demonstrated that, up to now, everyone who had a part in the matter of the grand carriage had behaved properly. The honor the Zhou king bestowed on Shusun Bao was so considerable that Shusun Bao did not think it was appropriate to flaunt it in front of his own ruler. And his ruler, having realized the delicate nature of this gift, had its ritual significance documented so as not to offend his superior. All this put pressure on the chief counselor to behave himself. So Jiwuzi acquiesced, and Shusun Bao went to his grave with dignity and splendor.

Even though this story ended well for the protagonist—his death was avenged and the state of Lu gave him a burial befitting his rank and reputation—it was not optimistic about the world as it was. Du Xie "left Lu as soon as the funeral was over." He had done all he could for his lord, using his knowledge of the Zhou political structure and of those rules that still applied. Now he had to look after himself in case the chief counselor planned to retaliate.

Du Xie was a smart man. He probably could have survived the violence and treacheries of Spring and Autumn politics if he had stayed. His skill in making grand speeches about things that mattered probably could have let him see others through their crises, but he felt he had done it long enough and was tired. So he fled.

Around the same time, in the state of Zheng, an eminent man by the name of Zichan was approached by the political governors after their ruler was killed by a cousin in a family brawl "on the street where the lamb vendors had their stalls." They asked Zichan to help them pull through this difficult period. "Do you think you are in my league?" he quipped. "Who knows how to put an end to the calamities in our country? If only those who are in charge could be strong and just, our troubles would not have started in the first place. For the time being, I am going to tend to my business." Only after the most prominent of the hereditary counselors offered Zichan his own job did Zichan begin to give the idea some thought. But he remained skeptical, telling the counselors, "The hereditary families are large. Many people need favors, so nothing can get accomplished." When he was assured that he "was free to govern as he liked," he decided to give it a try.

In the *Analects*, Confucius says of Zichan of Zheng: "He was respectful in the manner in which he conducted himself, reverent in the service of his lord, generous in caring for the common people, and just in employing them for work." People who knew Zichan thought that he understood propriety (*li*) and even under duress would not compromise any of its principles. Yet this same Zichan would bribe the powerful to get things done, saying, "It is hard not to be covetous, but once a person's desires are satisfied, then he is ready to get to work and get things done." During the Spring and Autumn period, there was probably no finer counselor than Zichan.

He had subtlety and flexibility, and was a genius at adapting to the situation at hand, "without swerving from the track." Yet words such as "devotion" and "scrupulosity" are not fit to describe him.

In the sixth century BC, there was no one in Lu who tried to do what Zichan had done for Zheng, and there was no one from the hereditary families who cared enough about Lu to invite an outside talent—someone with skills and learning—to help them steer their country away from disasters. Confucius' disciple Zigong, who was interested in "grading people," once asked Confucius what sort of men he "would consider as good enough to be in government." Zigong was hoping that if given a standard, he could better assess the political figures in Lu, who were his contemporaries, and he could weigh them against those with true qualifications. Confucius replied that men who are fit to be in government "have self-awareness in the way they conduct themselves and, when sent abroad, will not bring disgrace to the mission their ruler has entrusted to them." The conversation continued:

> "What would be the next best?"
>
> "Those who are good sons in the eyes of their kin and fine young men in the eyes of their neighbors and villagers."
>
> "And the level below that?"
>
> "Men who insist on keeping their word and seeing their action to the end. They have stones for brains and are inferior indeed. But I suppose you can say that they come next."
>
> "And what about those who are in public life right now?"
>
> "Unh? They are puny vessels, men with hardly any capacity. They don't even count!"

From this conversation, we learn along with Zigong what Confucius looked for in a counselor and why he would admire someone like Zichan and think so little of men who were enslaved to harsh and self-imposed principles. (He regarded the latter as having no more imagination than "stones.") His evaluation of the people who were running his government also reflects the political situation in

Lu during his lifetime. After Shusun Bao's death in 538, the feuding among the families became more trivial and more vicious. Jiwuzi and his heir died within a few years of each other, so a grandson, named Jipingzi, succeeded Jiwuzi as head of the Jisun family and the chief counselor of Lu in 530.

From the beginning, this counselor's behavior portended trouble. Just in the first year of his tenure, he managed to offend scores of people. Insiders found him unruly and intrusive. Outsiders did not trust him. One retainer even tried to overthrow him. Yet such warnings only encouraged him to take greater liberties with his power. Under his influence, crimes and misdemeanors would become rampant, and so would divisive feelings. By 517, they peaked. That year, the twenty-fifth year of Duke Zhao, a series of petty incidents would lead to consequences so damaging that the state of Lu could never again perceive herself in the same light as she had in the past and neither could others.

The first of these incidents involved a young widow in the Jisun clan. Enamored with a cook and not wanting to be found out, she accused her brother-in-law, who was also the guardian of her household and the chief counselor's uncle, of "trying to force himself on her." To give weight to her words, she had one of her maids beat her around the body and mark her with contusions. She also named another relative and her husband's retainer as being in collusion with her brother-in-law. Without first looking into the matter to see if this woman was telling the truth, the chief counselor, Jipingzi, had the retainer apprehended and swiftly executed. His uncle considered Jipingzi's action abominable. He said, "To have the retainer killed was the same as to have me killed," and he vowed revenge.

That same year, 517, the Jisuns and another large family, the Hous, came to blows over a cockfight. The Jisuns "fitted their birds with metal plates"; the Hous "fitted theirs with metal claws." When the Hous won, Jipingzi was furious and began to build a house for himself on their property. Jipingzi incurred the anger of a third family, the Zangs, when he gave shelter to a fugitive member of that household. Finally, he humiliated his own ruler, Duke Zhao of Lu. On the day of a state ceremony to honor Duke Zhao's father, Jipingzi conducted a similar sacrifice for his ancestors; and since he was more powerful than his ruler, "a crowd gathered at the Jisuns' to perform the *wan* dance" while only two dancers showed up at the duke's courtyard. Thus when Jipingzi's uncle suggested an insurrection and had his plan leaked to Duke Zhao, Duke Zhao was leaning toward endorsing it.

Duke Zhao thought that he might use the breakup of the Jisuns to assert his authority as the ruler of Lu. The Hous and the Zangs also threw in their support. The duke's advisor, Zijiazi, however, had a different view. He told Duke Zhao that he did not trust the men who were behind the plot, because they all held private grudges against the chief counselor, Jipingzi. He said:

> These small-minded men all rely on your luck to win this round. If you fail, it's your reputation that will suffer. So don't do it. The people of Lu have lost confidence in their rulers for generations, and there is no assurance that things will suddenly turn around for you.

Duke Zhao of Lu did not heed Zijiazi's advice. He charged into Jipingzi's palace with his own military officers, killing Jipingzi's brother, who was posted at the gate. Jipingzi climbed to the top of the terrace and begged Duke Zhao to reconsider. He asked his ruler "to conduct a formal inquiry" into his crime before "dispatching men with shields and spears to come after him," and to let him wait for the results of the investigation at a nearby river. Duke Zhao denied his request. Jipingzi then tried another idea on him. This time, he asked that he be held a prisoner in his hometown of Bi. Again his ruler said no. After Duke Zhao refused a third request, to let Jipingzi have safe passage out of Lu with an entourage of five carriages of men, the duke's advisor, Zijiazi, spoke. "Grant him his wish!" he said, and continued:

> He has been making political decisions around here for a long time. The poor rely mainly on him for sustenance, so he has a large

following. There is no way of knowing whether there is mischief-making after dark. So don't let the anger of the crowd accumulate. Once it has built up, and if you don't do anything to alleviate it, then it's going to intensify. With growing rage and dissatisfaction, people are bound to harbor seditious thoughts. Such thoughts will find sympathy and support from those who are seeking to create trouble. By then you will regret it.

Thus, in the voice of a sensible counselor, like that of the Duke of Zhou before him and of Confucius after him, Zijiazi was imploring his ruler to be mindful of his situation—of the potential "mischief-making after dark"—and to make a deal while he was still ahead. Again Duke Zhao did not listen to him. Meanwhile, members of the Shusun family were watching these events from the sidelines. After some discussion, they concluded that it would probably be to their advantage to have the Jisuns around rather than not, regardless of how they felt about Jipingzi. They agreed that "without the Jisuns there will not be the Shusuns," and so they sent reinforcements to Jipingzi's home, "to drive away" their ruler's "personal guards." It did not take long for the Mengsuns to join forces with the Shusuns and the Jisuns, leaving Duke Zhao all alone in his hope for redress and restoration. After his men were routed and when Duke Zhao was most desperate, his advisor Zijiazi pointed to one last way out:

> [Tell Jipingzi that] other people pressured you to act like this. Let them leave the country and take the blame. You, though, should remain in Lu. And Jipingzi will continue to serve you. He won't dare not to amend his ways.

Duke Zhao, however, "could not put up with the humiliation," and so he went to his family grave site, "bid farewell to his ancestors," and crossed the border to the state of Qi. Thus, for personal reasons, the ruler of Lu gave up his country, leaving the spirits of his ancestors to chance and his descendents in limbo. But the story of this man does not end until seven years later.

Zijiazi followed Duke Zhao to Qi and remained his protector. He would guard not just his ruler but all that was left of Lu's pride and sovereignty. When the Duke of Qi offered Duke Zhao a thousand hamlets consisting of twenty-five thousand households, Zijiazi asked his ruler to decline the gift, saying:

> Heaven does not bestow its emolument twice. If it wishes to be generous, it will not go beyond what was already given to the descendents of the Duke of Zhou. Lu should be enough! If you lose Lu because you have accepted the role of a subject with a thousand *she* of households in his possession, then who will try to get you reinstated as a ruler?

In the meantime, other followers of Duke Zhao wanted a formal covenant, "to affirm their purpose" and "to sort out the guilty from the guiltless." They also wanted to make a pledge that they would "not have anything to do with the present government in Lu." They asked Zijiazi to take part. Zijiazi refused, saying,

> I am not clever and cannot share with you your views. I feel that we are all guilty in what has happened [in the past few months]. Moreover, I might like to negotiate with those who are running things back home, in order to relieve our ruler from his present predicament.

Inside the government of Lu, the head of the Shusun family had the same idea. This man was Zhaozi, the person Confucius once praised as having acted justly and correctly by refusing to compromise the public interest on account of his private debts of obligation. Seeing that Jipingzi had shown signs of contrition, Zhaozi urged him to invite their ruler back and to put right all that was wrong. He also offered to go to the duke on Jipingzi's behalf, to discuss the terms of his return. Jipingzi agreed to the plan, but just as Zhaozi completed the negotiation, he changed his mind. In the winter of that year, on the fourth day of the tenth month, Zhaozi "went into seclusion and abstained from food and water." "He prayed to his ancestors, asking them for permission to end his life. By the eleventh day, he was dead."

The ruler of Lu was never allowed home; he spent his last years in a small town looking across the border. His advisor, Zijiazi, also did not return to Lu. After the duke died, the hereditary families established the duke's son as the next ruler. They begged Zijiazi to come back and work with them, but he refused to respond. Instead, he disappeared and is not heard of again in the history of Lu.

Counselors like Zijiazi and Zhaozi seemed to have lived in vain. The men they served commanded neither respect nor trust. Yet often it was because of their presence that others would even attempt any self-reform. Thus when a ruler's words were coarse and contemptible, when they seemed like "muck" as the *Zuo* writers put it, and when his constitution lacked altogether any moral drive, just the sight of him with one or two of his worthy counselors might inspire hope. But, of course, such perception is frail. The truly ignoble will remain ignoble, as Confucius observed. A few decades before Duke Zhao was forced out of Lu, a similar situation arose in the state of Wei.* After the ruler of Wei "had lived twelve hard years in exile," his old acquaintances noticed that nothing had changed about him—there was neither "anxiety in his countenance" nor "generosity about his words." Yet his better counselors stuck by him for years and negotiated terms for him—terms he could not keep. Eventually they would all leave him for faraway places—they would all vanish.

Confucius responded to the times in a somewhat different way. After he left Lu in 497, he would continue to offer his service, for the next fourteen years, to those he knew to be ignoble. He would listen to their talk, which was often no different from muck. In the end, he would come home and teach what he had learned. But never would he give up his belief in what good counselors could achieve even though they might seem to others to have failed.

Wei here refers to the state of Wei in the Spring and Autumn period, which is to be distinguished from the state of Wei later in the Warring States period. Some scholars in the West have romanized the Wei of the Spring and Autumn period as *Wey*.

CHAPTER THREE

Companions

ONFUCIUS WAS NOT ON HIS OWN DURING HIS FOURTEEN years of wandering. A handful of students and admirers followed him. It was rightly so that it should happen this way, for Confucius was on a quest to understand himself and his true calling, though, as with most quests of this sort, he did not plunge into it with that purpose in mind. Without his companions, it would seem, he would not have been as keen and lucid as he was to become in his later years. Without them, he could have been dead on the road, long before his work was coming to completion.

When Confucius took to the road, he was not running away from his past or from anything specific. He was not making a change because he had to. There was also no spiritual conversion in the background. His decision was, on the whole, a practical one. He was not like, say, his younger contemporary Fan Li. This man devoted most of his life to politics, and when he reached as high as he could get, he left that life behind and assumed a new identity somewhere else. Later Fan Li would flourish in trade and become one of the richest men in the Spring and Autumn history.

Fan Li ran away because he suffered from the sting of conscience. When he was in the service of the ruler of Yue, he maneuvered to have a model counselor from a rival state destroyed for no reason other than expediency, and the counselor died a horrible death. Remorse, however, did not paralyze Fan. He would travel to the east and then the northeast; he would apply his political skills to business deals, make millions and give away millions, and be content living the life of an openhanded merchant.

Men like Fan Li did not dawdle. They did not need companions to talk things through or interlocutors to force them to think more clearly. They had heart and they had good minds, and when they misbehaved, they wore their guilt on their sleeves and sallied forth to another stage of life. They did not seek conversations that treated the private self as a subject of reflection.

Confucius was different. He found even the act of engaging in a conversation a subject worthy of cogitation and discussion. He said, "There is something hopeless about a group of men spending time together all day, not touching on the subject of morality in their conversations and wanting only to show off their little cleverness." Confucius himself was fond of talking about rightful and virtuous conduct or morality, but he was discreet about whom to speak to. He pointed out that "not to speak to a person who is capable of absorbing what you say is to let that person go to waste. To speak to a person who is incapable of absorbing what you say is to let your words go to waste." He enjoyed conversing with young people. He thought the young were quicker, pluckier, and more original, and he saw them as having more generous sentiments in every respect, compared with men of his own age. Most of his companions on this journey were about thirty years younger than he was.

Confucius probably spent more time talking with Zaiwo and Zigong than with anyone else. Zaiwo liked to argue. Zigong was articulate and an elegant conversationalist. The *Analects* singles them out as followers of Confucius who "excelled in speech." Although Confucius preferred Zigong's company, he also needed Zaiwo, who was not always agreeable or easy to persuade. In the *Analects*, references to Zaiwo are sparse, but they give sharp impressions of his nature. He sleeps too much, talks back too much; he likes to think through a problem for himself and is smart and perceptive. Confucius was both irritated and anxious about Zaiwo—scolding and fretting like a father—because Zaiwo had bad habits and was careless with words. In one scene, Zaiwo is napping in broad daylight. Having learned this, Confucius lashes out: "Rotten wood is beyond carving, a wall of mud and dung is beyond plastering! What's the point of scolding Zaiwo?"

In another scene, Duke Ai of Lu asks Zaiwo about the material he should use to build an altar to the earth god. Zaiwo replies, "Rulers of the Xia dynasty used pine; Shang rulers used cedar; Zhou rulers used chestnut (*li*), saying that it made the people tremble (*li*)." The conversation took place at a time when Confucius had not yet returned to Lu. Later, when he heard about it, he remarked, "One does not explain away what is already done or try to retrieve what has already gone by. And one does not decry what is past." Like a number of Confucius' comments in the *Analects,* this one does not seem to bear any direct relation to the matter under discussion. Most scholars in the past tried to gloss over the problem, saying that Confucius was merely telling Zaiwo not to invent any "wild theories" about why the Zhou rulers used chestnut to construct their altars.

One nineteenth-century scholar, Liu Baonan, felt that Confucius' response to Zaiwo was much more complicated than it appeared. Relying on the history of this period, he believed that Duke Ai, son of Duke Ding of Lu, was seeking advice from Zaiwo, not just about the construction of an altar that had recently been burned down but also about how to handle the Three Families, and that Zaiwo's reply, "Zhou rulers used chestnut (*li*), saying that it made the people tremble (*li*)," was a coded message, urging Duke Ai to act aggressively. Duke Ai and Zaiwo had to "speak in a secret language," this scholar contended, because they were plotting to overthrow the Three Families. Meanwhile, Confucius either knew about the plan or saw through the pretext of their discussion. He told them that one cannot "retrieve what has gone by," meaning the power the rulers of Lu had once possessed; and that one should not "decry what is past," meaning the action and deeds from the past that had brought the ducal house to its present low.

If this scholar is right, Confucius probably stopped the two from carrying out their plot, but this did not put an end to the intense hatred and distrust Duke Ai and the Three Families had for each other. Nor did it deter either side from seeking ways to get rid of the other. According to the *Zuo Commentary*, in 468, a decade after Confucius' death, Duke Ai appealed to all the feudal lords he could reach to help him destroy the Three Families. He claimed that the families were trying to kill him. Nothing came of his plea, so he fled to a state in the south. The records do not even mention when or where he died.

In Liu's reading, Confucius anticipated that this might happen even though he would not live to see it. He was also perceptive about Duke Ai and about Zaiwo. Duke Ai "was incompetent, so should not take on more then he could handle." Zaiwo was too smart for his own good, but he was not glib or clever and would not, as other scholars have suggested, presume to know something when he did not. He had abundant intelligence but insufficient good judgment. He could be brilliant in debate but would, by the end, pique his opponent and weary his audience because he lacked tact or maybe sensitivity. One example is a conversation he had with Confucius regarding the mourning rituals.

Zaiwo argued that observing three years of mourning after a parent died was too long because it meant that one would have to put aside much else: "If a gentleman neglects the [non-mourning] rites for three years, those rites will be in ruins. [In the same way,] if he does not practice music for three years, music will fall apart." In Zaiwo's view, just as nature renews itself every year, so mourners should resume their work and play, and their other ritual activities, after a year. "A full year is already quite enough," he said:

> "And would you be able to eat rice and wear brocade and be at peace with yourself?" Confucius asked.
> "I would."

"In that case, do it by all means. But a gentleman in mourning finds no relish in tasty food, no pleasure in music, no ease even in his own home. So he does not eat rice and wear brocade. But if you have no problem doing it, then go ahead!"

The *Analects* tells us that at this point Zaiwo left the room and Confucius turned to others, saying, "How unfeeling Zaiwo is! A child does not leave his parents' arms until he is three. Three years of mourning is observed by all in the world. Did Zaiwo not also have three years of love and affection from his parents?"

The *Analects* rarely records what happens after a conversation is over. Rarer still is the above scenario, where the reader is allowed to hear what Confucius said in the absence of his principal interlocutor, Zaiwo. This heightens the tension, which was already apparent when Zaiwo was present; no one could fail to notice that the conversation circled around the words "ease" (*an*) and "unease" (*bu'an*), used in reference to whether or not one could feel comfortable about doing this or that during a period of mourning. It is impossible to guess why this conversation was handed down to us in this form. Since it was, it shows us that Confucius' relationship with Zaiwo was edgy—that Zaiwo was relentless and so could easily provoke anger or irritation in his teacher.

Zaiwo could make Confucius seem testy, but he could also propel him forward or in other unexpected directions. Another conversation in the *Analects* illustrates this side of their relationship:

Zaiwo asked, "If a truly humane man, a *renren*, is told that someone is stuck in a well, would he go down the well himself to see what he could do [not worrying about his own safety]?"

The Master said, "Why would he do that? A gentleman, a *junzi*, can go and take a look but he is not going to hurl himself into a trap. He can be deceived but not ensnared."

One can say that by phrasing his question in the way he did, Zaiwo was setting up a trap of his own for his teacher. A *renren*, a man with the deepest humanity and the noblest of character, represents the alpha example of moral achievement in Confucius' teachings. Zaiwo must have known that all too well, so he began with this man, and he asked Confucius would such a person descend into a well because he heard that someone was "stuck" there.

A *renren* is not dull-witted. He does not join the man in the well in order to give him solidarity. The mark of his character comes from the constancy he keeps in being able "to make an analogy from what is close at hand"—in being able to feel the anxiety and fear, the pain and pleasure of someone else from his own knowledge of such things. Lots of people possess the same ability, but they act on it by fits and starts. Zaiwo must also have learned this from his teacher, so it seemed reasonable for him to assume that a *renren* would lower himself into the well first before attempting to find ways to get the man in the well out: he would do this without thinking.

Zaiwo, I believe, was not taunting Confucius. Either he feared for the safety of a *renren* because such a man might set himself up to be duped; or he felt that Confucius fixed the standard too high—in fact, so high that one could not imagine a *renren* living in a world among real people. In his response, Confucius did not want to talk about the *renren,* as if he sensed where Zaiwo was leading him. Instead, he said, a *junzi,* a gentleman, a man of decency and propriety, would "go and take a look," but this person was not going to land himself in a trap. A gentleman can be deceived as all humans can be deceived, perhaps even more so, because he is more sensitive to human feelings and less likely to suspect what may seem reasonable. Still, he cannot be "ensnared."

Probably Confucius had in mind counselors such as Zijiazi. Many tried to mislead this man—above all, his own ruler, Duke Zhao—yet when the Duke of Qi offered Duke Zhao a portion of his kingdom, Zijiazi saw a trap and advised his lord to refuse the gift. Confucius could also have been talking about himself. In two instances, the chief stewards from two separate hereditary families sent for him as they were plotting their insurrections. Confucius wanted to go and have a look. His disciple Zilu tried to stop him. Zilu was worried, not that these places might turn out to be lion's dens, but that Confucius might emerge from them as tainted as the men he had been with. Confucius reassured him, saying, "White indeed is that which can withstand black dye." This could be another way of saying that he—Confucius—could be fooled into believing that these stewards would entrust him with the reorganization and the reform of their states but he could not be tricked into thinking that a swindler's way was the right way.

We have no record of Zaiwo's reply. But one cannot imagine that he would have wanted to return to the subject of *renren*. He used the idea as a lure, to get his teacher to talk about the more tangible—not what a perfected man but what a gentleman would do in a situation he described. Zaiwo achieved what he set out to do, so why would he want to hold on to the bait?

Zigong was another disciple who was skillful at drawing Confucius out. Since he was more attuned than Zaiwo to their teacher's temperament and style of instruction, one feels that their conversations gave Confucius more pleasure. The *Analects* says, "Zigong was affable" when "attending his teacher," which, however, does not imply that Zigong was dutiful or compliant. The two enjoyed being together and sharing thoughts about many things: poetry and politics, history and ritual practices, other disciples and each other. Confucius could be fiercely honest with Zigong, and Zigong would listen and then respond always to what Confucius had said, not to what his words could have implied. He did not fish for hidden judgments and he was not defensive. That was why they could converse so well.

The strongest word Confucius used to describe Zigong, which could sound like a reproof, is *qi*. *Qi* is a term for a vessel, a utensil, an object that serves a purpose. According to the *Analects*, it was Zigong who first asked Confucius: "What do you think of me?"

"You are a vessel [*qi*]," Confucius said.

"What kind of a vessel?"

"A *hu* or a *lian*, a vessel that holds offerings of sorgum and millet in the ancestral temple."

Some scholars read Zigong's follow-up question as a sign of anxiety. In their view, Zigong wondered whether this was indeed Confucius' opinion of him and whether Confucius could clarify what he meant, for, on another occasion, Confucius had also said, "A gentleman is not a vessel, not a *qi*"—that is, a gentleman can take on different kinds of problems and apply himself to many situations and so is not an object with a specific use. According to these scholars, when Confucius realized that his comment might have wounded Zigong, he tried to temper the effect and so described him as a sacred vessel holding offerings of grain in a temple. Such interpretations underestimated Zigong and Confucius, and simplified the nature of their relationship.

Zigong, I believe, knew that he was quick at acquiring a skill and quick at gaining mastery. He also knew that this strength could, in the end, stop him from reaching higher, letting him become satisfied in being the best in a profession or in several professions so that he would go no further. The *Analects* tells us that he was good at several things: speaking, grading people, and moneymaking. Which means that if he were put in government service, he could have been a splendid diplomat, a scout of fresh talents, or a shrewd financial manager. (When Confucius compared him to an implement in the state temple, he could have been telling Zigong that he thought highly of his administrative talents.) Once, a counselor from his home state of Wei said to Zigong: "What is important about the gentleman is the stuff he is made of (*zhi*), so why does he need to apply himself to the efforts of refinement (*wen*)?" Realizing that the remark was a jab at him, Zigong snapped back: "I am sorry to hear that you have spoken so about a gentleman," he said. "'A tongue can be faster than a team of horses.'" Then he added: "The stuff is not different from the refinement; refinement is not different from the stuff. The pelt of a tiger or leopard, shorn of hair, is not different from that of a dog or sheep."

If Zigong was convinced that "the stuff" of a gentleman was "no different from the refinement," it could be that he was defending his own reputation—that even though he was a man of many skills, whatever he learned would also influence his conduct and his deliberations. Confucius seems to support Zigong's view of himself in a statement he made comparing this disciple with another one, Yan Hui, a man he thought came closest to being perfect. As Confucius put it,

> Hui is almost there yet he lives in poverty. Si [Zigong] does not accept his lot. He is good at making money, and [because of it] is given to assessing a situation and weighing the favorable against the unfavorable, and is often right in his speculations.

Zigong does not resign himself to his circumstances. To change them, he has learned to make money, and in so doing he has also become shrewd and observant, which, in turn, informs his thought and actions, his judgment and predictions. Thus "the stuff" he is made of is not different from his "refinement." Did Confucius prefer Yan Hui over Zigong? Yes, we know this from other evidence. But here he simply says, Yan Hui is Yan Hui, and Zigong, Zigong— one has nearly fulfilled his moral potential but "is often poor," while the other will not bow to his situation and so has gained many skills and an analytical mind. Confucius appreciated both.

Another day, Confucius asked Zigong:

> "Who is the better man, you or [Yan] Hui?"
> "How dare I compare myself with Hui? From learning one thing he understands ten. After I've learned one thing, I understand only two."
> "You are not as good as he is. Neither of us is good as he is."

Confucius might have regarded Yan Hui as a better man, better than everyone else he knew and better than himself, but he prized Zigong for holding his own. He directed more questions to Zigong than to anyone else, as if he was looking for another point of view or anticipating a surprise. With Zigong, he could also expect their to-and-fro to take on a life of its own. In one instance, Zigong asked:

"What do you think of the expression 'Poor yet not obsequious, wealthy yet not arrogant'?"

Confucius replied, "That is fine, but better still, 'Poor yet joyful, wealthy yet loving the rites.'"

Zigong continued, "The *Book of Odes* says, 'Like bone filed, like tusk smoothed, / Like jade carved, like stone polished.' Is this what you mean?"

Confucius said, "Si [Zigong], only with you can one discuss the *Odes*. Tell you something and you can see its relevance to what is not said."

The conversation begins with one subject and ends with another. Confucius provides the initial thrust by making Zigong's original statement sharper and subtler. This prompts Zigong to declaim a few lines from a poem, which, Confucius feels, catches the spirit of the occasion and is the pith of the matter. And he praises Zigong for having gotten it on his own. It is not an exaggeration, therefore, when he says, "Si [Zigong], only with you can one discuss the *Odes*."

What about Yan Hui, then? Why could Confucius not talk to him about the *Odes*? Yan Hui possessed a finer sensibility than Zigong and, measure for measure, was far superior. Yet Confucius had more affinity with Zigong, so it was not out of mere modesty that he said to Zigong, "Neither of us is as good as [Yan Hui]." He realized that Zigong was his kindred. Both had to pick up skills to get by and acquire learning to refine the stuff they were born of; both were prone to question themselves and others concerning what they knew and did not know; both were restless and so could not easily find peace. Yan Hui was different from them.

Confucius was suspicious at first of Yan Hui's affability and calm, and of his apparent lack of intellectual interest in having a disagreement. He said: "Hui is no help to me at all. He is pleased with everything I say." And: "If anyone can listen to me with unflagging attention, it's Hui, I suppose." When these doubts led him to ask whether Yan Hui was perhaps "stupid," he took a look at what Yan Hui did "in private" and found that this disciple was indeed able "to give play to" what he had learned—that "he was not at all stupid."

Yan Hui was the anomaly among Confucius' disciples. He was pleased with everything his teacher said but he was also pleased with "living in a shabby neighborhood on a bowlful of millet and a ladleful of water." Unlike Zigong or, for that matter, most people, he was content with any circumstances of life. Poverty did not vex him because he could not keep his mind off things he considered to have greater importance. What the philosopher Mencius once said about the ancient ruler Shun, I believe, also applies to Yan Hui:

> When Shun dwelled in the depths of the mountains, he lived amongst trees and stones, and had as companions deer and pigs. Then the difference between him and an uncouth man of the mountains was slight. But when he heard a single good word, witnessed a single good deed, it was like water causing a breach in the dykes of the Yangtse or the Yellow River. It swells up and overflows, and nothing could hold it back.

Yan Hui was born with similar proclivities and the same compulsion to move toward the good. Confucius described him as someone who "for three months at a time does not lapse from benevolence," while "others attain benevolence by fits and starts." Yan Hui could hold on to benevolence because nothing could hold him back from it. Others came to it sporadically because they found the effort strenuous.

Of all the disciples of Confucius, Yan Hui was also the most eager to learn and the most constant, driven by the same love for the good and the same feeling of inevitability. He himself spoke most forcefully on this subject—about his rush and his desire for learning. The *Analects* says:

> Heaving a sigh, Yan Hui said, "The more I look up at it, the higher it appears. The more I bore into it, the harder it becomes. I see it before me. Suddenly it is behind me. But my teacher knows how to coax me to move forward, and he does it a step at a time. He

expands me with literature and culture and pulls me in with the rites. I cannot quit even if I want to, but having done all I can, it still seems to stand way above me. I don't know where to start, however much I may want to."

Yan Hui was on a quest, with his teacher next to him or just ahead. He listened to him "with unflagging attention" and "without ever disagreeing" with him. Even his teacher became doubtful of Yan Hui's potential until he observed the urgency with which Yan Hui applied himself to what he had learned. As Confucius would eventually realize, it was the looking up higher and the boring deeper and it was the frustration of going at it on one's own and an unwillingness to give up that allowed Yan Hui to move from one thing to ten. Yet despite his drive and his gift of perspicuity and understanding, Yan Hui needed instruction from someone who knew how to urge him on and rein him in—and he needed not just this man's "good words" but also his presence on the long journey, which was often lonely.

We are told that when Confucius was in danger of being killed in a place called Kuang by a hostile crowd who mistook him for the very unpopular Yang Hu, Yan Hui was not by his side; he "had fallen behind." When Yan Hui finally caught up with him, it was Confucius who expressed relief, seeing that Yan Hui had not met with any mishap. He said to him, "I thought you were dead." To this, Yan Hui replied, "With you alive, how would I dare to die?"

Yan Hui did die before Confucius. When Confucius first heard the news, he was so bereft that even his followers were concerned, for it seemed as if he had abandoned all restraint—any sense of proportion—in his grief for Yan Hui. And when told that this was how he behaved, Confucius replied, "If not for Hui, for whom should I show so much sorrow?" Years later, Confucius would say to others that with Yan Hui gone there was no one who could take his place— no one who had his temperament and who loved learning as much as he: "Yan Hui never displaced his anger on someone else and he did not repeat a mistake twice." Confucius also believed that his disciples were closer to him when Yan Hui was alive, implying either that others gravitated toward him because they were fond of Yan Hui or that he himself was calmer, gentler, and more agreeable because Yan Hui was around. It is possible that through memory Yan Hui had grown in stature. He became the only person, in Confucius' mind, who could have fulfilled all the moral potential that was possible in a human being. But this is the kind of wishful assumption we make about those who die before their time is up.

Confucius lived with these regrets until his own death. Still, it was better for Yan Hui to go first. What Yan Hui said to his teacher after the crisis in Kuang—"With you alive, how would I dare to die?"—seems to imply that Confucius needed him more than he needed Confucius. Was this true? The most astute and most compassionate critic of Confucius—a thinker from the fourth century BC called Zhuangzi—gave this question a lot of thought. The relationship between the two men that Zhuangzi projects in his writings combines a sympathetic reading of what he knew about them with his own reflections on how to reconcile the impermanence of the human condition with our stubborn resistance to letting go old attachments. In one of Zhuangzi's scenarios, Yan Hui says to Confucius:

> When you walk, I walk. When you canter, I canter. When you gallop, I gallop. But when you break into a kind of sprint that does not even leave a trace of dust, all I can do is to gaze after you from the space you have left empty.

Here, Zhuangzi has Yan Hui talk metaphorically about what they share and do not share in the march of life. Yan Hui says he can "speak," "make distinctions," and even "discuss the Dao, the moral way," just as his teacher can, but he can only "gaze after" his teacher in wonderment when he sees that he can "command trust without words," "embrace all without ever being partial," and "draw others to him without the trappings of high office." In his response, Confucius sidesteps the point Yan Hui has just made; instead, he concentrates on the sadness he heard in Yan Hui's voice when he talked about separateness. Separateness leads to separation and the pain of watching the familiar dash off and disappear—this is what Confucius imagines Yan Hui to be saying. He does not explain or even mention Yan Hui's worries about the disparities between them. He tells his disciple:

> I have gone through life linking arm in arm with you. Now you have lost sight of me, how can you not despair? Yet you probably saw only what was visible about me. But whatever is visible is already gone. For you to come to look for it as if it still exists is like looking for a horse after the fair is over. In my thinking of you, I have utterly forgotten you. In your thinking of me, you have utterly forgotten me. Even so, why should you repine? Although you have forgotten the old me, there is something of me you will not forget.

The conversation probably existed only in Zhuangzi's head, yet it is an astonishing example of art imitating life.

After Confucius had absorbed the shock of Yan Hui's death, he seemed reasonable and calm. Yan Hui's father asked Confucius to sell his carriage so that he could buy his son an outer coffin. Confucius refused. His disciples gave Yan Hui a lavish burial despite their teacher's objections. Confucius was disappointed. He thought that neither an outer coffin nor an expensive funeral was appropriate, given the fact that Yan Hui came from a poor family. Besides, such displays bear no relationship to the indiscernible—to what one will not forget.

When Confucius himself was gravely ill, and for a while it appeared that he might not pull through, Zilu told the disciples who were present to act as Confucius' retainers. Confucius had no official position at the time, and Zilu was worried that he might die as an unemployed scholar and be buried like one, without the formalities accompanying the death of a minister.

Confucius had earned such a status under Duke Ding, but when he gave up his job, he also relinquished all the privileges the position entailed. A former minister was not the same as a minister and should not be regarded as one. This was what the ritual rules of the Zhou prescribed, and until this person was appointed to another post of ministerial rank he remained a *shi,* a common gentleman, and, because of his learning, an employable man. Without an office, a common gentleman was not entitled to have retainers.

A few days later, Confucius' condition improved. He upbraided Zilu for "having practiced chicanery for much too long" and said:

> By pretending I had retainers when I had none, whom were we trying to deceive? Heaven? Besides, would I not rather die in the arms of a few good friends than in the arms of retainers? And even if I could not have a minister's burial, it was not as if I was dying by the wayside.

The early sources stress that Zilu was a *yeren,* "a man of the field," not a *guoren,* "a man of the city." These two categories, *yeren* and *guoren,* were established long ago, during the early years of the Zhou conquest. Those who went east with their vassal lords to settle in the new territories were called *guoren,* "people of the city" or "people of the state." They lived in fortified towns, paid their military and civil duties, had some weight in political decisions, and were members of the state. Those who were already in the territories when the settlers arrived were called *yeren,* "people of the field." They lived in the surrounding countryside. The garrisoned states to which they were attached might exact some military service from them but did not allow them the status of members. *Yeren,* therefore, had no political sway; at the same time, however, they were left alone to carry on the way of life they had always known.

The mounting pressure for military and financial resources would change things. By the middle of the Spring and Autumn period, about a century before Confucius' birth, several larger feudal states began to integrate the people of the field into their political structure. Certain distinctions between *yeren* and *guoren* would vanish, while others would endure. Zilu, for instance, was probably a full member of the state of Lu—he had considerable influence when he was a retainer in the Jisun family—yet he remained a native with a native's resistance to the settlers' niceties and even their fineries. The early historian Sima Qian tells us that when Zilu first met Confucius he was aggressively attired—wearing a "cockscomb cap" and a "boar-skin belt"—and "he was rude to Confucius." In this account, it was Confucius who "first tried to influence Zilu with the practice of the rites," and when Zilu was ready to accept his instructions, other disciples had "to intercede for him to have him admitted into their group." Once admitted, Zilu, who was only nine years younger than Confucius, became his attendant and self-appointed guardian.

The early sources also stress that Zilu was from Bian, a district in Lu reputed to have produced the bravest man in the Spring and Autumn history. In one story, this man was said to have faced two tigers on his own, and to have struck and killed both. People were so terrified of him that soldiers of the opposing army dared not pass through Bian when they were sent on an expedition against Lu.

Either valor was endemic to Bian, or many men of Bian felt compelled to live up to the fame their hero had given to their home place, for Zilu also came to be known among Confucius' disciples as the one who loved valor and who was most likely to get involved in acts of valor. And it was to him Confucius would emphasize that it was not enough just to be "trusty," "straightforward," "brave," and "unbending." A person may have these attributes, which may seem honorable and worthy, but without a love of learning, Confucius says, problems will begin to emerge for the protagonist: he will keep his word "for the wrong reasons," or be so forthright that he "becomes a menace," so brave that he "foments anarchy," and so unbending that he "is simply mad."

Once, in the presence of Zilu, Confucius said to Yan Hui, "Only the two of us are able to act when we are employed and to live in reclusion when we are let go." Anxious for Confucius not to forget him, Zilu asked, "But if you were to lead the Three Armies [of Lu], whom would you take with you?" His teacher replied:

I wouldn't take anyone who would try to wrestle a tiger with his bare hands and walk across a river [because there is not a boat]. If I take anyone, it would have to be someone who is wary when faced with a task and who is good at planning and capable of successful execution.

Since Zilu asked, Confucius told him plainly enough that he would not take him if he was on a military campaign, just as he would not want Zilu to accompany him if he was at the end of his road. He felt that even though Zilu was more courageous than others, his lack of fear probably would do more harm than good.

If Confucius seems slightly dismissive of Zilu, it was not because Zilu was a rustic. He knew from the start that Zilu was churlish and was nevertheless willing to accept him as a disciple. In fact, Confucius said that he would not deny instruction to anyone who wanted to learn, whether or not this person could pay: "just a bundle of dried meat as a gift for our first meeting will do." Confucius also expressed no opinion of those disciples who were "men of the field" or those who came to him "already refined and gentlemanly." When he talked about their differences, it was in the context of how he could best teach them: "I would guide the men of the field with rites and music first, and I would hold off rites and music for the gentlemanly type until much later."

Confucius' problem with Zilu, therefore, was not that he was rough and unhewn but that he was pushy and violent and quick to take offense. Even Zilu recognized these tendencies in himself, but he did not quite see them as defects—this was another problem he had. He said he feared that before he could do anything about what he had heard, he might hear something else. The haste and scrappy energy with which Zilu moved through life lent him some charm; otherwise he was difficult to like. And his lack of self-awareness could win one over or wear one out, depending on the situation. This is one reason why Confucius found Zilu both endearing and insufferable, and felt unable to turn him away. So he led him a step at a time, supplying him with knowledge Zilu could not acquire on his own.

When Zilu asked Confucius one day whether one should act as soon as one learned that something needed to be done, Confucius said, "As long as your father and your older brother are alive, you are not in a position to act in such a way." Later he told someone else that he intended these words only for Zilu: "He had the fire of two, so I tried to hold him back." When Zilu wanted to know "how to serve the spirits of the dead and the gods," Confucius chided, "You can't even serve men properly, how can you serve the spirits?" Again, not knowing when to stop, Zilu pressed on: "May I then ask about death?" "You can't even understand life, how can you understand death?" Confucius snapped.

Perhaps because there were too many such scenes where Confucius could seem disparaging or cutting when speaking to him, other disciples began to treat Zilu in a similar manner. The *Analects* identifies the precise occasion when this happened. On that day, Confucius said: "What is Zilu's lute doing in my room?" Those who heard him understood him to say Zilu was not good enough to appreciate his subtler teachings and his grander thoughts and so had no place in his inner room. Afterwards, they began to shun Zilu. When Confucius realized this, he provided a correction, saying, "Zilu may not have entered the inner room, but he has ascended the hall."

Zilu did not have Zigong's intellectual agility or Yan Hui's strong—even unbreachable—desire to know the good, but he was one of those rare persons who "would not feel ashamed standing next to a man wearing fox or badger fur while himself dressed in a tattered gown padded with old silk floss." He was also so reliable that in a court of law he would have "to speak only a few words to bring a legal dispute to a conclusion." Yet Zilu could never be much more than a topflight retainer. He was neither "grasping" nor "malign"; he was generous and brave and would never betray those he loved or anyone to whom he felt bound by a sense of duty. However, Confucius told him, "This is hardly the way to be good."

Confucius had known this disciple for a long time, and he realized that the code of honor Zilu lived by could dull his judgment and rein in his perception if he continued to believe that "there are people [to govern] and altars to the gods of grain and soil [to serve], so why must we study rituals and music, poetry and history before we are said to learn?" Confucius feared for Zilu because of the extreme measures he might take and what he could do to others and to himself. He predicted that Zilu would not "die a natural death."

Zilu's death was indeed unnatural and pointless. It also proved, among other things, that his education had failed him. He had gone his own way in being "trustworthy," "straightforward," "brave," and "unbending," and he died looking slightly like a madman. The episode is recorded in the *Zuo Commentary*. It was in 480 BC, the year before Confucius' death. Zilu was serving as a retainer in the very powerful Kong family in the state of Wei (which had no relation to the Kong family of Confucius). Sometime earlier, the ruler had driven out his own heir apparent and put the disgraced man's son in his place. When the ruler died, the grandson succeeded him on the throne while his own father still lived in exile. Eventually the father plotted with his sister to dispose of his son. He understood the risks, for he would have to come back to Wei in disguise and stage an insurrection, and until the coup was put in motion, he would not know just how many men might be on his side. But he also saw a reasonable chance of success. His sister was the widow of the former lord of the Kong family. She had in her service a group of family retainers loyal only to her. Her own son was the new head of the Kong family. He was also the ruler's cousin, and, in principle, the ruler's closest ally. But being young and timid, he could easily succumb to his mother's pressure and betray that trust. On the appointed day, everything went according to plan. The displaced heir apparent "muffled himself in a woman's robe," went past the guards in front of the Kong mansion, and found his way to his sister, Lady Bo. Then:

> Lady Bo, having finished her dinner, took a halberd and led the way for the group, with the heir apparent and five men, all armed, following after and carrying a pig. They cornered Lady Bo's son in the privy and forced him to swear an alliance with them [using the blood of the pig to seal the oath].

When the senior steward of the Kong family "received word of a revolt," he picked up the Duke of Wei in his carriage, and the two fled to the state of Lu. Meanwhile, Zilu and another disciple of Confucius, Zigao, who was also a retainer in the Kong family, heard the news. Zilu wanted to go into the city where the fighting was taking place. Zigao tried to stop him, saying, "It's too late. Don't get mixed up in the trouble!" Zilu would not bend. He said to Zigao, "I earn my living from them—I cannot hope to escape their trouble." So with no sound reason (except perhaps to rescue the young lord of Kong from his mother and uncle, who probably did not wish to do him harm), Zilu hurled himself into the trouble he did not cause and could not affect. Soldiers loyal to the displaced heir apparent cut him down and chopped him into mincemeat.

Confucius knew that Zilu would die violently if he chose to live only by the way of a retainer, however noble it might appear. Before the uprising took place, he had had a conversation with his disciples about the politics in Wei. His disciples wondered whether he was on the side of the displaced heir apparent or that of his son. Confucius spoke circuitously about the matter. It was Zigong who concluded, "The Master was not on the side of the son."

Evidence suggests that on his long trip abroad Confucius had more followers with him than just these four. While Zilu and Yan Hui guarded him throughout most of the fourteen years he was away and Zigong and Zaiwo for about half that time, there were others who stayed with him for shorter periods, a few months or a few years at a stretch. Ran Qiu was one such disciple. According to some sources, the Jisun family offered Ran Qiu a job in 492. He probably did not respond right away, but before Confucius came home in 484, Ran Qiu was already well situated in the political hierarchy of the Jisun family. This man's name was often linked with that of Zilu even though the two had little in common. Zilu rushed to get things done, while Ran Qiu was inclined "to hold back"; Zilu was decisive, while Ran Qiu commanded many skills; Zilu was boorish, while Ran Qiu was smooth and accomplished; one was a soldier and the other a politician. Confucius pointed out most of their differences but insisted that these two were also "most likely to succeed in government." And when asked whether they would make great ministers, he replied: "The term 'great ministers' applies to those who serve their lord in a moral way. If they simply could not, then they would stop. Zilu and Ran Qiu are men appointed to fill the ranks of a supervisory staff in a hereditary family." Though they might be dutiful to their employers, Confucius continued, "still, there are things they would not do. They would not, for instance, kill their fathers or their rulers [when ordered to do so]."

There was one follower of Confucius who could have been a great minister. This man, Zhonggong, had the markings and the making of someone great. Confucius said at one point, "Zhonggong could be given a seat facing south," which meant that Zhonggong could become a true king should he be put in the position of a ruler. Zhonggong's father, we are told, was either lowly or low-down. Mindful of this fact, Confucius compared Zhonggong to "a bull born of plough cattle" that had "a sorrel coat and well-formed horns." "Would the spirit of the mountains and rivers allow it to be passed over," Confucius asked, "even if we felt it was not good enough to be used in a sacrifice?"

Confucius gave Zhonggong higher praise than anyone, with the possible exception of Yan Hui. Yet the *Analects,* the most reliable source on the disciples, yields only a few slivers of information about this man. Consequently Zhonggong remains the most enigmatic of the group. Bad luck or chance could be the explanation for his near anonymity. Or if one is given to skepticism and suspects human machination, one could imagine the younger disciples or editors of a later generation deliberately suppressing whatever records they had about him. After Confucius died, jealousy and competition were known to have caused sharp divisions within his followers. But if this was true, why not remove everything? Why leave a trace of a man? Why let his spell survive?

During his years of wandering, Confucius never considered his followers part of a school, certainly not of his school, for he had none. He put himself on the road without the nudging of gods or visions. He needed a proper job and did not think he had much to preach about. Zigong, Yan Hui, and possibly Zaiwo followed him because they loved learning as much as he and thought that he had a deft hand at leading them forward, not by the nose but like a master driver, spurring them on and reining them in, down the path of human life. Zilu followed him as a retainer would—loyal and loving and learning a little about refinement whenever he was willing. Ran Qiu was probably going along for the ride, looking for opportunities in case Confucius landed a prime spot. Thus when the Jisuns summoned him, he headed home. Zhonggong is a mystery, so we cannot even surmise. He could be the sixth man, and there could be more.

CHAPTER FOUR

Wanderings

CONFUCIUS SPENT A LONG TIME ABROAD. THOSE YEARS, from 497 to 484, are a challenge for the historical imagination. We have a few facts about them but far too many gaps, some of which even the imagination has to strain to fill in. Over the centuries, scholars have combed the sources for any track of his movement and any flicker of revelation, and they have concentrated on these questions: When was Confucius where, and how long did he stay? Who were his hosts or sponsors, and how did he let himself be known to them? Why did he leave a place? Was it restlessness or frustration, or did other people want to see him gone? In what straits did he find himself? What were the important moments on this journey, and if he happened to say something in those moments, how do we understand what he said? Could he have meant more than what he said?

Records of Confucius' travels are scattered throughout the *Analects* and in the writings of philosophers who lived in the two hundred and fifty years after Confucius' death. But they appear either as fragments or as isolated episodes, and most of the episodes are either too tidy, too self-conscious, or too well-crafted to be authentic. Sima Qian was the first historian to string the pieces together as a continuous narrative. He added flair and drama whenever he felt they might improve his story; he was also liberal in providing transitions and patching up holes. Aside from the overwriting, and the overcompensation for questions that could tarnish Confucius' good name, there are also logistical problems in Sima Qian's account. According to the itinerary this Han historian sketched out, Confucius must have covered thousands of miles on foot and stayed for various durations, and sometimes more than once, in seven separate states. Why, one might ask, would Confucius want to pick up and move so many times? Why would he want to risk unfriendly approaches in uncharted places and the possibility of illness and starvation in the long stretches between towns when he could have settled down somewhere that, in time, might prove to be agreeable? Even for a man who was restless by nature, would it not have become apparent, after a while, that one place was as good as another? Sima Qian did not try to answer these questions. He wanted to fill his story with action and adventure, and so he kept Confucius in motion.

A more reliable source is the philosopher Zhuangzi. He lived two hundred years earlier than Sima Qian and so two hundred years closer to Confucius' time. Zhuangzi simplifies the journey. Instead of shuffling Confucius around and trying to fit him into scores of locations, as Sima Qian later did, he places Confucius in four states: Wei, Song, Chen, and Cai. The *Analects* also mentions that Confucius stayed briefly in She, a district under the jurisdiction of Chu. Thus, if we follow these sources, Confucius started out in Wei, went through Song to Chen and Cai and possibly to Chu, and, on his way back, stopped by Chen and spent a few more years in Wei before returning home to Lu. This would mean that he did not, as Sima Qian suggests, leave a place and then come back, sometimes repeating this three or four times, and he did not behave like a man who could not make up his mind about what to do and where to spend his life.

In his account, Zhuangzi also suggests that this was not the first time Confucius went abroad. We know that Confucius spent some time in the neighboring state of Qi, and that this could not have occurred on the trip in question. According to the *Analects*, Duke Jing of Qi once asked Confucius about government, and Confucius answered, "Let the ruler be a ruler, the subject a subject, the father a father, the son a son." The same ruler had considered giving Confucius a job but dithered over the questions of how high to raise him and how much to pay him, and in the end gave up the idea altogether, saying, "I am too old. I am afraid I cannot use his talents." Consequently, we learn, "Confucius departed."

From his relationship with Duke Jing, it seems that on his visit to Qi, Confucius was already known outside of his home state, in the larger world of politics; therefore, he could not have been in his thirties or even in his forties because at that age he was still in the private employment of a hereditary family. This would put him in Qi around 505, when the browbeater Yang Hu was rough-riding everyone in Lu. Confucius could have gone to Qi to avoid further confronation with Yang Hu.

On the trip with which we are concerned, Confucius went west, straight for the state of Wei, which was about a hundred and twenty miles away. He did not even consider going northeast, to Qi. The Qi ruler who had once expressed some interest in hiring him was now dead, and Confucius' relationship with this man's son was not amicable. Three years earlier, at the covenant in Xiagu, he had made the new duke of Qi look inept and poorly schooled in decorum, like a rustic, or worse, like someone who could not distinguish Zhou culture from the ways of the barbarians. Consequently he did not expect to be treated well or even equitably if he showed up in Qi. Wei was different. Confucius said in the *Analects*, "The two governments of Wei and Lu are like brothers."

The royal ancestors of Wei and Lu were Kangshu and the Duke of Zhou. They were brothers by the same mother and brothers on the most amiable terms. According to the *Zuo Commentary*, a counselor of Wei had once advised his own ruler not to react too rashly and too forcefully to a transgression Yang Hu had committed against their state. He said, "Among the children of King Wen and [his wife] Taisi, only the Duke of Zhou and Kangshu got along well. If you imitate the behavior of a petty thug, will you not be falling into his trap?" Yang Hu was the "petty thug." He was not a descendent of the Duke of Zhou: his power was ill-gotten, and his ways did not represent the ways of Lu. Thus, the counselor of Wei asked his ruler not to respond to this man's action—not to stoop to Yang Hu's level—but to follow their ancestor's example and to treat Lu in a brotherly manner.

Lu and Wei were brotherly in other ways. During the Spring and Autumn period, it was common knowledge that the two states were never short of men with integrity and political talent. If a person with some position had acted ingloriously, say, in the state of Qi, he would be very reluctant to go to either Lu or Wei because he would not be able to face the counselors in those places.* Confucius himself boasted: "With one great change, the state of Qi can resemble the state of Lu. With one great change, [the government of] Lu can embody the way [that is moral and good]." Qi was inferior to Lu from the start, because its founder, though a capable man, was inferior to the founder of Lu—who was the son of the Duke of Zhou—inferior in character and in his political vision. However, five hundred and fifty years later, the ruler of Lu had become no different from the ruler of Qi. Being a descendent of the Duke of Zhou no longer allowed him any advantage: he was not superior in either probity or proficiency, and he had only ordinary perception. Confucius realized this, but he still believed that with one profound change, things could turn around in Lu—that the people of Lu would be able again to look forward to the kind of stability only a virtuous government could create. He was optimistic because he had faith in "the talented gentlemen of Lu." In fact, he felt that more of them had the promise of being good counselors than any other group of men, and good counselors were his hope in an age of moral rot and political misrule.

---

*Dilu Zifang from the state of Qi is an example. He was the family retainer of a Qi minister. Even when his life was in danger, he refused the help of an enemy of his lord because at the time he was thinking about fleeing to Lu or Wei. He said to others, "If I were to have private ties with the enemy while I am in the service of my lord, I wouldn't be able to face the gentlemen of Lu and Wei [when I see them]." See *Chunqiu Zuozhuan zhu*, Duke Ai, 14th year; Yang's edition, pp. 1685-86.

The history of counselors in Lu—men like Zhaozi and Zijiazi—might have given Confucius faith and a reason to believe that things could change for the better in his native state. Yet when he was a guest in the state of Wei, he showed the same kind of optimism about the political situation there. The ruler of Wei at the time was Duke Ling. Confucius talked openly about the moral depravity of this man. When someone asked him how it was that "such a ruler did not lose his state," Confucius replied that it was because the state of Wei had the right person "in charge of foreign guests," an honest priest "looking after the ancestral temple," and a capable general "responsible for the military affairs." "This being so," he said, "how can this ruler lose his state?"

In time of crisis, the people of Wei, like the people of Lu, had always relied on good counselors to help them avert catastrophe. And though Wei was not his home, Confucius was familiar with those counselors—the whole roster of them, even those born a few generations back. The ones he cited by name possessed these qualities: one was "straight as an arrow whether or not a moral way prevailed," another "took office when the moral way prevailed and let himself be rolled up and hidden away when the moral way did not prevail," a third one was so generous in spirit that he "recommended a retainer in his household to the position of a state counselor," thus letting his subordinate "serve side by side with him."

When Confucius first arrived in Wei, he, like any employable professional, was waiting to see whether a suitable offer might come along. That is why when Zigong asked him, "If you had a beautiful piece of jade right now, would you put it away safely in a box or try to sell it for a good price?" Confucius replied, "I will sell it, I will sell it. I am just waiting for the right offer." After living in Wei for ten months without any prospect, he decided to travel to Jin, a neighboring state to the west, perhaps to explore the opportunities there. Before Confucius reached the border, he was summoned by a retainer from a hereditary family in Jin who planned to use the family's stronghold to stage a revolt. For a while Confucius thought of going, but then he decided to retrace his steps back to Wei.

After his return to Wei, Confucius became anxious about finding a job there. It was possibly around then that he paid a visit to the ruler's wife, Nanzi, an oversexed woman with a scandalous reputation that was richly deserved. In the *Analects,* we are told that when Zilu learned about the visit, he "was not happy." Confucius, however, swore to him, "If I have done anything wrong, may Heaven forsake me, may Heaven forsake me!" The historian Sima Qian simply could not resist the dramatic possibilities in these two lines and so retold the story his way:

> The wife of Duke Ling, Nanzi, sent someone to Confucius with this message: "When a gentleman from anywhere in the world wishes to be friends with my lord, he will have to come and see me first. Now I would like to see you." Confucius declined at first but then changed his mind, for he had no choice.
>
> The lady was sitting behind a *ge*-hemp curtain [when he arrived]. Confucius entered the room. Facing north, he got down on his knees and placed his hands on the ground. He bowed with his head touching his hands. The lady returned the formality from within the curtain—the jade pendants on her girdle tinkled as she bowed.
>
> Confucius later said, "I did not want to see her, but, out of propriety, had to pay her a visit." Zilu was not happy. Confucius swore to him, saying, "If I have done anything wrong, may Heaven forsake me, may Heaven forsake me!'

In his version, Sima Qian gives Nanzi a speaking part and a chance to carry out her act. Her performance is especially pleasurable because it is within the confines of proper behavior. Yet we may still prefer Nanzi in the *Analects*. There she is a subject that requires no explication. Just a visit with her put a strain on Confucius' relationship with Zilu. Such was her power.

In his defense of Confucius—that he went to see Nanzi because he "had no choice"—Sima Qian also undermines the significance of Confucius' meeting with Nanzi and of Confucius' reaction to Zilu's displeasure. In the absence of an apology, we may ask what could have made Confucius so uptight and skittish that he had to swear a dark and solemn oath in order to give his disciple peace of mind. A more recent scholar offers a simple answer, which is more persuasive than Sima Qian's. When Confucius was in Wei, this scholar says, he was desperate for a position in Duke Ling's government, and so when he went to see Nanzi, some, including Zilu, thought that he had tried to push his way to the top through private influence with the duke's wife. This can be corroborated with another conversation found in the *Analects:*

> Wang Sunjia [the military commander of Wei] once said to Confucius, "What do you think of the adage, 'Better to flatter the god of the kitchen hearth than the god of the southwest corner in the inner room'?" Confucius replied, "The saying has got it wrong. When you have offended Heaven, there is no spirit you can pray to."

The "southwest corner" is the darkest spot in a room where there is no window or any source of light; it refers to Nanzi, who sits in the inner palace. The "kitchen hearth" is an open space where people gather to have a meal or a chat; it refers to Wang Sunjia, who lives and works in the public arena. Wang implies that it is probably more effective for Confucius to go to him rather than to Nanzi if Confucius is looking for a place in Wei politics. Confucius' response is not unlike what he said to Zilu: If you have done something wrong—if you have offended Heaven—there is no god you can appeal to; if you have done no wrong, then you can swear an oath without the fear of Heaven's retribution. The principle applies to all, himself being no exception.

Confucius might have had nothing to hide from men or from the gods, but he still wanted a counselor's job. No one, I believe, described as well as Mencius just how distressed Confucius would become whenever he was unemployed. Mencius said, "According to some accounts, when Confucius was not in the service of a ruler for three months, he became extremely anxious, and when he decided to leave for another state, he always took a present with him [in case he was summoned to an audience]." A gentleman would be extremely anxious in such a situation, Mencius continued, because without a position in government, he would not have any land, which, in turn, would mean he was not entitled to have sacrificial animals and sacrificial vessels. Thus he would not be able to offer a sacrifice and to host a feast: for "a gentleman to lose his position is like a feudal lord losing his state," and "after three months of not being in the service of a ruler, others would begin to offer their condolences."

Descriptions of Confucius in the *Analects* concur with what Mencius told us about him, but they also give us more clues about why he could not keep still. An elderly man once asked Confucius: "Why are you so restless? [Do you move around] for the sake of trying out your skills of persuasion?" Confucius responded: "I dare not practice any skills of persuasion. It is just that I worry that the world is so stubbornly ignorant." He also told others: "There is nothing I can do with a man who is not constantly saying, 'What am I to do? What am I to do?'" Yet the person who understood his peripatetic leanings better than even Confucius himself was a border warden from Wei. Being a minor official, this man had to ask for an interview when he learned that Confucius was passing through his district. After their meeting, he said to the two or three disciples who accompanied Confucius on this trip: "Why do you worry about him not having an office? The world has long been without a moral way. Heaven is about to use your master as the wooden tongue for a bronze bell." What this border warden realized was more than what Confucius at the time could have grasped about himself. He said that it was Heaven's wish to have Confucius travel the empire and arouse people like the tongue of a bell—that Confucius was destined to be a teacher, not an official. Heaven could have used the border warden to proclaim a prophecy, so the assertion seemed more knowing than any human insight. Yet because of this, a person as firmly human as Confucius was going to put up resistance. Thus he continued to worry about "not having an office."

According to Sima Qian, when Confucius lived in Wei, he stayed with Qu Boyu, the man he revered most in that state. Unlike Confucius, Qu was not eager for employment, and he did not seem worried about anything except for the consequences he might have caused by being partial or myopic. Even his servants realized this. Once Confucius asked a man who worked for Qu what his master had been doing. The servant replied, "My master wishes to make fewer mistakes, but he has not been able to do so." The philosopher Zhuangzi takes this idea to another level. He seems to think that Qu possessed an awareness that was keener, even more alert, than what the editors of the *Analects* described. In his estimation, Qu knew that everything about himself was questionable, not only his character but all his stances, no matter how sound they might appear or how dear they were to him. Zhuangzi exaggerates this point in his writing so that we will not forget Qu Boyu:

> Qu Boyu has been going along for sixty years and has changed sixty times. There is not a single instance in which what he called right in the beginning he did not in the end reject. So now there is no telling whether what he calls right at the moment is not in fact what he called wrong during the past fifty-nine years.

Being a guest of Qu Boyu would have lent Confucius prestige. But by the time Confucius reached Wei, Qu would have been in his nineties and probably would not have warmed to the thought of having Confucius and his disciples stay with him indefinitely. In fact, Confucius' own comments about Qu in the *Analects* suggest that he maintained a measured distance from this man, who was nearly forty years his senior. He would get the news about Qu from a messenger the latter sent to him. The distance might have been generational, or it might be an indication that Confucius was a little afraid of Qu—of his awesome reputation and of his judgment.

Confucius' follower Mencius seems to know a lot about who played host to Confucius when Confucius was in Wei. The subject came up when someone asked Mencius whether it was true that Confucius stayed with a court doctor, someone who specialized in gangrene and boils. Mencius calls the story "the work of gossips and busybodies." Court doctors were not widely admired in Chinese society—certainly not in early China—but they were favorites of rulers because they could soothe the pain and quiet the worries of their patients, or claimed that they could. Duke Ling of Wei was very attached to the doctor in question, which explains why men of ill will wanted others to believe that Confucius had been a guest of such a man. The scenario would suggest that Confucius was so hungry for a job in Duke Ling's government that he was ready to accept the help of a toady. His visit with Nanzi must have fueled the same busybodies, giving them something to do, something to talk about; but in that situation, even his disciple Zilu and the military commander Wang Sunjia began to waver in their judgment of him, not knowing for sure if Confucius' action was completely honorable.

Mencius had an easier time responding to stories about Confucius that were clearly uncharitable. He simply dismissed them as malicious and unfounded. But when asked whether Confucius had accepted the hospitality of the court doctor from Wei, Mencius pointed out that if Confucius had wanted private influence he could have used the help of someone who was on even more intimate terms with Duke Ling than the man who looked after the duke's gangrene and boils. That person, Mi Zixia, was a famous courtier in the Spring and Autumn period. One source said that Duke Ling, for a while, was so enamored with Mi that he regarded Mi's every transgression as having a noble intent. Mi Zixia was also married to the sister of Zilu's wife. According to Mencius, Mi had told Zilu that if Confucius let him act as host and sponsor, then "the office of the counselor of Wei would be his for the asking." But when Zilu related this to his teacher, Confucius just carried on with his business: "He advanced in a manner that was appropriate and withdrew in a way that was morally right. And whether or not he succeeded in what he was doing, he always said, 'This is what it has to be.'" Mencius' argument is that if Confucius accepted any special favors, he "would not have tried to do everything right and accepted the outcome as what it has to be."

If we believe, as Mencius did, that Confucius refused to shortcut his way to power, it probably took him a long time to get a position in Wei. His reticence could not have helped him catch Duke Ling's attention. Besides, around this time, things were not going well in Wei. Early historians attributed the problems in Wei to the indiscretions of Duke Ling and his wife Nanzi. According to these historians, Duke Ling was a well-known cuckold in his own country and abroad. Nanzi was carrying on an affair with her brother, a prince from the state of Song, and instead of putting a stop to it, in 496, the year after Confucius arrived, Duke Ling summoned her brother to Wei "in order to please her." Not long after, the heir apparent of Wei, son of Duke Ling by another wife, was sent on a mission to the state of Qi, and "while passing through the countryside of Song, he heard a rustic man singing this song, 'Now that you satisfied your randy sow, / Time to send home our handsome swine.'" This song so humiliated the heir apparent that he tried to have Nanzi murdered. The plot was bungled, and Duke Ling, unable to punish or to part with Nanzi, dispatched his soldiers to go after his son. The heir apparent fled to the state of Song and did not come back to claim his rights until thirteen years later, after his own son had succeeded the father that drove him out. The succession crisis in Wei would later claim the life of Confucius' disciple Zilu.

This chapter in the history of Wei does not quite do justice to what we know about Duke Ling. According to most accounts, he was not an easy victim despite the siren hold Nanzi had on him. The *Zhuangzi* tells us that Duke Ling "drank wine and wallowed in pleasure, paying no heed to the government or the state"; that "he went hunting and gaming with nets and stringed arrows, ignoring his obligations to the other feudal lords"; "that he had three wives with whom he would bathe in the same tub." It appears, therefore, that Duke Ling was himself a randy swine to his randy sow. He was also the man Confucius hoped to serve.

We do not know how Confucius landed a job with this ruler or whether his position was at all important. Confucius probably saw Duke Ling very rarely. Only one meeting between Confucius and Duke Ling is recorded in the *Analects*:

Duke Ling of Wei asked Confucius about military formation. Confucius responded, "I know something about the use of ritual vessels but have not learned anything about commanding the troops." The next day Confucius decided to leave Wei.

Confucius must have waited a long time to have an audience with this ruler, and then decided to leave Wei because from the question Duke Ling asked he could tell that he was counseling the wrong man. Duke Ling was interested only in winning wars, while Confucius could teach him only the civilizing ways of the rites.

However, Sima Qian, in his account, not only exaggerates this ruler's estimation of Confucius' worth and the frequency of their meetings, but also imagines the rift to be personal—the result of inattentiveness on the part of Duke Ling and a casual slight:

Duke Ling and his wife [Nanzi] were sharing a carriage with the eunuch Yong Qu as their escort and Confucius as Yong Qu's assistant. Confucius said, "I have yet to meet a man who loves virtue as much as he loves the enthralling sight of a beautiful woman." Angry and humiliated, he left Wei.

The episode is a familiar one. Sima Qian tells us that Confucius left Lu for similar reasons, and that as he was going, he chanted this song:

> A woman's tongue can send a man to flight.
> Her insinuations can send him to his doom.
> So why not wander here and there,
> Until I am finished my allotted years?

Was this how Confucius felt about women? Did he really think that women were the ruin of men—of their lives and careers, and of their chance to live a virtuous life? Or did Sima Qian invent this? In his biography of Confucius, Sima Qian usually tucked Confucius' comments about women into the conclusion of a chapter. The comments would follow some account about how Confucius had failed to get the ruler interested in carrying out his duties as a ruler. From Sima Qian's reporting, we have the impression that whenever Confucius could, he would point to a woman and say it was her fault, so that he would not be so disappointed in himself. But a sharp and cognizant person like Confucius must have known that most of the rulers of his time were more susceptible to the influence of those who lived by their wiles and charm than to the influence of those who lived by their integrity and wit. He must also have known that the influence could have come from a man or a woman.

The history of the Spring and Autumn period did not lack women with irreproachable character and a strong point of view. One was Duke Ling's adoptive grandmother, Ding Jiang. Ding Jiang was the principal wife of Duke Ling's grandfather, but since her only son died before his time, she was made the adoptive mother of Duke Ling's father. When the hereditary families of Wei forced her adopted son into exile because he had been callous and shortsighted, this man instructed the priest in the ancestral temple to inform his forbears that he was fleeing the country but that he had done nothing wrong. When Ding Jiang learned of what her adopted son had told the priest, she said:

> Since there are no gods, whom shall we notify? And if there are gods, we cannot insult them by telling them a lie. Our ruler has done wrong, so how can we say that he is not to blame? He abandoned his counselors and schemed with his minions. This is his first crime. His father appointed his own counselors to be his tutors and guardians, yet he failed to show them any respect. This is his second crime. I attended to his father's every need, waiting on his father with towels and comb, yet he treated me boorishly as if I was a [leftover] concubine. This is his third crime. Tell the ancestors that he is fleeing. But don't say to them that he has done nothing wrong.

It is understandable that the true and laudable would admire a woman like Ding Jiang. Her speech rivaled those of the great counselors of the past, but, as every fine gentleman in the empire knew, it would not have any effect on a man like her adopted son, whether he was the ruler in the palace or an exile in the wilderness.

Confucius did not comment on the lady Ding Jiang, or if he did, we do not have any record of it. But he did have something to say about women like her. One such person was a woman from the Gongwen family. She was the mother of a Lu counselor. According to one account, after this counselor died, "his wife and consorts cried as they paced the [rooms and] hallways; they cried until they lost their voice." Their mother-in-law admonished them, saying,

> When a man chooses to forgo his home for a life outside, other men will be willing to die for him. But when a man prefers to stay right at home, it is the women who will be willing to die for him. My son has died young, and from what I can see, I fear that he will be known for his love of the inner quarters.

This woman then instructed the young widows who decided to remain in her household and not to remarry:

> Don't look wan and sallow. Don't cry buckets of tears. Don't beat on your chest. Don't put on a pained look. And when choosing your mourning clothes, don't exceed what the rites prescribe. Understate it. Find quietness and calm through the propriety of your conduct. This is the way to bring my deceased child to light.

We are told that when Confucius heard this, he said:

> There is no female intelligence superior to that of a middle-aged married woman. There is no male intelligence superior to that of a middle-aged married man. The female intelligence of this woman from the Gongwen family is such that she cuts off her emotional attachments and shortens the rituals in order to make eminent the virtues of her son.

In an earlier version of this story, instead of describing the nature of this woman's intelligence—that she is able to part with her attachments and minimize the rituals—Confucius simply remarks that "her female intelligence is like that of a man." From these two versions, one can perhaps understand something about Confucius' views on female and male sensibilities, certainly more than what one can learn from Sima Qian on the subject. For Confucius, it seems, a salient feature of an intelligent man is that he is able to moderate his suffering and outrage—that he is not tedious and not easily sidetracked from fulfilling a more important purpose. Confucius thinks that an intelligent woman can conduct her life in the same way, but if she does, she is more man than woman.

Confucius could not have arrived at these judgments from what he remembered about his own parents. His father died when Confucius was a toddler and so could not have left any impressions on him. Confucius had many more years with his mother, but she never reached middle age. And from the few reports we have of her, she seems to have been a taciturn and private woman. Nothing in her conduct suggests that she could have resembled the woman from the Gongwen family had she lived to see Confucius become a counselor. In the *Analects*, Confucius does not describe his parents and does not hint at his feelings about them. Yet we know that what he said about the joys and the difficulties of being a son must have come from an intimate knowledge of such things, unless, of course, he possessed an uncommon ability to internalize what he had seen and heard and what other people had told him about their mothers and fathers.

Confucius was silent about his parents and relatives, and about his forbears. His travels, however, brought him back, quite by chance, to the ancestral home of his father in the state of Song. Given the family history of the Kongs, it could not have been comfortable for him to be there. About a hundred years before Confucius was born, the head of a rival family, the Huas, murdered the head of the Kongs, took possession of this man's wife by force, and then drove the Kongs out of Song. The first time Confucius set foot in Song was probably in 492, just after his lengthy sojourn in Wei.

Duke Ling had died the year before, which may explain why Confucius left Wei. But as we are told in both the *Analects* and Sima Qian's biography, Confucius had made up his mind to go even while this ruler was alive because Duke Ling was interested mainly in fighting and fornicating. Still, Confucius allowed himself a long time before deciding that he had again chosen the wrong man to serve, and even after he resigned, he bided his time. The death of Duke Ling made Confucius' situation more urgent. The new ruler was the old ruler's grandson. Confucius did not know him and did not approve of his decision to accept his grandfather's position, since the new ruler's father was the legitimate heir and was still at large. Now Confucius felt he had no reason to linger.

Confucius was met with violence not long after he crossed the border into Song. But who could have been behind it? The Huas, by this time, had all but disappeared from Song politics. In 522, their head made a public show of contrition for the family's past transgressions, and then, two years after that, nearly all the Huas left Song for Chu. Thus they could not have been a source of trouble for Confucius. Several early works mention that when Confucius was in Song it was Huan Tui who tried "to kill him." The *Book of Mencius* reports that "Confucius was not happy in Lu and Wei" and so left these places, and that while Confucius was "passing through Song" on his way to Chen, "Huan, the minister of military affairs in Song, tried to waylay him, and, as a result, he had to travel in disguise." The *Book of Zhuangzi* says: "They tried to chop down a tree on him in Song, thus causing him great distress." The *Analects* simply quotes Confucius as saying, "Heaven has given me this power—this virtue. What can Huan Tui do to me!" Sima Qian appropriated something from all three and wrote this story:

> Confucius came to Song from Cao, and while he was practicing the rites with his disciples under a tree, the military commander of Song, Huan Tui, with the intent to see Confucius killed, uprooted the tree. Confucius stepped aside. His disciples said to him, "Let's get out of here!" Confucius replied, "Heaven

has given me this power—this virtue. What can Huan Tui do to me!"

We do not know whether Confucius had passed through Cao to get to Song. He could have gone directly to Song from Wei or journeyed east to Cao first and then south to Song. If he was in Cao, he probably did not stay long. But when he reached Song, did he already know that an ambush was waiting for him, or was the ambush truly a surprise? While Zhuangzi and the *Analects* did not say one way or the other, Mencius suggested the first scenario, and Sima Qian the second. In Sima Qian's hand, the scene becomes zany and surreal: Confucius conducts rituals with his students under a large tree; Huan Tui comes from behind and plucks up the tree, not chopping it, which would have been easier if he wants the tree to fall; the tree falls, but not on Confucius because Confucius has shifted his position; his students urge him to leave right away, and he seems unfazed, uttering the line recorded in the *Analects*.

None of the early writers explained Huan Tui's relationship to Confucius or why he wanted Confucius dead, though a character sketch of Huan Tui appeared in the history recorded in the *Zuo Commentary*. As a young man, he was his ruler's favorite. When he coveted four prized horses, his ruler wrested them from their rightful owner and gave them to him. When he was thinking of fleeing the country because his enemies had been making his life unpleasant, his ruler "cried until his eyes were swollen" and begged him not to leave. The year Confucius happened into Song, Huan Tui was an imposing figure there, probably even more powerful than Yang Hu when his career was at its peak, for Huan was the minister of military affairs in his state while Yang was merely a retainer in a large family. Thus if Huan Tui planned an ambush to have Confucius done away with, he did not have to carry it out himself. His soldiers could easily have taken care of it for him. Mencius' version, therefore, not Sima Qian's, seems more plausible here: Confucius anticipated danger and took precautions so as not to be conspicuous.

But we still do not know why Huan Tui hated Confucius so much that he wanted him dead. Since no early writings discussed this, any attempt at an answer would have to be conjectural. One recent scholar links Huan Tui to Yang Hu through a counselor from the state of Jin because this person had at one time or another looked after the interests of both men. The scholar claims that Huan Tui was acting on behalf of Yang Hu, and that Yang Hu had been tailing Confucius throughout his wanderings and was waiting for a chance to strike when Huan Tui offered his help. While the thread in the proposed scenario does not lead to any hard evidence, it does suggest that during this period of Chinese history there was a strong bond among those who took bold strides in politics and were undaunted by the size of their risks or the degree of their impropriety. These men had formidable enemies and many of them, but they looked out for one another.

The other claim about Yang Hu is more problematic. Ever since he was banished from the politics of Lu, Yang Hu had been exploring his options in other regional states, busy creating a broader, though more tenuous, political network. He was, in a way, everywhere during the period Confucius was living abroad. Thus if one wants to show that he was trailing Confucius all this time, one can use the records selectively and have the two be at same location frequently enough to construct a conspiracy theory out of it. But Yang Hu was ambitious and wily. He would not have pursued just one goal even if he considered Confucius to be his nemesis—about which there is, of course, no proof.

Yet the two men did cross paths, and their lives overlapped in ways that were beyond their own doing. A few years earlier, we are told, when Confucius was passing through a town called Kuang in the state of Zheng, a mob gathered around him, and for a while it seemed that he was going to die at their hands. That this incident happened at all was due to Yang Hu, even though Yang Hu was somewhere else and did not do anything to encourage it. Most early writers agreed that the crisis in Kuang was a case of mistaken identity: Confucius looked like Yang Hu, which was unfortunate because the people of Kuang held a grudge against Yang Hu. According to the history in the *Zuo Commentary,* in 504 the Lu army seized Kuang from the state of Zheng. To curry favor with the ruler of Jin, Yang Hu, who was the de facto power in Lu at the time, had two counselors from his state present to Jin an unknown number of captives from Kuang. His indiscretions must have offended the people of Kuang so sorely that they wanted to kill him the first chance they got. Thus when Confucius came to Kuang, they hemmed him in, thinking that he was Yang Hu.

Sima Qian put one more character in this scene to make even more persuasive the argument that the men of Kuang mistook Confucius to be Yang Hu. According to him, when Confucius "was passing by Kuang, he had as his attendant a man called Yan Ke," who had once been in the service of Yang Hu. And as they approached Kuang from its outskirts, Yan Ke, "pointing [to a section of the city wall], said to Confucius, 'The last time I entered this city, I did so through that gap.' When the people of Kuang heard this, they thought that [Confucius] was Yang Hu from Lu."

The *Analects* also mentions the incident at Kuang, but its emphasis is not on what happened but on what Confucius declaimed when the people there had him surrounded. It says:

> Confucius was in a tight situation when he was in Kuang. He said, "With King Wen dead, is it not so that his cultural vestiges are invested in me? If Heaven intended this culture to be destroyed, it would not have let the descendents [of King Wen] take part in it. Since Heaven has not destroyed this culture, what can the people of Kuang do to me?"

Here is Confucius at his best—self-possessed and confronting the world on his own with a mixture of confidence and bravado. We hear echoes of a remark he made earlier with regard to Huan Tui, but now he clearly states his purpose. He says that he inherited the work of King Wen and was helping to keep it alive, and that Heaven gave him the potential to find his strength, and once he had done so, it was ready to stand by him. Heaven is, therefore, daemon and the source of divine sanction; but in the case of Confucius, the two are often indistinguishable.

Four centuries later, the incident at Kuang took on a different significance. The Han dynasty writers worried more about how to tell the story well than how to understand what Confucius said. They also wanted Confucius to seem more impressive, more resourceful, so they adjusted the premise and made his situation even more distressing than it had been. One of these later accounts says:

> Because Confucius looked like [Yang Hu], an enemy of Yang Hu [thinking that Confucius was indeed him] armed his soldiers and ordered them to surround Confucius' home. Zilu was furious, and just as he was about to go out and confront the hostile troops, Confucius stopped him, saying, "What shallow understanding you have of what is humane [ren] and what is right [yi]! It would be my fault if I don't learn history and poetry and if I don't apply myself to music and the rites. It would be destiny, and no fault of mine, when I am not Yang Hu and people mistook me for Yang Hu. Why don't you sing a melody and I will do the harmony?" Zilu sang, and Confucius harmonized. After three rounds, the soldiers dispersed, and the siege was over.

According to this Han writer, it was, therefore, with "the sound of strings and singing" that Confucius persuaded the crowd in Kuang "he was not Yang Hu": "he did not have to resort to words to defend himself."

Sima Qian proposed yet another scenario. According to him, Confucius sent his followers to Wei, asking them to find employment with a counselor called Ning Wuzi, and through Ning's intervention, Confucius "was released." This story had to be fictitious because by the time Confucius was in Kuang, Ning had been dead for decades. Nevertheless, during those fourteen years when he was away from home, Confucius occasionally did rely on his disciples to get him the kind of political influence that a counselor like Ning could have had. He says in the *Analects,* "When I was in a rut on the road from Chen to Cai, none of my followers was in the service of a counselor." Mencius is even more explicit on this point: "The reason why Confucius was in straits between Chen and Cai was that he had no friends at court."

After leaving Song, Confucius lived in Chen for about three years. A reference in the history of the *Zuo Commentary* places him in Chen by 492. That year, the record says, there was a fire in the state of Lu, and when Confucius heard that the fire had destroyed two ancestral temples, he remarked, "It must have been the temples of Duke Huan and Duke Xi." His stay in Chen was probably uneventful, and we have no record of his activities there. In 489, "the state of Wu sent an expedition against Chen to settle an old grudge." The threat of a long war and the promise of a good job in Chu prompted Confucius to leave Chen for Chu. But as he and his disciples were making their way there, they found themselves trapped somewhere in the wilds of Chen or Cai with nearly no provisions left, and for a while it appeared that they might starve to death.

The early writers felt that the crisis in Chen or Cai was the most important chapter in the journey. For them, the episode was about confronting darkness and the void, slowly and on an empty stomach, with no visible enemy. The *Analects* says:

> In Chen, when the provisions ran out, [Confucius'] followers had become so weak that none of them could rise to their feet. Zilu, with a resentful look, said, "Does a gentleman find himself in circumstances as bleak as these?" Confucius responded, "A gentleman would persevere even in a situation [like ours]. It is the petty man who would not be able to withstand it."

Two centuries later, the Confucian thinker Xunzi would rework this dialogue, placing more emphasis on the fact that there was no reason why a man of integrity would not find himself in distress. In Xunzi's version, Confucius says:

There are plenty of people, not just myself, who have not met the opportune time. Consider the angelica and the orchid that grow in the deep forest. That no one is there to smell them does not take away their fragrance. The same applies to the learning of a gentleman: he does not learn in order to be known. Thus, in extreme straits, he will not be vexed; in times of anxiety, his purpose will not diminish.

The Daoist philosopher Zhuangzi takes the scene in Chen or Cai to another level:

Confucius was in trouble between Chen and Cai, and for seven days he ate no cooked food. His left hand was propped against a withered tree, his right beating time on a withered limb. The rapping of the limb provided an accompaniment, but it was without any fixed rhythm; there was melody, but none that fitted the usual tonal categories of *gong* or *jue*. The drumming on the tree, the voice of the singer had a pathos to them that would strike a man's heart.

Yan Hui, standing with his hands folded respectfully across his chest, turned his eyes and looked inquiringly at Confucius. Confucius, fearful that Yan Hui's respect for him was too great, that his love for him was too tender, said to him, "Hui, it is easy not to feel the afflictions of Heaven, but hard not to feel the beneficence of men. There is no beginning or end. Heaven and man are one. Who is it, then, who sings this song now?"

In these accounts, the disciples are too weak from hunger or from the thought of losing their teacher to come to terms with their distress, and so it is Confucius who tries to help them. Confucius in the *Analects* urges Zilu to hold on to his integrity. In the *Xunzi* he tells the same disciple that misfortune can visit the noblest of men if he lives in the wrong time, yet nothing of his labor is lost because his quest is not for the pursuit of a name or even of a good ending. Confucius in the *Zhuangzi* tries another tack. He says to Yan Hui that if we can feel lightly the afflictions of Heaven, why not the beneficence of men? "Heaven and man are one," he continues, and so even though his own singing has "a pathos" to it, it is no different from the music of Heaven, a singing that is neither happy nor unhappy. "Who is it, then," he asks, "who sings this song?"

Sima Qian took something from all three accounts and created his version of "the crisis in Chen or Cai." He first put Confucius and his three disciples in a hostile environment: after the men of Chen and Cai learned that Confucius was on his way to Chu, they became worried, scared that his service in Chu might endanger the future of their own countries; so they had him "surrounded in the wilderness." Sima Qian's version continues:

> Confucius could not go anywhere. His provisions ran out. His followers became so weak that none could rise to their feet. Confucius went on teaching and singing—his spirit was not at all defeated.... Yet when he realized that his disciples looked resentful, he called Zilu to his side and asked him this question: "The *Odes* says, 'I am neither rhinoceros nor tiger, yet I pace back and forth in the wilderness.' Is our way wrong? Why have we come to this?" Zilu replied, "Perhaps we are not yet virtuous, and so people do not trust us. Perhaps we do not yet have knowledge, and so people do not put our ideas into practice." Confucius said, "Is this really so? If the virtuous are always trusted, how do you explain [the tragic end of] Bo Yi and Shu Qi? If those with knowledge are always put to good use, how do you explain [the violent death of] Prince Bigan?"
>
> After Zilu left, Zigong came to see Confucius. Confucius put the same question to him. ... Zigong replied, "Your way is too great. The world is unable to contain it. Why don't you modify it and make it a little simpler?" Confucius said to him, "A good farmer can work as hard as he can but does not always reap a harvest. A fine artisan can produce wonderful craftsmanship but is not always appreciated. A gentleman can be cultivating a [superior] way for himself; he can outline and summarize what he has learned, and gather all the strands and sort them into [interlock-

ing] principles. Yet people will not always accept what he can teach them. Now it seems that you are not pursuing [learning and] self-understanding. Rather, you seek to have your ideas gain acceptance. Your goal is not far enough!"

After Zigong left, Yan Hui came to see Confucius. Again Confucius put the question to him. . . . Yan Hui replied, "Your way is too great. The world is unable to contain it. Even so, you push to have it put into action. But what is wrong if the world cannot contain it? It goes to show that you are a superior man. It is our disgrace if we fail to cultivate the higher way. It is the ruler's disgrace if we have done all we can and he doesn't put our way to use." Confucius smiled and said, "You are right, son of the Yan clan! If you should ever become rich, I will manage your money."

The antagonists Sima Qian put in his story probably did not exist. The men of Chen and of Cai were inimical toward each other and so could not have worked together to try to stop Confucius from reaching Chu. A more likely scenario is that Confucius and his disciples wandered into the wilderness without a clear sense of where they were going or a plan to fall back on in case they were in trouble, and other people had simply forgotten about them. To confront a death that is without consequence is sad and lonely but also less clouded. This was how Sima Qian wrote the scene, even though he thought it would be flattering for Confucius if an adverse circumstance were forced upon him by men who were jealous of his talents. But once Sima Qian got going with his three-part conversation even he had forgotten the enemy. And it was his genius that he let the conversation unfold as if it were these four men's last, without the bother of an outside world.

First Zilu responds to Confucius' question. He judges his teacher by how other people react to him. If other people do not trust him and if they are reluctant to implement his ideas, Zilu thinks, then it must be Confucius who does not have perfect character and sufficient knowledge. Zilu would be willing to die for his teacher, yet he cannot be absolutely sure that Confucius is virtuous and his way is right. Just as he wants Confucius to have a counselor's death and a counselor's burial, he wants to see public approval of his teacher before he can let go of his own doubts. Confucius' response is curt: Why should a good man be trusted and why should the ways of the learned be put to use? He rebukes Zilu for trying to work out the cause and effect of human behavior with simple equations.

Zigong, on the other hand, is certain that Confucius' way is greater than all others. But, he feels, it is too big to fit into this world. He would like to see Confucius reduce it a little—lower his standards a little—so that others may begin to think that they can embrace it as well. Moreover, Zigong himself could apply his skills at rhetoric and sales to help Confucius promote a more appealing version of his teachings. In response, Confucius points out that his teachings have nothing to do with giving pleasure or looking agreeable. He says he would not consider himself to have failed if his way was not accepted; he would worry only that he had not done his best to cultivate it.

Only Yan Hui understands Confucius on his own. He also thinks that Confucius' way is too large to fit into this world, yet he is unperturbed. He says: "What is wrong if the world cannot contain it? It goes to show that you are a superior man." The conceit may seem forward, but it gives Yan Hui a reason to keep going. After all, he was Confucius' fellow quester and closest companion, as Zhuangzi observed years later. His purpose was the same as Confucius', and so, unlike Zilu and Zigong, he had no other distractions, no political ambitions of his own or moneymaking schemes.

Confucius, however, does not praise Yan Hui for standing by him. In Sima Qian's imagination, he smiles and says, "You are right, son of the Yan clan! If you should become rich, I will manage your money." Yan Hui could never have become rich. He was content living in a shabby neighborhood on millet and water. But should Yan Hui suddenly take a liking for moneymaking, Confucius says that he would lend him his help. His declaration of loyalty is lighthearted and stated at a desperate hour. This is Confucius' show of detachment.

No one knows how Confucius got himself out of his troubles. Sima Qian claimed that Confucius "dispatched Zigong to Chu" and that the ruler of Chu sent his own men to have Confucius escorted out of the wilderness. For some time now, scholars have been skeptical of this story, but no other explanation has emerged. We know that Confucius reached Chu because two conversations he had with the governor of She, which was a district of Chu, are recorded in the *Analects*.

The district of She had originally been a part of Cai. In 493, the ruler of Cai decided to move his capital east to be nearer to Wu, which was his ally at the time. The area around She was, therefore, left to its own devices. Two years later, the government of Chu took control of She, and its representatives encouraged the people of Cai, who had decided not to move east with their ruler, to come and settle in She and to recognize Chu as their new overlord. When Confucius arrived in She, the governor had just been assigned there, his subjects were essentially a foreign people, and he was a long way from his own political base in Chu. In their first conversation, the administrator asked Confucius, "What is considered good government?" Confucius replied, "[A government is good] when those who are near are pleased and those who are far away are drawn to it." The advice was appropriate to the governor's circumstances at the time. Surely he was hoping to keep his new subjects content and to inspire more settlers to come. The *Zuo* writers say that the governor remained in his position for twelve years. In 479, he went home to help put an end to a cycle of violence that had been consuming the Chu court, but once he had finished doing so, he returned to She to retire.

When Confucius was in She, the governor also shared with him a criminal case that had come to his attention or had come under his jurisdiction. In their conversation, the governor mentioned the circumstances of this case but not his opinion of it, so one suspects that he was waiting to hear what Confucius had to say. He told Confucius: "Right here, in my native place, there is a man called Upright Gong. When his father stole a sheep, he bore witness against him." Confucius replied: "In my native place, those who are considered upright are quite different from this man. Fathers cover up for their sons, and sons cover up for their fathers. Being upright lies therein."

Upright Gong was only the son of a common thief, yet what he did resulted in one of the most talked-about cases in Chinese history. Moral philosophers and legal historians were drawn to it just as they were to the story of the Duke of Zhou and his two contemptuous brothers. Like the earlier episode, it raised issues concerning the individual's relationship to society: whether it is possible for a person to fulfill both his love for the family and his social responsibilities, and what happens when the two clash.

It is not clear whether "Upright Gong" was already a celebrated case by Confucius' time or whether its importance grew out of the conversation recorded in the *Analects*. Confucius did not consider this man upright because, in his part of the world, "fathers cover up for their sons, and sons cover up for their fathers," and in this, he said, one finds what is upright. The eighteenth-century scholar Cheng Yaotian offered what, I believe, is the most forceful defense of this view. In his essay "Talking about Public Spirit," he writes:

> Someone making an irrevocable statement says: "Once there is true public spirit [*gong*], then private feelings and private motives [*si*] will no longer exist." One cannot believe that this statement is taking the idea of public spirit to any higher ground. In fact, I would argue that it does not have much to do with the idea. It is the kind of teaching that treats all things with equal humanity and encourages love without distinction.

Cheng is also deeply suspicious of the man who claims that he acts solely for the good of the public:

> When everyone else acts out of private motives, and one person makes a show that he does not, is this then truly a case where private motives do not exist? If even the sages find it difficult to realize what is called "public spirit," and one person finds it easy, does it mean that this person has made simple what everyone else considers as difficult? Has he gotten what he claims to have?

In this scholar's view, such a man either is seeking a reputation of being public-minded or he is not human. For, if he is human, he would naturally have more love for his family than for anyone else, and more love for his own son than for his brother's son. To have preferences is an inherent condition of being human and is the reason why even the wisest and the most virtuous "find it difficult" to attain a goal as noble and considerable as "public spirit." Without this condition, Cheng argues, no matter how upright or public-minded an action might seem, it has no real integrity; and this is how he understood Confucius' remark that "uprightness lies therein." He writes, "[It means that] one has to use [the fullness of] one's private feelings to realize what is impartial and what is for the public good."

Confucius never used the relationship of private to public to articulate what he meant by "upright." He was firm in his judgment of the man who betrayed his father, yet he left room for a reader like Cheng to find relevance in it for himself. No one knows what really happened to Upright Gong after he turned his father in. There are at least two conflicting reports, both from the third century BC. The first is found in the writings of the legalist thinker Hanfeizi. He says that the local official had Upright Gong put to death because "in his attempt to be upright while in the service of his sovereign, this man had wronged his father." Hanfeizi finds the official confused and incompetent. The second source, *Mr. Lü's Spring and Autumn Annals,* tells us, however, that just as the authorities were about to have Upright Gong's father executed, the son asked to take his father's place; and that just as Upright Gong himself was about to be killed, he said to the officials who were present: "I informed on my father when he stole a sheep. Am I not trustworthy? When my father was about to be put to death, I asked to die in his place. Am I not filial? Now I am both trustworthy and filial, and yet you want to have me killed. Is there anyone else left in this country whom you don't want to execute?" Anticipating Cheng Yaotian some two thousand years later, the Confucius of *Mr. Lü's Spring and Autumn Annals* remarks, "How odd this thing that Upright Gong called 'trustworthy'"! Was it not just a name he hoped to gain by selling out his father?"

The district of She was as far south as Confucius had gone before he decided to turn back. He must have left She around 487. If he was homesick, this was not the first time. When he was living in the state of Chen, he said at one point, "Let's go home, let's go home! Our young men back home are spirited and fresh (*kuang*). They are brilliant fabric but don't know how to shape their material." As an idea, *kuang* goes beyond being spirited; it is being wildly spirited and sublimely wild. Once, a disciple of Mencius asked his teacher: "When Confucius was in Chen, why did he miss the wildly spirited men of Lu?" Mencius said: "Confucius himself had remarked, 'Not being able to be within the reach of those who never swerve from what is appropriate and sufficient, one has no choice but to turn to the wildly spirited and the overly cautious.'" In Chen, Confucius' thoughts turned to the wildly spirited. Yet one suspects that he was always attracted to those who were slightly off the mark.

In She, he came very close to meeting Jie Yu, a wildly spirited man, known to the world as "the Madman of Chu." The *Analects* says:

> As Jie Yu went past Confucius' door, he sang, "Phoenix, phoenix, / How your virtue has declined! / What has gone by cannot be made right. / What is to come may yet be overtaken. / Leave off, leave off, / Dangerous are those in office today."

In this song, Confucius is the phoenix—not a phoenix in full splendor but one whose power "has declined"—from years of travel, perhaps, and the lonely chase of things good and noble. The madman tells Confucius, "Leave off, leave off," for one cannot correct the mistakes of the past or anticipate new ones in the future. He warns also of the perils of politics: "Dangerous are those in office today." We are told that when Confucius heard this song, he rushed to the gate, hoping to have a word with this man, but Jie Yu had already vanished.

Why was Confucius so eager to speak to Jie Yu if he was the phoenix of the two? What did he want from Jie Yu that his own belief could not have satisfied? And why did Jie Yu hurry away from him? What did he fear? These are the questions early texts like to pose, regardless of their teachings, and they are not always playful ones, the kind skeptics like to contrive to rattle their readers. Zhuangzi, the genius in a skeptic's disguise, recorded a longer version of Jie Yu's song that some scholars have thought to be closer to the original. In it, the singer offers more clues about himself and a sharper point of view. He says to Confucius:

> In times like the present, it is already hard work just to avoid punishment. Good fortune is light as a feather, yet no one knows how to hold it up. Misfortune is as heavy as earth, yet no one knows how to stay out of its way. Enough, enough, this looking after people with the force of your integrity. / Dangerous, dangerous, this picking your path and then setting off. / Brambles, brambles, don't spoil my walk. / I walk a crooked path—don't hurt my feet.

In Jie Yu's view, Confucius was phoenix and bramble: supremely noble and a menace. He chose too carefully and pushed too far, in a time when it was "already hard work just to avoid punishment." And Confucius? What did he think of Jie Yu? He knew, of course, that Jie Yu was not raving mad, just so spirited that he could not walk a straight line. He knew also that Jie Yu had something to offer: a way out of his despair and a way out of the dangers humans created in a human world. Jie Yu was the tempter in the wild, but there were others like him, whom Confucius might or might not have met on his way home from Chu.

As examples of such people, the *Analects* mentions two tall and imposing men, Changju and Jieni, working in the soft and oozy field.

> Confucius went past them and then sent Zilu to find out where the ford might be.
> Changju asked, "Who is that man driving the carriage?"
> Zilu replied, "It's Kong Qiu."*

---

*This is, of course, Confucius' name—family name (Kong) plus given name (Qiu).

"Is it Kong Qiu of Lu?"

"Yes."

"Then he knows where the ford is."

Zilu then tried [the other man] Jieni.

Jieni asked, "Who are you?"

"Zhongyou."*

"Then you must be a disciple of Kong Qiu of Lu."

"I am."

"The world is in chaos, yet it is full of people, wandering here and there [trying to find someone who might use their talents to set things right]. [The turmoil continues and so] why bother to seek another ruler when you have given up this one? Why change? Moreover, why do you want to follow someone who kept running away from men [who turned out to be the wrong ones to serve]? Why not follow someone who has run away from the world altogether?"

Zilu went to tell Confucius what these two men had said.

Confucius seemed lost in thought for a while. Then he spoke: "We cannot flock with birds and beasts, can we? Whom can I be with if not with other human beings? The world has a moral way, [I know,] so I will not let those two change my mind."

Immediately following this entry, the *Analects* records another encounter Zilu had with a third stranger. The second episode could have happened around the same time as the first, along the stretch from Cai to Chen, where birds and beasts were more at home than humans. In this scene, Zilu gets separated from Confucius. He meets "an old man carrying a basket on a staff over his shoulder." Zilu asks this man whether he has seen his master.

The old man said, "You look like someone who neither has toiled with his limbs nor is able to tell one kind of grain from another.

---

*This is Zilu's given name.

Who can your master be?" He then planted his staff in the ground and started to weed.

Zilu stood, cupping one hand in the other, showing his respect.

The old man invited Zilu to stay for the night. He killed a chicken and cooked millet for his guest to eat, and he introduced him to his two sons.

The next day, Zilu resumed his journey, [and when he met up with Confucius again] he related what had happened. Confucius said, "[The old man] must be a recluse." He then sent Zilu back to find him. When Zilu got there, the old man had already gone somewhere else.

The scene ends with Zilu's remarks:

There is no way of knowing what is appropriate and what is right if one does not enter public life. If the old man knows not to abandon the etiquette between old and young, how can he let go of the moral responsibility between ruler and subject? By keeping himself unsullied, he has brought confusion to an important human relationship. A gentleman takes office in order to understand the rightness in that relationship. As for putting the moral way into practice, he knows all along that it is not possible.

Confucius said that he could not let the recluses change his mind no matter how enticing their way might seem, for he was human and could not live among birds and beasts. Zilu told us more. He said that Confucius knew all along that it was hopeless for him to put "the moral way into practice," yet he still had to get himself involved in public life, in order to understand what was right at that level of human relationship. In both episodes, Confucius and the recluse each held on to what he believed—each was beyond persuasion—yet the *Analects* would like us to believe that this was all right, all right for them to go their separate ways.

A paragraph later, in the *Analects,* we find a list of men who withdrew from society in order to preserve their integrity. Confucius weighs their characters. He draws subtle distinctions among them, and he has nice things to say about all. The men in one group "did not modify their purpose and did not bring disgrace upon themselves." Those in another group might have "modified their purpose and suffered from disgrace but their words were morally sound and their conduct never sidled from their thought." Those in a third group "lived in seclusion and said whatever they liked; they were immaculate in character, and in giving up the world, they acted with expediency." Confucius concludes: "But I am different from all these men. I have no preconceptions about what one can or cannot do."

Confucius did not have to tell anyone that he was different. He displayed his singularity in many ways, sometimes quite unexpectedly. In the first years of his exile, he learned to play the stone chimes. One day a man, carrying a basket, went past his door and heard him striking the chimes.

> The man said, "This playing is fraught with a heavy and careworn heart." He continued, "How squalid this *keng keng* sound! If no one understands him, then he should just keep what he believes to himself and that is all: 'If the water is deep, then just wade across it. If the water is shallow, lift your hem and cross it.'"
>
> Confucius, in response, made this remark: "[This man sounds like he knows what he wants.] If he is so resolute, then he should not have any difficulties."

The man with a basket was surely a recluse. The early commentaries identify such men as "worthies who had decided to hide from the world." The charitable man Zilu met years later in the wilderness of Chen or Cai also carried a basket. These men are all resolute. They all know to adjust the length of their garment to the depth of the water—letting themselves steep in the world when virtue is high and plenty, and lifting themselves up when virtue is shallow and scarce. Confucius sees their point and commends their decision, but he also thinks that if these men are so clear-eyed about what to do and how to act, then they "should not have any difficulties" at all. He, however, is different. His love for the human race is born out of the squalid, and his relation to the world does not change because of the moral climate. He demands no terms, and he has no certain ideas about what is permissible and what is not.

A contributing editor of *Mr. Lü's Spring and Autumn Annals* had Confucius give this self-description:

> A dragon drinks from the clear water and swims in the clear. A yellow *chi* dragon drinks from the clear water but swims in the turbid. A fish drinks from the turbid and swims in the turbid. I am not as good as the dragon but not as lowly as the fish. Am I not then a *chi*?

This Confucius was being modest. He knew how difficult it had been to drink from a clear pool and swim in the mud, and how much easier if he had decided to live an immaculate life in an immaculate place. He knew he could have been a dragon but chose to be a *chi*.

CHAPTER FIVE

Return

ONFUCIUS WAS BACK IN WEI BY 485. FOUR YEARS OF HIS
life, from 489 to the end of 486, are unaccounted for: he either was
in enforced idleness in the south or was slowly making his way back
to the north. Meanwhile, his disciples Zigong and Ran Qiu had gone
ahead and accepted jobs in Lu. They were young and full of promise,
and so Confucius did not mind letting them go.

In Wei, Confucius befriended a powerful counselor called Kong
Yu. Kong Yu had serious troubles at home. His wife was carrying on
an affair with a manservant in the household, but the truth about
them did not surface until Kong Yu died, so he was spared any public humiliation. However, while he was alive, Kong Yu fomented
controversies his own way. Sometime before 485, he put pressure on
a junior counselor to marry his daughter when this man already had
a wife, and had the wife's sister as his secondary consort. After the
younger colleague consented to a divorce and a new marriage, to
Kong Yu's daughter, he still could not part with the former sister-in-
law, and so he set up house with her in a district near the capital. At
the time, everyone knew that this junior counselor carried on his life

"as if he had two wives." His indiscretion so enraged Kong Yu that Kong decided to take back his daughter and confront his son-in-law "with force." Just before an assault was to take place, he paid a visit to Confucius, to see if his friend felt that he was doing the right thing. What happened next cannot be clearly established, but it seems that as soon as Kong asked whether he should take up arms against his son-in-law, Confucius became so enraged that he told his own carriage driver "to hitch up and take him out of Wei without delay."

Confucius' reaction to Kong Yu's appeal for advice is baffling. Here was a man with a high official position seeking the counsel of someone without a position because of the latter's superior virtue. What was there to object to? Moreover, Confucius was known to have had a favorable opinion of this man. In the *Analects*, he says: "[Kong Yu] was quick and eager to learn. He [was a person of high status, yet he] was not ashamed to ask advice from those of low station." If Kong Yu was as worthy as his friend described him, why, then, when he asked this friend a question in good faith, did the latter find this so offensive that his immediate response was to flee? What Kong Yu said next, as he was trying to get Confucius to stay, may offer a clue. He declared: "How dare I act [against my son-in-law] to satisfy myself! I was merely trying to protect the state of Wei from any further disasters."

It appears that when Kong Yu first informed Confucius of his plan to attack his son-in-law, Confucius saw it as an act of personal vengeance, which, in his view, could never put an end to a feud or teach anyone a lesson. He said: "To attack the wrongful act but not the person who performed it, is this not the way to reform the depraved? To let a sudden fit of anger make you forget the dangers you risk for yourself and for those who are nearest and dearest to you, is this not misguided judgment?" Besides, when the principals were "men in government," their private wars could have unrectifiable consequences and involve many more people, including those who had nothing to do with either side of the conflict. "Men in government," Confucius said, "should not reward on account of private favors or punish on account of personal grudges." Kong Yu may have guessed why Confucius was angry and so expressed shock that he could be so misunderstood: "How dare I act [against my own family] to satisfy myself!" Confucius was probably too clever to be swayed by his friend's rhetoric; still, he showed signs of wavering. And just as he "was thinking that he might stay after all," a summons from the Lu court arrived with either the gift of a handsome sum or the promise of a good salary. "Thereupon," the *Zuo Commentary* says, "Confucius returned home." The event took place in the winter of 484, and the person who arranged it was probably Ran Qiu.

Ran Qiu had been in the service of the Jisun family since his own return to Lu, and he had swiftly made himself indispensable. There was a further boost to his standing in 484, just before Confucius came home. In the spring of that year, two commanders from the state of Qi moved their troops alarmingly close to the border of Lu. The head of the Jisuns, also the chief counselor of Lu, Jikangzi, asked Ran Qiu how he should respond to this hostile gesture. This was after he had learned from the two other hereditary families that they were not interested in committing their troops should a war break out. Ran Qiu reassured him, saying, "The number of soldiers and chariots in your family alone well surpasses what the enemy dispatched. So what is your worry? With the political power of Lu solely in your hands, it is easy to understand why the other two families are reluctant to fight. This being the case, if you do not face down the Qi army, which has come to attack us, you will be bringing disgrace upon yourself while making it impossible [for our ruler] to be included in the roster of the feudal lords."

So it was in this way that Ran Qiu tried to cajole and shame the Jisuns into action. And while the Jisuns were still struggling to find the courage to confront the enemy, Ran Qiu put himself in charge of the Left Army, which, nearly eighty years before, the family had appropriated from the state for their own use. He asked Guan Zhoufu to be his charioteer and Fan Chi to be his lieutenant. When his superiors objected to his choice of Fan Chi, saying, "He is too young," Ran Qiu replied, "He knows how to give orders."

Ran Qiu was right to take Fan Chi with him. Together the two led the Left Army to what turned out to be a decisive battle for Lu. The *Zuo* writer says: "The Qi army was coming at us from Jiqu, and our soldiers were unwilling to cross a gully to meet them head on. . . . Fan Chi tells [Ran Qiu], 'It's not that our men are unable [to confront the enemy]. It's that they do not yet trust you. Shout the order to charge three times, and then be the first to cross the gully.'" When Ran Qiu did exactly as Fan Chi advised, his troops followed him without the slightest hesitation: "they chopped off eighty enemy heads and threw the opposing side into complete disarray." By the end of the day, the Qi army was forced to turn back.

Ran Qiu must have earned so much merit in the war against the Qi that if he had asked his superiors to make a proper offer to his teacher to entice him back, they would have been inclined to oblige. The Han historian Sima Qian tells us that after the enemy troops were routed, the chief counselor Jikangzi asked Ran Qiu about his knowledge of the art of warfare: "Did you acquire it or were you born with it?" Ran Qiu said, "I learned it from Confucius."

Jikangzi asked, "What sort of person is Confucius?"

Ran Qiu replied, "He is someone who will use force only when there are good reasons to do so; and someone who has no regrets if his plan is broadcast to the people and made plain to the gods and spirits. And if by following his way, I were to gain a territory of one thousand *she*-units of household, my teacher would not want any part of it."

Jikangzi said, "If I want to send for him, would that be all right?"

Ran Qiu answered, "If you want to send for him, then [once he is here] do not use the means of a petty man to make him feel constricted. If you can manage that, then it will be all right."

Ran Qiu might have acted in concert with his classmates to get Jikangzi interested in Confucius, who, without such coverage, might have been just another counselor from the past. Zigong by now had gained a reputation as an expert on rites and diplomacy. On several occasions, the heads of the Three Families and the ruler of Lu called upon him to extricate them from situations or propositions that they felt were unfavorable to their standing in the world of interstate politics. In 488, for instance, four years before Confucius' return to Lu, the ruler of Wu demanded a meeting with the ruler of Lu at a place called Zeng; and as soon as everyone got there, he extorted from the representatives of Lu one hundred domestic animals as gifts for the people of Wu. His chief counselor then insisted that his counterpart from Lu also be present at the gathering, saying that "if the two rulers ventured a long distance to come here, surely it would be improper for the counselors to stay home." The chief counselor of Lu sent Zigong to formally decline the invitation. Once Zigong reached Zeng, his response to the counselor from Wu was crisp and elegant: "The conduct of our counselor can hardly be regarded as being in compliance with the rites. However, he acted in anticipation of what a powerful state [like yours] might do to a weak one [like ours]. A powerful state [like yours] has imposed its will on other regional states without any consideration for the rites. Once you have disregarded the rites, is there any limit to what you might do?"

No one wrote about the welcome Confucius received, but there is no doubt that he arrived home with a respectability he had not known before. The success of Ran Qiu and Zigong could have helped to boost his image as a man with smart political sense and uncommon pedagogical skills. But Confucius was also someone who had been a long time on the road: he had seen a lot and heard a lot; he had survived the violence of nature and the ferocity of court politics. Thus even before he entered the city gates, plenty of young men in the capital of Lu were considering studying with him. Among them was Fan Chi, Ran Qiu's right-hand man in the conflict against the Qi.

Other circumstances were also in Confucius' favor. Duke Ding and his counselor Jihuanzi, the two men who drove him out in 497, had long been dead, as were most of the old guards in their coterie; and now, in the eyes of the present ruler, Duke Ai, and his counselors, Confucius was their "state's elder" (*guolao*). The larger world, however, was a harsher and gloomier place: conflicts among the regional states occurred with greater frequency and many more casualties, and Lu had become even more disjointed than Confucius remembered. During the war, Duke Ai's uncle, twin brother of Duke Ding, told the keeper at the gate just moments before he was cut down by the Qi soldiers in the suburb of the capital: "We are inundated by troubles and weighed down by levies. Our leaders are unable to plan for the future. Our men are unwilling to die for our country." His commentary reflects accurately the underside of Lu, which might not have been within Confucius's ken in the first few weeks of his arrival.

Toward the end of 484, the Jisun family wanted to collect land tax from their tenants, and they dispatched their chief steward, Ran Qiu, to Confucius to sound out his views on the matter. Confucius, however, despite Ran Qiu's repeated pleas for some sort of an answer, would only say, "I don't understand a thing about it." Finally his student declared: "But you are our *guolao,* our elder statesman. I am waiting to hear from you in order to know what to do. So why don't you say something?" Confucius "still did not respond."

Confucius realized that his thoughts on the issue were not what the Jisuns wanted to hear. He also felt that to let Ran Qiu bear his message would not be wise or fair, for it would confound Ran Qiu's own stance on the tax proposal and put him in a difficult position with his employers. For these reasons, he refused to give Ran Qiu an answer. Privately, however, Confucius told him:

> The gentleman gauges his action according to the spirit of the rites—when conferring a benefit, he tries to be generous; when performing a service, he aims for what is most appropriate; when imposing a tax, he is sparing.

Once they were alone, Confucius also let Ran Qiu know his assessment of the Jisuns:

> If they do not measure their actions by the spirit of the rites and are consumed by desires that cannot be satisfied, then even taxing

the people by the crop yield on their land will not be enough for them. Moreover, if the Jisuns really wanted to do the right thing, there is always the standard set by the Duke of Zhou. Now if they want to act as they please, why come to me?

Here "the standard set by the Duke of Zhou" refers to the *fengjian* system this counselor instituted at the founding of the dynasty, wherein the relationship of a regional ruler and his subjects was based on mutual support, not on material transactions: people contributed to the ruler and the state through their work on the public land, while the ruler made sure that his people would never be deprived of their basic sustenance. In Confucius' view, that relationship was ideal because it demanded reciprocity in the form of moral obligation and public service. But, he said, to ask the people for payment in kind instead of payment in service would spoil the relationship, for once the ruler began to accumulate a private hoard, he would not know when to stop, and the people would naturally feel unhappy and would be reluctant to volunteer their service in a time of need.

In 484, the situation in Lu was further complicated by the fact that the ruler had no authority to collect revenue. He had given away most, if not all, of his administrative districts to the Three Families even before they took possession of his army in 562. Thus by the time the Jisuns wanted to impose a land tax on the tenants living on their land, the rulers of Lu had long been relying on the "tributes" sent by the families as their income.

The Jisuns did not invent the land tax. The concept had been around for a long time. The rulers of Jin, Qin, and Chu had all tried it and found it gainful. The idea was first introduced in Lu in 594, before its rulers were stripped of their power and property. Since no tax records of Lu from the Spring and Autumn period have survived, it is difficult to know how often and how widely it was implemented. Early scholars of the *Spring and Autumn Annals*, however, found the policy deplorable. The *Zuo Commentary* says: "It is against the spirit of the rites and the rules of propriety. To increase his wealth, a ruler should not collect more grain from his people than what he receives through the labor he borrows from them." Another commentary of the same Lu chronicle explains that since land tax was collected in addition to, not in lieu of, the grain produced on the public land, "the state extracted all it could from the people for its own benefit." This was also Confucius' opinion, and so, in his private conversation with Ran Qiu, he reminded his disciple of what would be an acceptable measure when imposing a tax. Violation of this "universal standard," he warned, would often mean that it would benefit the few to the ruin of many. Ran Qiu, we learn, "did not listen to his teacher." By the spring of 483, the *Spring and Autumn Annals* states, "The land tax was administered."

The *Analects* tells us what happened next:

> The wealth of the Jisun family exceeded that of the Duke of Zhou and still Ran Qiu helped them add further to that wealth by raking in the taxes. Confucius said, "He is no disciple of mine. You, my young friends, may attack him openly to the beating of the drums."

Confucius had good reasons to be enraged. The Jisuns constituted the largest landowner in Lu, with more administrative districts under their control than all that the rival families had in total. This meant that the land tax they reinstituted in 483 must have caused widespread hardship. In the meantime, nature also turned savage. We learn that in the winter of 483, there was a locust plague, and that two more followed the next year. The combined effect of these afflictions must have made Confucius extremely testy.

The *Analects* records several other occasions in which Confucius lost his temper with Ran Qiu. When another disciple, Gongxi Hua, was sent on a mission to Qi, Ran Qiu offered to look after Gongxi Hua's mother. He asked Confucius how much grain he should send to the elderly lady while her son was away. Confucius told him, "A *fu*." Ran Qiu asked for more. Confucius said, "A *yu*." Ran Qiu gave her a *bing*, many times more than a *fu* or a *yu* of grain. After hearing about this, Confucius remarked, "Chih [Gongxi Hua] went off to Qi, drawn by firm-fleshed horses and sporting a light-fur gown. I have heard it said, a gentleman is busy finding ways to help the poor and desperate—he does not try to top up the supply [in the storehouse] of the rich."

In yet another instance, Confucius learned that Jikangzi intended to "set out offerings and perform sacrifices on Mount Tai." This was an ostentatious act of infringement—a kind of ritualistic usurpation—since the Zhou king alone was entitled to conduct rites to Mount Tai and Jikangzi was only a counselor to a feudal lord. Confucius right away asked Ran Qiu whether "he could put a stop to it," given Ran Qiu's close relationship to this counselor and the occasional success he had had in getting the counselor to bend his way. Ran Qiu gave an uninterested response—"There is nothing I can do"—which prompted Confucius to say, in that case, then, Mount Tai would not accept the sacrifices anyway because the circumstances were fraudulent.

According to the record of his own words, Confucius seems to have been more disappointed in Ran Qiu, and less forgiving of this disciple, than he was toward all others who had come to study with him. This is curious. Ran Qiu, after all, was a great success. He accomplished more in government than any of his classmates and more than Confucius had hoped to achieve for himself. He was also the first to take charge of an army when unfriendly approaches threatened his country, and the first to charge into an enemy formation when no one else was willing. Ran Qiu had talent and political instinct. And he was plucky, a real soldier. Yet he lacked moral courage: he was not brave enough to contradict the wishes of his superiors. Confucius picked up on this when he remarked that Ran Qiu, like Zilu, was capable of serving "on the supervisory staff of a hereditary family" but "incapable of serving his lord in a moral way." Ran Qiu, on the other hand, admitted openly to his teacher, "It is not that I am not pleased with your way, but rather that my strength gives out." To this Confucius replied, "Those whose strength gives out collapse along the way. You draw a line first [to tell yourself how far you want to go]."

Whenever Confucius urged Ran Qiu to dissuade his lord from behaving badly or doing something wrongfully, Ran Qiu's immediate reflex was to recoil—to blurt out an excuse such as "I can't do anything more about it." He set the limit before he allowed himself to find out if his strength would indeed "give out." In Confucius' mind, this was moral cowardice against which he could do little to help except to take Ran Qiu seriously each time he came to him for advice. Confucius realized that in the end it was Ran Qiu who had to find the courage to act as he saw was right even when he was under fire or under pressure from above.

By this time, Confucius' own influence in the political world was limited. People might defer to Confucius as their elder statesman, but such a calling carried little weight in government and among the decision makers of Lu. An audience Confucius had with Duke Ai in 481 makes this point. Earlier that year, a counselor of Qi, Chen Heng, created a succession crisis in his country. First he got rid of his rivals in court; then he took his ruler by force to a district he controlled and had the ruler put to death. This was not the first time counselor Chen killed a ruler. A few years back he had dealt with the father of this ruler in the same way. Now, with the father and the son both dead, he put a grandson in their place. The *Zuo Commentary* says:

> On the sixth day of the sixth month, Chen Heng from the state of Qi slew his ruler Ren. Confucius fasted for three days [before going to see Duke Ai]. Three times he implored the ruler to initiate a punitive action against the state of Qi. Duke Ai said, "Qi has sapped our strength for so long now. If I were to follow your advice and attack them, what do you think might be the outcome?" Confucius replied, "Chen Heng murdered his ruler. At least half of the people from Qi oppose him. Our men plus at least half of theirs can certainly quash their army." Duke Ai said, "Why don't you tell the Jisuns what you propose to do?" Confucius declined. After he withdrew, he told others, "Since I take my place after the counselors, it was my duty to speak out."

According to the account of this episode in the *Analects*, Confucius actually went to see the Jisuns as well as the Shusuns and the Mengsuns. The families were not interested in what Confucius had to say. (One would imagine that they were pursuing the same ends as their Qi counterpart.) This gave greater specificity to Confucius' thinking; so after his request was denied, Confucius said, "Since I take my place after the counselors, it was my duty to speak out."

In both versions, Duke Ai was evasive. But even if Confucius had managed to convince him that it was morally right and practically sound to punish Qi for the extreme irregularity in their political procedures, Duke Ai still could not have done anything, since all the soldiers and arms were in the hands of the Three Families. Nevertheless, his response to Confucius, "Go and tell the Jisuns"—or, in the *Analects* version, "Go and tell the Three Families"—reveals a deep sense of the hopelessness he felt about his situation and about himself. The ruler accepts his lot and is too weak to do anything about it. And as for Confucius, he probably did go and see the Three Families, for it would be unthinkable for him not to comply with the command of his ruler. Confucius was politically responsible and ritually observant, and even when the world around him had succumbed to the pressure or the lure of expediency, he held on to a few rules: he would purify himself before seeing the ruler; and he would approach the counselors in earnest, entreating them to rectify a wrong, though he knew that nothing would come of it.

In conduct and speech, therefore, Confucius did not veer from what he considered to be the fundamentals of order and civility. As he got older, his work came to seem Sisyphean—repetitive and without effect—and fewer and fewer people bothered to notice the trouble he took to do things right. Still, he always aimed high. He never jumped a step or gave his work up even when he could guess the result and feel the futility of his labor. We have other records of his conversations with Duke Ai, but this one alone catches the dignity and stubbornness of an old and tired Confucius just before he bowed himself off the political stage. The ruler, so plainly impotent, is also the right foil.

Confucius' conversations with the chief counselor, Jikangzi, were all business. Jikangzi asked about government, and he wanted to know which of Confucius' disciples were suitable for office. Confucius told the counselor essentially that he—Jikangzi—was responsible for the behavior of his people. "If you are not grasping," he said, "then no one will steal even if stealing carries an award." The two men were candid, but what they said to each other lacked tension and distinction because neither was making much of an effort. Perhaps even Confucius had come to accept that this was the end of an era—the end of a tradition that the Duke of Zhou and the Duke of Shao had begun at the court of King Wu and King Cheng; the end of authentic debates in government about law and rites, responsibilities and interstate politics, war and the conditions of peace.

Privately, however, things were different. Conversations Confucius had with his disciples were never short of edge or energy. They give the impression that he had taken a sharp turn in his life, redirecting his attention from politics to teaching, from counseling the prince to nurturing the young. It is possible that he had been brooding for quite some time about making such a move. When he was living in Chen, he had already considered returning to Lu to help "our young men back home to shape their material." But once he was back, he placed all his hope on the young. He said, "How do we know that the generations to come will not be the equal of the present?"

The smartest and the most promising among the younger group of disciples was Zizhang. Zizhang asked difficult questions: What is "keen discernment"? What is "clouded judgment"? How do we "take virtue to a higher level"? When can we say that a man of education possesses "a gentlemanly adroitness," and what is the difference between such a man and a man who sets out to achieve fame? He also asked about "the marks of benevolence"; how to get on in the world; how to get on the track of an official career; and the moral requisites for serving in government. Zizhang's interests were wide, and he liked to burrow around, which made him the ideal interlocutor for Confucius—a good whetting stone.

Some of the shrewdest and finest observations Confucius made about human nature and self-understanding came out of his conversations with Zizhang:

> Zizhang asked, "What is keen discernment?" Confucius said, "When slanders that seep under the skin and grievances that cause pain do not drive you to an immediate response, you may be said to have keen discernment."

> Zizhang asked, "Is it possible to know ten generations hence?" Confucius replied, "The Shang dynasty built on the rites of the Xia dynasty. What was added and taken away can be known. The Zhou dynasty built on the rites of the Shang. What was added and taken away can be known. Whoever may succeed the Zhou, [their rites and culture,] even a hundred generations hence may be known."

> Zizhang asked, "How would you characterize a good and decent man by the path he follows?" Confucius answered, "This man is not slavish to a path others have trodden, but neither does his path lead to the inner recesses [of moral knowledge]."

> Zizhang asked, "What must an educated man be like before he can be said to possess a gentleman's adroitness in all he does?" Confucius said, "You tell me first what you mean by possessing a gentleman's adroitness." Zizhang replied, "A person that everyone would know, whether he is in the service of the state or in the service of a hereditary family." Confucius said, "You are talking about fame, not about possessing a gentleman's adroitness. A person who is gentlemanly and adroit is by nature fair-minded and upright, and he is bent on aiming at what is right. He also listens to what others have to say and is observant of their expressions and moods. He is ever mindful of not being high-handed. Such a man possesses a gentlemanly adroitness whether he is in the service of the state or in the service of a hereditary family. A person who covets fame takes on the appearance of benevolence,

which is belied by his deeds, and he is not troubled by his hypocrisy. Surely people would know him or his reputation whether he is in the service or the state of in the service of a hereditary family."

Zizhang asked, "How does one take virtue to a higher level, and how does one know that one's judgment is clouded?" Confucius replied, "If you hold on to doing your best and being trustworthy in words as your principle and try always to direct your intent and action to what is right, you will be taking virtue to a higher level. When you like a person, you want him to live. When you dislike that person, you want him to die. To wish a person to live at one moment and to wish him to die at the next, this is clouded judgment."

Zizhang has a special appeal for readers of the *Analects*. He was interested in the keenest and the most difficult of moral questions, and he was interested in himself. Zizhang was not only self-absorbed, he was unembarrassed to let his teacher know that he wanted to advance in the world and that he intended to put himself on a salary track. Some scholars have claimed that in response Confucius always tried to lead Zizhang back to self-cultivation. This was true to a degree. "To get on in the world, whether in your neighborhood or in the land of barbarians," he said to this disciple, "you must impart sincerity and trust in your words, and integrity and respect in your deeds." Yet when he noticed that "Zizhang was studying with an eye to an official career," he offered him this advice:

Use your ears well and widely, and leave out what is suspect; speak with caution about the rest, and you will make few mistakes. Use your eyes well and widely, and stay away from potential perils; act with caution even after the perilous are kept at bay, and you will have few regrets. To make few mistakes in your speech and to have few regrets in your action, these are the keys to securing a career as a salaried official.

Here Confucius was giving Zizhang preferential treatment. He knew that Zizhang's goal was motivated entirely by pragmatic considerations without any trace of a moral intent, yet he did not seem to mind; in fact, he allowed Zizhang a few professional secrets. Maybe Confucius appreciated Zizhang's honesty, for, unlike Ran Qiu, who liked "to gloss his remarks," Zizhang was clear about what he wanted and was unapologetic.

Zizhang was also "wildly spirited," "with a proneness for going too far"—an attribute Confucius could not really commend but was nevertheless drawn to because it held the promise of "brilliant material." As it turned out, Zizhang did not disappoint his teacher. He was brainy and articulate, and from the account of one classmate, he also had "a grand presence." But as another classmate observed, "Although Zizhang is difficult to emulate, he still has not realized his moral potential (*ren*)." And the challenge Zizhang offered Confucius was how to guide his gift of fluency and agility so that it did not glide into glibness. A good example is the way Confucius handled Zizhang's question of how to decide whether a person possessed "a gentlemanly adroitness." Confucius first established how Zizhang understood adroitness. In Confucius' view, what Zizhang described was mastering the skills of being smooth and ready and of giving the appearance of having distinction. These skills cannot bring about the ease with which a person of "gentlemanly adroitness" conducts his work. It is not difficult for a clever man like Zizhang to learn the skills of a glib man, but the art of adroitness is a different matter. To master the art, Confucius says, a person must be partial to the concept of fairness; he must want it so much that he tries for it in all he does; and he must, at the same time, be aware of what other people say and how they respond to him lest he becomes unbearable in their eyes through believing that what he does is good for them.

We learn from the *Analects* that Zizhang "wrote down on his sash" what his teacher said to him, as if to let the latter's words weigh him down and tug him in when he got carried away. Among his classmates, there was one, Zixia, who was his opposite. The *Analects* implies that the two did not see things eye to eye, or rather that they understood their teacher differently. On the subject of making friends, Zixia said, "You should make friends with those whose characters are acceptable and reject those whose characters are not." Zizhang said, "This is not what I have heard. The gentleman respects the worthy and is generous toward the common people. He speaks highly of the good and is compassionate toward those who have a hard time trying to be good. If indeed I am a man of great worth, whom would I not embrace? If I am a person of no worth, others will for sure reject me. If that is the case, how can I reject them?"

Both men thought that they were relaying what their teacher had taught them about how to make friends. How, then, do we explain the disparities? Was Confucius inconsistent in what he said, or did either disciple misread or inflate what he said? In his own words, Confucius seems to maintain both positions. On one occasion, he said, "Do not make friends with those who are not as good as you." On another occasion, he said, "Love all, but stay close to those who are truly humane." In the first instance, Confucius was thinking pragmatically about education—only a person who is nobler and better will have something to teach you. In the second instance, he was speaking broadly about educating the young—teach them not to abandon a single person but to gravitate toward the morally superior when making friends. Zixia grabbed hold of one aspect, and Zizhang the other, and through their translations Confucius could seem at once intolerant and magnanimous, squeamish and carefree.

Confucius had once compared the two in this way: Zizhang "overshoots the mark," while Zixia "falls short." Falling short suggests the pace of a snail or a turtle, and it could mean dull-wittedness or a dogged determination to see things to the end. In Zixia's case, it must have been the latter, for he saw virtue in being slow and methodical. Others mocked him. A classmate observed that Zixia could teach his own students only about "sprinkling and sweeping [the ground]," "responding to calls and replying to questions," and "advancing and retreating [when receiving guests]," but, the classmate pointed out, "these are only details." Zixia thought differently about details. He did not worry whether they would lead to a larger vision or add up to a deeper insight. For him, everything learned is gained, but only "a person who each day acquires something that he lacks and after a month still remembers what he has gotten" can be said to have truly learned. Here Zixia might have been thinking solely of the analogy Confucius had once used comparing leveling ground to learning: "In leveling ground, even though I flipped only one basketful, progress is made because I have gone ahead and done it." On its own, however, the analogy invites an austere and narrow reading of what Confucius said about the good and the joy of learning, and why he, Confucius, was never tired of learning.

Zixia's description of learning sounds a lot like book learning— knowledge one can commit to memory and "gather up in a thick pile." His worries were about not being able to hold on to the knowledge gained; and so he opted for a program and a routine to cultivate good habits in conduct and in scholarly work. Thus, even though Zixia said "one should study widely," he also stressed the importance of sticking to the main track: "There must be a lot to see along the byways, but do not wander off because a person might get bogged down if he has to journey a long way." He took a similar view of asking questions. "Ask scores of them about what you do not understand," he said, "but give consideration only to matters within your reach and your capacity to manage." Learning within these confines leaves little room for the unexpected, for exploration and the imagination. It also allows little time for reflection, for mulling over what is learned and deciding which part, if any, is worth retaining. Confucius said, "If a person merely learns and does not think, he will be in a snare; if he thinks but does not learn, he will be in danger." Maybe Zixia was never in danger of being "in a snare," but his thoughts about learning betrayed the anxiety of someone who worked too hard and too willfully at it. He said, "Artisans live in their shops to master their craft; the gentleman steeps himself in learning to perfect the way." Zixia, in a way, was the artisan kind of gentleman—he lived in the shop of learning "to perfect the way" and rarely let himself out to take some air.

Confucius, however, was a different kind of gentleman. Contemporaries observed that "when he was singing in the company of others and liked someone's singing in particular, he always asked to hear it again before joining in." Confucius learned without the burden of intent and without the need for specificity, which so consumed his disciple Zixia. Yet when he heard a beautiful voice or a beautiful interpretation of a note or stanza, he wanted to listen to it again so that he could take in every note. Confucius might not have been thinking of the ultimate good when learning from this voice, but some elevation must have been gained as he found himself soaring.

This is not to say that Zixia did not know the joy of a sudden lift in his shop of learning. Like any scholar who loves his work, he had good reasons for not wanting to leave his shop. Confucius said that Zixia "excelled in his knowledge of literary sources and in scholarship." Some historians later would credit Zixia with developing a strategy of reading, especially reading the laconic and the abstruse, and they would place him ahead of other scholars as the precursor of the interpretative traditions in Chinese classical studies. Perhaps they exaggerated Zixia's importance, but a conversation about a stanza of poetry recorded in the *Analects* might have given them grounds for their claim. In this conversation Zixia asked Confucius:

"What is the meaning of these lines: 'Her entrancing smile, dimpling, / Her beautiful eyes so black and white. / Distinct colors upon a white background.'?"

Confucius replied, "Colors are put in after the white."

"Does the practice of the rites, in a like manner, come afterwards?"

Confucius said, "It's you who have drawn my attention to such a reading. Only with you do I feel I can discuss the *Odes*."

This was not the first time that Confucius told a disciple, "Only with you do I feel I can discuss the *Odes*." He paid Zigong the same compliment when Zigong chanted a few lines that, Confucius felt, resonated with a point he had just made about the refinement of human character. In praising Zixia, Confucius may have forgotten that he had commended someone else with the same words. Or he may have meant to say, "Only with you do I feel I can discuss the *Odes* in *this particular way*"? Or did he make the statement deliberately, in order to bring his discussion with Zixia to a close? For it seems that Confucius was not terribly interested in the kind of inquiry that absorbed Zixia. Zixia was searching for the precise reading of just three lines from a poem. Confucius offered him some direction, but when Zixia wanted to pursue it further, Confucius held back, saying that it was Zixia who had steered him to such an interpretation. For someone who "liked to ask questions about everything," it is remarkable that Confucius did not want to know anything more about what Zixia was thinking. Maybe he simply did not care for this disciple's approach.

The poem from which Zixia lifted his three lines celebrates the wedding of the daughter of the Duke of Qi to the ruler of Wei—the union of two powerful families at the beginning of the Spring and Autumn period. It is a simple song: the bride is "elegant and slender; / brocade she wore under an unlined coat." The description continues:

> Hands soft as rush-down,
> Skin like lard,
> Neck white as the tree grub,
> Teeth like melon seeds,
> Forehead chiseled like a cicada's and brows arched
>   like moths.
> Her entrancing smile dimpling,
> Her beautiful eyes so black and white.

As the splendid lady "comes to court" in a carriage "screened by fans of pheasant-feather," the singer tells the great officers of Wei "to retire early" and reminds them: "Do not fatigue our lord."

The lady vanishes in the reading we have from Zixia—not her smile, perhaps, or her beautiful eyes, but her magic and the promise she brings. Impressed only with her application of makeup— "Distinct colors upon a white background"—Zixia tried to turn a

conversation about a poem, or the lady in the poem, into a disquisition on the practice of the rites. Confucius said that the *Odes* "can
give the spirit exhortation" and "the mind keener eyes," that the *Odes*
"can make us better adjusted in a group" and "more articulate when
voicing a complaint." He also told his son: "Unless you learn the *Odes*
you won't be able to speak" and "Unless you apply yourself to what
you have learned from the Zhounan and Shaonan poems in the *Odes*,
you will be as if standing with your face toward the wall." An education in the *Odes* did not mean just familiarity with the poems, or being
able to manage a theorist's control over a word or a line in a poem by
turning either the word or the line into a point of digression for one's
own sake. Confucius applauded Zigong for his knowledge of the *Odes*
because he was able to declaim so effortlessly a few lines from a poem
and let the sentiment of those lines fit the spirit of their discussion.
Zigong was speaking in the voice of the *Odes;* his relationship to the
poems was incidental (an occasion inspired his recitation). The same
cannot be said about Zixia. One can well imagine Zixia becoming an
expert in the *Odes* or a didactic pedant using the *Odes* for moral
instruction. (This, in fact, is the hallowed position Zixia occupied in
the pantheon of scholars on the *Odes*.)

What was Confucius' judgment of the two approaches? There is
no doubt that Confucius loved learning for its own sake and encouraged it in disciples who were inclined toward scholarship. Yet he also
showed a strong resistence to placing knowledge outside the self.
This was especially true toward the end of his life when he decided
to plunge into teaching just a few good men. And here is the paradox: just as he was leaving the world of practical affairs—giving up
politics for good—he was teaching most forcefully his belief that the
proof of a true education may be found in the adroitness—in the
ease and fluency—with which one can translate knowledge into
action, ideals into policies, and poems into the language of one's own
thought.

In the last years of his life, Confucius withdrew into a place of his
own. Given his strong aversion to the idea of abandoning the hub-
bub of the human world for some peace in a quieter spot, he proba-

bly would have had a hard time admitting this. At one point he told Ran Qiu, "Were there affairs of the state, I would get to hear them even though I am no longer employed in government." Confucius always "used his ears widely" and "his eyes widely," but after he had come home to Lu, he kept his mind remote, far from the distractions that war and politics could have brought him. One day Zilu asked what he had set his heart on. Confucius replied, "To make the old feel at home, to have the trust of my friends, and to have the young drawn to me." On another day, Confucius asked Zilu, Ran Qiu, Gongxi Hua, and Zeng Dian how they would go about doing things if someone appreciated who they were and knew what they could accomplish.

> Zilu quickly offered a response: "If I were to govern a state of a thousand chariots that was squeezed between two powerful states, worn out by unwanted warfare, and made even weaker by famines, I would be able, within three years, to give the people courage and let them know the right way to put their lives in order."
>
> Confucius smiled.
>
> "And Ran Qiu, what about you?"
>
> "If I were put in charge of a place measuring sixty or seventy *li* square, or even fifty to sixty *li* square, I would be able, within three years, to meet the people's needs. As for the practice of rites and music, I will have to leave them to the gentlemen."
>
> "What about you, Gongxi Hua?"
>
> "I am not sure if I can do this well, but I am willing to learn. I would like to be a minor official, assuming the role of either an assistant in ritual affairs at the ancestral temple or a junior diplomat, dressed in a black robe and ceremonial cap, at a conference of the regional rulers."
>
> "And you, Dian?"
>
> Zeng Dian had been playing the zither. Now he was coming to the end. With the last note still vibrating in the wind, he put down his instrument, stood up, and said, "What I would like to do is different from what we have just heard from these three."

Confucius said, "There is no harm in that. We are all telling each other what's on our mind."

Zeng Dian replied, "In late spring, after the spring clothes have just been made, with five or six young men or six or seven young boys, I would like to go bathing in the River Yi and enjoy the breeze at the Rain Prayer Altar, and then come home singing."

Confucius sighed and said, "I am for Dian."

One can read a lot into this scene. Over the years, followers of Confucius from the right and the left did exactly that. Some claimed that the conversation was fabricated and then appended to the *Analects* by a rival school, most likely the Daoists, either as a tease or as proof that even Confucius at the end had come around to their point of view—that even he had given up the state, the ancestral temple, music, and ceremony, to join them in the immaculate water. Others, such as the sixteenth-century thinker Wang Yangming, insisted that a kin in spirit at "a playful moment" drew out in plain sight a Confucius at his truest. Wang said that "the other three disciples had useful talents," but Zeng Dian alone "was self-possessed wherever he might be," whether he was "among the barbarians" or "in the middle of a crisis." Wang's reading tallies with what we (along with Zilu) learned about Confucius' secret self—what he wanted most and what gave him satisfaction. Yet if we were to settle on this view, we would not be able to explain why for so long Confucius had been singularly stubborn in his search for political opportunities to fulfill his ambitions. His resignation—and the calm that ensued—was a late thing in his life. It was not, however, a form of surrender, although the world was in bigger trouble than before. Even the musicians were leaving Lu. The *Analects* says:

Zhi, the Grand Musician, left for Qi; Gan, musician for the second course of the banquet, left for Chu; Liao, musician for the third course, left for Cai; Jue, musician for the fourth course, left for Qin; Fang Shu the drummer walked down to the Yellow River; Wu, player of the hand-drum, walked down to the River Han;

Yang, the Grand Musician's deputy, and Hsiang, who played the stone chimes, walked down to the sea.

The musicians fled, some going as far as the sea, because the moral order that relied on the efficacy of rites and music had fallen apart. Confucius did not join the exodus. He found his peace right at home, though home was a more solitary place than before. His only son died at around this time. Yan Hui and Zilu soon followed him. One would imagine Confucius depressed. But this was not so. He was still going with his own gait, and to the more discerning eyes, his steps had a spring not seen before. Being around the young must have helped, but Confucius had also gained more knowledge of himself.

Teaching

ONFUCIUS WAS NEVER TIRED OF TEACHING BUT WAS nervous about being perceived as someone who took teaching as his calling. He liked teachers, but most of them were archers, musicians, stone-chimers—men who became indistinguishable from what they had mastered. Confucius had deep respect for these men. He did not explain why, but the *Analects* tell us how he behaved in their presence. On one occasion, a blind musician, Mian, came to call.

> When he approached the steps, Confucius said, "Here are the steps." When he reached the mats, Confucius said, "Here are the mats." When everyone was seated, Confucius told him, "This is So-and-so and that is So-and-so."
>
> After Mian had gone, Zizhang asked, "Is this the way to speak to a [music] teacher, a *shi*?" Confucius replied, "This is the way to assist a [music] teacher."

In the world of craftsmen, no one would have presumed to call himself a teacher, a *shi*, before others had approached him first, entreating him to pass on to them his skills. A teacher was a master: he had to be proficient in something—music, drumming, archery, charioteering. This was the assumption Confucius shared with his contemporaries; and so anyone advertising himself as a teacher without a command of any precise art would have been looked upon as suspect. Partly for this reason, Confucius remained reluctant to take the title of teacher until late in his life, when the people of Lu, having decided that his knowledge could be an aid to government, sent for him.

Even though on his return to Lu Confucius still could not claim to have mastered the art of government, the political successes of Zigong and Ran Qiu established him as someone who knew how to instruct others on acquiring the skills they needed. Consequently he gained the reputation of being a master in the art of teaching, but he did not intend it to happen this way, and he never tried to gather a group of young men around him so that he could have material to work on. The few who followed him into exile did so at their own discretion, with the understanding that he lacked specific prospects. What they learned in those years of travel was not something they could have gotten from lectures or any kind of formal lessons. They would have been hard put to express in words what that education was like. But they knew that being with him changed them: they were better prepared for government service and the hurly-burly of politics; even more important, they gained an interior and keener perspicacity. This was what Confucius wanted—that he should inspire his young companions to become stronger, quicker, and more reflective than they had been when they started their journey together. He was never tired of teaching if teaching was meant to enlighten and to illuminate (*mingxiao*). Yet he did not believe that one could or should package it into a profession. The irony, of course, is that in the eyes of other people he did precisely what he did not think was possible or suitable: he became a teacher.

On the subject of teachers, he said: "Even when walking in the company of two men, I am bound to find my teachers there. Their good points, I would try to emulate; their bad points, I would try to correct in myself." And when someone asked Zigong, "From whom did Confucius learn?" he replied, "From whom does Confucius not learn?"

"The way of King Wen and King Wu has not crumbled to the ground. It is lodged in all human beings," explained Zigong. "The superior person absorbed what is of greater importance. The less than worthy absorbed what is of minor importance. So from whom does Confucius not learn? Moreover, how could there be a constant teacher for him?"

Just as Confucius did not recognize any one person as his permanent teacher, he did not wish others to put him in that postion no matter how earnestly they might have petitioned or how flattered he may have felt by their appeals. Besides, he thought, a teacher could only point out one corner of a square: the rest was up to the students. "If a student does not come back with the other three [corners] after I have shown him one," Confucius said, "I will not repeat what I have done." Education, in his view, must begin and end with the person who seeks to learn. A teacher cannot make it happen. A person must desire it so strongly that he goes and looks for a teacher, and he must realize that in applying the skills and knowledge he has learned, he is also reaching an understanding of himself. Confucius said, "I have never refused to teach (*hui*) anyone who approaches me on his own with a bundle of dried meat [as a gift]." And of those young men who came to him for instruction, the ones who did not suffer the anxiety and anguish of learning did not have Confucius on their side. He told us that he would not give these students a "boost" or a "start" should they be stuck, for they would not be genuine seekers if they did not know "the frustration of trying to solve a difficult problem" or "the frenzy one would get into when trying to put an idea into words."

These predilections of his explain why Confucius was suspicious of Yan Hui at first and why, later, as he understood him better, he came to feel that he could never have another student who loved learning as much as Yan Hui. Yan Hui might appear to be accepting everything Confucius said, but a closer look showed that he understood learning as a private thing—that no matter how skillful his teacher might have been in nudging him forward or pulling him in, the journey was his; he was on his own.

Confucius would go further. He would say to his best students that not only were they on their own but under certain circumstances they also had to hold their own even at the risk of contradicting him. It was entirely permissible to do this, he thought. "When encountering matters that involve [the basic principles] of humanity," Confucius said, "do not yield even to your teacher."

This statement could have serious ramifications. One Han dynasty scholar, Dong Zhongshu, gave full play to the political when he was asked why the historian of the *Spring and Autumn Annals*—a voice whose moral authority remained uncontested in what was becoming the Confucian tradition—praised a military commander who had clearly disobeyed the orders of his ruler and taken matters into his own hands. Why was this not "an act of usurping the ruler's authority"?

The story was a well-known one in the history of the Spring and Autumn period. The ruler of Chu sent his military commander to the capital of Song to gather intelligence about a place his army had put under siege; he wanted to know whether the people of Song had the stamina to hold on to their city, because his own men were running out of energy and supplies. Once the general got there, he realized that the people of Song were so desperate that they "were forced to exchange children" and eat the children of strangers to keep themselves alive. The sight so shocked him that he decided to come to their aid. When he returned to his camp, he told his ruler that he had informed the enemy of the truth about their situation—that the Chu forces, too, had depleted their resources. This left his ruler no choice but to abandon the siege.

The ruler of Chu did not punish his general, because this man had become indispensable to him. But why should historians be charitable to someone who had undermined the command of his sovereign and sided with the enemy? To this question, the scholar Dong Zhongshu replied, "It is because [the military commander] had a heart that could not bear the sight of extreme suffering. This man simply could not let a whole country of people become so hungry that they were forced to devour each other." Dong felt that if the situation pertained to the most fundamental questions of humanity, it was all right "to overstep certain fixed principles in the ritual order." He said: "Those who advocate kindness would try to be compassionate to as many people as possible. Those who are humane are guided by what is natural. [The commander] Zifan was simply responding to the promptings of his heart when he sympathized with the people of Song, and so he gave no thought to the possibility that other people might perceive his action as a form of usurpation." And to strengthen his defense of Zifan, Dong cited Confucius as his support: "'When encountering matters that involve [the basic principles of] humanity,' Confucius said, 'do not yield to anyone.'"

Here we see just how dangerous Confucius' remarks could be, especially out of context and in a partial citation. A sloppy reader might be led to think that the heart has the highest moral authority, but this was not Dong's or Confucius' position. Dong was a fierce backer of the emperor and of the state. He could not have had sedition in mind, and the extreme conditions in his example would have protected him from any suggestion of such. For who, in this general's circumstances, knowing what he knew about the horrifc suffering in Song, could have allowed his army to inflict even more injury just because he could not bring himself to disobey the order of his ruler? If there were such a man, how could he be considered human?

Confucius was more astute on the subject of the heart. He was more careful about letting the heart handle moral questions because he realized that the heart often competed for mastery against judgment or reflection. Thus he told Zizhang, "When slanders that seep under the skin and grievances that cause pain do not drive you to an immediate response, you may be said to have keen discernment." Keen discernment was what Confucius hoped his students would use when faced with a moment that shook their hearts. The best student, he felt, was someone who, on the strength of his clear judgment, could refuse to go along with his teacher should the teacher insist on a different point of view; and the right teacher would want his student to break away because he knew that this was all he could do for his student. Confucius accepted this paradox. He thought that this was a plain way to describe his idea of teaching.

Whenever Confucius talked in the first person about teaching—"I teach without growing weary," for instance—he always used the word *hui*. He could have used another word, *xun*. They both mean "to teach." A first-century dictionary defined *hui* and *xun* in this way: *hui* is to teach "by way of imparting light" or "throwing light" (*xiaojiao*); *xun* is to teach "by means of giving a lesson or a lecture" (*shuojiao*). Since *xun* does not appear in the *Analects*, it is possible that Confucius was not disposed toward making long disquisitions or speaking in front of an audience. There is also *jiao*, a more general word meaning "to teach." The same dictionary explains *jiao* as "to emulate," but only in the case of a subordinate emulating the example set by a superior. Thus Confucius said: "After a good ruler has instructed (*jiao*) his people for seven years, then he is ready to employ them in war"; "To send people to battle without first instructing (*jiao*) them is no different from throwing them away"; "To execute a man without first teaching him (*jiao*) [how to reform] is a cruel act." And when the counselor Jikangzi asked how he might get the people of Lu motivated when he tried to point out to them the virtues of respect and of doing one's best, Confucius replied, "Exalt the good—make them the examples—and teach (*jiao*) the backward, and the people will spur each other on." *Jiao* implies an unequal relationship—one bestows and the other receives—and the teacher in this relationship could not have been a teacher of Confucius, for Confucius found his "even when walking in the company of two men."

Confucius did not care to have a teacher chosen for him and did not wish to receive instructions he did not request. That kind of education may very well work for the common lot, but he preferred to discover on his own who might be a suitable instructor and who might not. This was the high opinion he had of himself. And when others looked up to him for guidance, he told them that all he could do was "to draw some light (*hui*)" into a dark corner so that they could see more clearly: whether or not they made use of the light was up to them.

Yet Confucius said to Zilu, "When I tried to enlighten you, did you get it? To say that you know something when you know it and to say that you do not when you do not know it, this is true knowing." What was Zilu meant to get? Few Chinese asked this question, though many could quote what Confucius said to Zilu. Was it the difference between truthfulness and deception? Did Confucius think that Zilu had not been altogether honest about what he knew and did not know and so urged him to do better? But even if a person intends to be truthful about what he knows, how can he be sure that what he thinks he knows is not, in fact, a delusion?

Certainty of what one knows is hard to achieve, and harder still to defend, because what seems true may turn out to be fake. Confucius himself "loathed purple for usurping the place of vermillion," "the songs of Zheng for corrupting elegant, classical music," and "the smooth-tongued for creating chaos in a state." By being a close semblance, the color purple, the songs of Zheng, or the glib tongue can pass for the genuine article. If Confucius recognized the difficulty of distinguishing one from the other, how could he expect someone like Zilu, who was far from being keen-sighted, to see their difference? Moreover, if he truly feared the consequences of mistaking the imposter for the authentic—which he did—why did he feel that all he could do as a teacher was "to draw some light" into a dim spot in the student's skull? Was Confucius being inordinately modest about his teaching? He said that he could only point to a corner of a square, but did it take years of study to absorb just the one corner? What did his students say about their education? Was there a curriculum, a program? Could they put into words what they understood about his teaching? And if they wanted "to enlighten" their own students, would they be able to do it?

One disciple observed that Confucius instructed in four categories: literature and culture, conduct, doing one's best, and being trustworthy. Yan Hui tells us that Confucius tried to enrich him "with literature and culture" and pull him in "with the rites" before leaving him on his own to to carry out his quest. Confucius' son, Bo Yu, tells us that his father did not teach him "anything special," even though others thought that Confucius might, since Bo Yu was his only son. Bo Yu, however, did remember two occasions during which his father brought up the subject of his education:

> One day, my father was standing there by himself. As I crossed the courtyard with quickened steps, he said, "Have you studied the *Odes*?" . . . Another day, my father was again standing there by himself. As I crossed the courtyard with quickened steps, he said, "Have you studied the rites?"

Confucius told others that he was a transmitter, not an innovator—that he "was fond of antiquity and had faith in it." His disciples and his son seem to attest that this was indeed the case. They all agreed that what he taught was knowledge of the past as culture and ritual practice. But once he had imparted what he knew, how could Confucius be sure that instead of spurring his students on as he had hoped, this body of knowledge would not in fact deluge them, leaving them dazed and dampened? He himself had said: "If you simply learn but do not think, then you will be bewildered. But if you simply think but do not learn, you will be in danger." The knowledge he passed on, therefore, could not have been knowledge garnered wholesale but knowledge he had distilled by way of thought. When Yan Hui asked how to govern a state, Confucius said:

> Follow the calendar of the Xia dynasty, ride in the carriage of the Shang, wear the ceremonial cap of the Zhou, and as for music, embrace the music of *shao* and *wu*. Ban the music of Zheng and keep a distance from glib men. Glib men are dangerous.

The right calendar, carriage, and cap were not just correctives to the indecorous and the vulgar. They could anchor a government and the state. Such were the powers of the ritual objects if they were the right ones; and only the right ones, Confucius thought, could withstand the trials of time. Thus his preference for the Xia calendar, the Shang carriage, and the Zhou ceremonial cap was not arbitrary: like the men who helped to keep three dynasties "to the straight path," these objects, too, had been "put to the test."

In addition to ritual objects, Confucius also mentioned music as a source of influence that could keep a dynasty "to the straight path." Again, he appraised music in the same way he assessed men, a subject that always received his closest scrutiny. On the question of friends, for instance, Confucius said:

> You stand to benefit from three kinds of friends, and you are bound to suffer from three kinds of friends. You stand to benefit from friends who are forthright and upright; friends who are generous and forgiving; and friends who have a breadth of knowledge and experience. You are bound to suffer from friends who are given to being partial; friends who are too amenable; and friends who are disposed to being glib.

Confucius was aware of just how easy it was to mistake a person who was judgmental for someone frank, and a person who was eager to comply for someone compassionate; the confusion could occur, he said, even with those you thought you knew well enough to consider friends. Yet he believed that there was a clear way to tell them apart. Both types can be firm and flexible, but one exercises his discretion responsibly, while the other is merely shifty. One relies largely on his learning and the acumen he has gained from learning to help him find what is right, while the other acts only for the sake of expediency. Confucius called one "the gentleman" and the other "the petty man." He said:

> A gentleman cherishes a true friendship; he will never try to lobby you to join a party or a clique. A petty man tries to enlist you as a fellow partisan; he is not after true friendship.

> A gentleman is agreeable without being an echo. The petty man echoes without being agreeable.

The gentleman is easy to serve but difficult to please. He will not be happy if in trying to please him, you veer from the proper way, but when it comes to employing the services of others, he does so within the limits of their capacity. The petty man is difficult to serve but easy to please. He will be happy even though in trying to please him you have transgressed, but when it comes to employing the services of others, he demands all-round perfection.

Petty men can easily come under the influence of plausible men because they are susceptible to pleasing words. But they themselves are often plausible because, as Confucius observed, they "understand profit"; so, in the act of pandering, they can expect a gain. Thus it is odd for Confucius to compare the music of Zheng to a glib tongue. Both make sounds that give immediate pleasure. But a man with a glib tongue has self-interest in mind, and so is dangerous. Surely the same cannot be said about the music of Zheng. In his conversation with Yan Hui, Confucius implied that this music could be the ruin of a state. Did he exaggerate its negative sway?

The music of Zheng was lewd music. The early sources say that the men and women of Zheng liked to gather by the riverbanks and sing songs "to stoke each other's fire," and that these songs "gladdened the senses" and "the fancy pluck-work" of the instruments "quickened their desires." Confucius objected to this music because it was lustful, not because it was about love. In fact, his favorite poem from the *Odes*, "Fishhawk," recounts the courtship of a prince and a "gentle maiden, pure and fair."

> *Watercress grows here and there,*
> *Right and left we gather it.*
> *Gentle maiden, pure and fair,*
> *wanted waking and asleep.*
>
> *Wanting, sought her, had her not,*
> *Waking, sleeping, thought of her,*

On and on he thought of her,
He tossed from one side to another.

The yearning in "Fishhawk" could not have been any less consuming than that in the songs of Zheng. But here the stricken prince does not make a crude display of his feelings toward his beloved. He enlists the help of the men and women in his community, and together they make music to hearten her and gladden her:

Watercress grows here and there,
Right and left we pull it.
Gentle maiden, pure and fair,
With harps we bring her company.

Watercress grows here and there,
Right and left we pick it out.
Gentle maiden, pure and fair,
With bells and drums do her delight.

Of the tone and sentiment expressed in this poem, Confucius said, "There is joy yet no wantonness, sorrow yet no self-injury."

The music Confucius loved best was the ancient music known as *shao*. Musicians first performed it in the court of Emperor Shun. *Shao* tells us the story of Shun's succession—of Emperor Yao's decision to abdicate in favor of a man "who lived in the depths of the mountains" but whose love for virtue was like the rush of a torrent. The music was not desire, not passionate music. But the gods and spirits were drawn to it; the birds and beasts, too—they all succumbed to its power. The *Classic of Documents* describes one such performance in the presence of Emperor Shun: "When the nine movements came to a close, the male and female phoenix descended in pairs from their mountain trees [to the court below]." Confucius heard this music for the first time during his visit to the state of Qi. Of this experience he said, "I never dreamt that the joys of music could reach such heights." The pleasure stayed with him, and while it did, everything else seemed pallid. "For the next three months," we are told, "Confucius did not notice the taste of meat." Some said that it was the court's master musician who played the *shao* for him.

Others accepted another story:

> When Confucius had just arrived at the outer gate of the capital of Qi, he met a boy. The boy tapped on a *hu*-flask [and sang]. For a while, the two traveled side by side. The child had sharp eyes, an infallible heart, and proper demeanor. Confucius said to his driver, "Hurry, [don't lose sight of this child]! Just now he was playing the music *shao*."

We, of course, would like to believe the second story. We want Confucius to come under the spell of a child's singing rather than that of a court musician's playing. But evidence suggests the reverse, that Confucius loved the idea of perfection not as first sound or first word but as a realization of something beautiful with all the weight of human endeavors. And if he seemed enraptured and comforted by music, it was not that the music filled a deep yearning but that it embodied the peace of a political order. Thus even when speaking of ancient musical forms, he felt compelled to rank them:

> Confucius said of the *shao* music that it was both perfectly beautiful and perfectly good, and of the *wu* music that it was perfectly beautiful but not perfectly good.

Wu was the music of King Wu. The work complemented the exploits of this ruler, which were heroic and glorious but still fell short of being "perfectly good" because King Wu had to conquer the world before setting it in order. Emperor Shun, on the other hand, never had to brandish a weapon or raise a single army. His ascension to power was a peaceful one: he won the world through the force of his integrity. Hence the beauty of his music acquired a moral tone.

Confucius saw music as the culmination of culture and its most fitting metaphor. When he talked about music, he concentrated on the distinct elements in a pattern (*wen*), the patterns that defined a movement, the transition between movements, and the fluency that transcended the concerted effort of playing in unison. He told the master musician of Lu:

> We are able to know this much about music. It begins with playing in unison. And when it goes into full swing, [the sound] is pure and harmonious, [the notes] bright and distinct, and [the passages] are linked and fluent until the music reaches the end.

Confucius' follower Mencius took the idea further. He proposed that we look at Confucius' achievement in light of a grand symphonic event. He began by pointing out that other men, too, were capable of remarkable feats—the severely scrupulous, for instance, and the politically responsible. The severely scrupulous always tried to keep themselves immaculate and so would "only take office when order prevailed," while the politically responsible were devoted to public service, and so would "take office whether order prevailed or not." Both were wanting, thought Mencius, in spite of their merit: the stickler would be reluctant to take on political responsibilities unless he had "the right person to serve and the right people to rule"; the undemanding might have a hard time maintaining his dignity if he was willing to work in any situation, even with men of tarnished reputation. But only Confucius, Mencius thought, could advance or retreat, serve or not serve, "all according to the circumstances," because his actions were timely; so, like a symphony perfectly brought together, "from the ringing of the bells at the beginning to the sound of jade tubes at the end," there was an "internal order" in his performance.

To act in a timely way is not the same as to act with an eye to expediency. The difference lies in whether a person has truly applied himself to learning or not. Someone might give the impression that he can take charge of a whole community of people and look after the spirits of their altars, but, Confucius said, without a rigorous education, he may be persuaded to follow the way of the slick and the sly. For this reason, Confucius was deeply suspicious of anyone with a reputation of being "the village goody man." Such a man, he said, "is the enemy of virtue." Mencius gives a fuller explanation:

[The village goody man] says, "What is the point of having noble ideals? Words and deeds take no notice of each other anyway. . . . So why keep saying 'The ancients, the ancients.' And why must you walk alone? You are born to this world, so try to be a part of it. And you will do fine if you seem friendly to everyone." Thus he fawns on the world with flattery. Such is the village goody man. . . . [Confucius thought that this man was "an enemy of virtue" because] if you want to censure him, you cannot find any evidence of his wrongdoing, and if you want to attack him, you cannot find a clear target. He is in tune with the prevalent custom and blends in with the sordid world. When in a state of repose, he appears to be conscientious and trustworthy. When actively engaged with the world, he appears to be principled and immaculate. People all like him, and he thinks he is in the right.

According to Mencius, Confucius had said, "Of those who pass by my gate without entering my house, the only ones that cause me no regret are the village goody men."

When Confucius was the minister of crime in Lu, he sentenced such a man to death. This person, Shaozheng Mao, walked with the crowd, preached to a crowd, and was a crowd-pleaser. The Han historian Sima Qian stated that Shaozheng Mao "created political disorder" and so Confucius had him executed. But what sort of disorder? Sima Qian did not explain. Was it at all like the uprising of 498? Confucius himself was a culprit in that affair. But if he did not consider his involvement wrong, and he was the minister of crime at the time, Shaozheng Mao's doings must have been a lot more serious. Or were they? Some scholars maintained that Confucius had considered Shaozheng Mao a rival—both were vying for students—and so, they argued, by getting rid of Shaozheng Mao, Confucius was merely eliminating a competitor. In the writings of

Xunzi, a Confucian thinker of the third century BC, there is another version of the story:

> [While serving as the minister of crime, for a while,] Confucius was also the acting counselor of Lu, and within seven days of holding court, he had Shaozheng Mao executed. His disciples came forward and asked him, "Shaozheng Mao was a famous man in Lu. Yet the first thing you did when you took charge of government was to have him put to death. Did you not make a terrible mistake?" Confucius said [to his disciples], "Sit down, and I will tell you the reasons. Now there are five odious predilections humans can possess, and robbing and thieving are not amongst them. The first is having a penetrating but pernicious mind. The second is being partial yet stubborn in conduct. The third is speaking falsehood and loving disputation. The fourth is having the capacity of a fine memory but retaining only the bad and the ugly. The fifth is being inclined to wrongdoing yet never short of justifications. A person with just one of these tendencies would inevitably end up being executed by a gentleman. Yet Shaozheng Mao had all five. Moreover, wherever he happened to be residing, he had enough appeal to draw a crowd of followers around him; and whenever he opened his mouth, he had enough slickness to disguise his depraved nature and to hoodwink his audience. This man was so powerful that when he turned right and wrong on their heads, no one could call his bluff and bring him down. He was a hero to petty men and so he had to be put to death."

Xunzi took what he understood about Confucius and used it to help him construct this scenario and an argument that he hoped could settle any doubts people might have about Confucius' treatment of Shaozheng Mao. And he projected onto Shaozheng Mao those qualities Confucius despised most in a man. Thus, in Xunzi's story, Shaozheng Mao could draw a crowd with wayward charm; he could persuade the world that right was wrong; and he was so forceful that even after people had exposed him as a fraud, they could not bring him down. This man was the opposite of Confucius: he was Confucius' moral opponent but not his professional rival.

To lend further support to Confucius' position in the case of Shaozheng Mao, Xunzi provided as precedents seven other examples from history in which a fair-minded king or counselor had seen through the deception and malevolence of a man and then had that man executed. Among the seven men Xunzi named as being equal in villainy to Shaozheng Mao, Deng Xi stands out as the most relevant to our understanding of this episode in Confucius' life. Deng was either a legal expert or a publicist representing some private interest. One early account says that this man "maintained ambiguous assertions and never ran out of arguments to support them," and that at the end "he was arrested and executed." Other accounts concur both on this profile of Deng and on the circumstances of his death, but they do not agree on who was responsible for his demise. The *Zuo Commentary* named Sichuan, while all the other early sources pointed to Zichan, someone Confucius had described as "generous," "judicious," and "a gentleman." Both men were counselors from the state of Zheng: Sichuan was a contemporary of Confucius; Zichan was a generation older. The *Zuo Commentary* says:

> Sichuan of Zheng had Deng Xi killed and then adopted the laws that Deng Xi wrote on the bamboo slips. A gentleman gave his assessment of Sichuan: 'In handling this case, Sichuan did not do his best. If there is someone who can benefit the country, then the right thing to do is to help him get rid of his vices . . . . When you think of someone, you even love the tree he once sat under. It makes all the more sense that if you utilize someone's policies, then you should take pity on his life. Sichuan was quite incapable of encouraging the talented [to participate in government].

No "gentleman" came to Deng Xi's defense in other sources because in those sources it was Zichan who was responsible for his death, and Zichan, in the Chinese mind, was the most judicious of counselors. Thus we are meant to assume that Deng was beyond reform. But how bad was he? This is difficult to establish because the stories about him exist only in piecemeal fashion and they do not add up to the life of a single person. According to one account in a collection of essays from the third century BC, Deng was a legal expert with his own practice: he "charged his clients a long robe for a major case and a short robe for a lesser one," and because he was driven by commerce and his clients by the desire to win their cases, together they managed "to destroy any standard of right and wrong." This created "great confusion in the state of Zheng" and "so much distress for Zichan" that at the end this counselor had no choice but to have him executed.

Another account in the same text says:

In the state of Zheng, many people liked to post their writings [along the main routes and byways]. Zichan ordered it to be stopped. Deng Xi began to pass out slips of his writings. Zichan again ordered it to be stopped. Deng Xi then began to attach his writings to other things he sent out. The infinite number of ordinances was matched by Deng Xi's infinite number of attempts to circumvent them.

The author goes on to observe that "this is to confuse what is permissible with what is not," and adds:

When people cannot distinguish what is permissible and what is not, then the government will have to resort to reward and punishment to maintain order. And as the use of punishment becomes more pressing [in a society], the descent into chaos will also accelerate. This is what a state should avoid doing at all costs.

Although these two stories differ on the specific charges against Deng Xi, they do agree on the nature of his crime: he forced even the most reasonable authorities to respond frantically and unthinkingly to his doings and so he was the one who gave them grounds for arbitrary rule.

Did Shaozheng Mao's behavior fit the same pattern? It appears that way, but he was more treacherous than Deng Xi. Shaozheng Mao was capable of many levels of deceit, just like Deng Xi, but his trump was his clever disguise—he was not a wolf in sheep's clothing but a sheep with a wolf's heart. He personified what Confucius despised most, since he closely resembled something good but if one could see the heart or the kernel of him one would find the very opposite. A story from the second century brings this point into sharper focus:

> Shaozheng Mao lived in Lu and was a contemporary of Confucius. The disciples of Confucius came in droves and left in droves. Only Yan Hui refused to go near [Shaozheng Mao's gate] because he alone knew that Confucius was a sage. But all his other disciples had abandoned him for Shaozheng Mao, whose instructions they now sought. A person could not know that Confucius was a sage and Shaozheng Mao was a specious man if he had not followed Confucius and apprenticed with him for a long time. For this reason, even Confucius' own disciples were muddled.
>
> [Sometime later,] Zigong said to Confucius, "Shaozheng Mao was a famous man in Lu. So why did you have him executed as soon as you were put in charge of government?" Confucius snapped him short. "Go away!" he said. "This is not something you are able to understand." If even Zigong with his talent was not able to recognize who was a true sage, the ordinary scholars must have been lying when they claimed that they could do it.

Parts of this version read like a reworking of Xunzi's. The mood is sadder, though. Confucius' disciples came and went "in droves"—everyone, with the exception of Yan Hui, left Confucius for Shaozheng Mao. Even Zigong, who had been at his teacher's side for years, could not tell the real thing from a fake. But the incident did not take place. It could not have, for only a handful of followers, not "droves," were attached to Confucius when Shaozheng Mao was alive. Still, had it happened, Confucius would have been reluctant to drive anyone—especially Zigong—away if that person had not yet steadied his gaze and was still vacillating between the true and the false, seeing both as "yeses."

Confucius himself never claimed to have absolute knowledge of anything. Others might find him taller and steadier than anyone they had met, but he knew that he had to work through every problem carefully and sedulously to find certainty. He said:

> Do I possess knowledge? No, I do not. A rustic put a question to me, and my mind was a complete blank. I kept knocking at the two sides [of the question] until I got everything out.

Confucius had knowledge but not an overarching theory with ready answers. Thus he regarded every question put before him, even the question of a "rustic," as new; and so he would clear away everything and begin with a blank space—a limpid mind—promising only that he would give the question all his thought and attention until he "got everything out." According to the *Analects*, Confucius stayed away from four things, and "theory-making" was one. He also did not believe that anything could be "beyond doubt" or any rule should be "immutable," and he refused to force his opinion on anyone or put himself above anyone. However, working only with the assuredness of an uncertainty principle did not stop him from having firm judgments about human conduct and human character. In the case of Shaozheng Mao, his verdict was also dead serious.

Confucius was more compassionate toward robbers and thieves if he thought that they had potential for reform. He gave his own daughter in marriage to a man who once had been "in fetters." He said, "Even though the law treated this man like a criminal, he did not do anything wrong, and would, in fact, make a suitable husband."

Shaozheng Mao, on the other hand, did not break any law or attempt to circumvent it, and he was not even a provocateur like Deng Xi: he did not ask for what he got. Furthermore, he gave no indication that his action was either social or political—that it was a response to the human condition or a reaction against any regime or authority. If we can trust the descriptions of this man in the early sources, it seems that Shaozheng Mao had no principles to defend, probably not even self-interest to protect. He enjoyed the act of subverting reason and impairing the ability of man to see what was right and what was just. This, in Confucius' view, constituted a capital offense. For it was a deliberate attempt to dull the distinctions between humans and beasts and, in fact, to turn humans into beasts. Moreover, because Shaozheng Mao performed his act by sleight of hand, his audience would have been too spellbound to notice what was taken away from them. They would have fought hard and nobly had they known the object of his game. Thus it was not even fair play.

Shaozheng Mao, I believe, was Confucius' toughest enemy, tougher than Yang Hu, Jihuanzi, Huan Tui, the men of Kuang, and even the wilderness of Chen or Cai. Xunzi called him the paragon of petty men—their champion and hero. One can perhaps say that Confucius taught in order that the young men around him could see through the cover of men like Shaozheng Mao and recognize just how dangerous their game could be. But did he overreact to what may have been epistemological exercises or the sportings of skeptics? Skepticism as a teaching would have been an anachronism in the age of Confucius. Another century had to elapse before men like Hui Shi and Gongsun Long would come along and elevate it to an art. Had Confucius been a man of the fourth century BC, he might have felt frustrated if he was forced to debate these men, but he would have not put either Hui Shi or Gongsun Long in the same pack as Shaozheng Mao. As we know from his political career, Confucius was willing to call on lawless men—Gongshan Furao and the like—if he felt that working with them might give him an opportunity to accomplish something good and ambitious. But he could never let himself go near Shaozheng Mao. In fact, if Shaozheng Mao had passed by his door without stopping in to have a talk, Confucius would not have felt any regret.

Zigong was wrong, then, when he said "From whom does Confucius not learn?" He was also wrong to assume that every person had a part of King Wen and a part of King Wu in him. Surely his teacher would have disagreed. Pointing to Shaozheng Mao, Confucius would have said that this man possessed no trace of King Wen or King Wu, or of anything human. Confucius, because he thought that life was sacred, had to be certain of his judgment before handing Shaozheng Mao over to the executioner.

Confucius always exercised great caution in matters that straddled life and death, the *Analects* says, and such matters would include war and illness and the purification rituals practiced before one made offerings to the ancestral spirits. In gauging human character, too, Confucius liked to take his time to think through a person's strengths and weaknesses; he also needed prodding "to get everything out." When a counselor of Lu asked him whether his disciple Zilu was benevolent, Confucius replied, "I don't know." The counselor pressed him for an answer, and Confucius finally said: "Zilu can be put in charge of levying troops in a state of ten thousand chariots. But whether or not he is benevolent, I cannot say." The counselor then asked about Ran Qiu. Confucius said: "Ran Qiu can be employed by a hereditary family with a hundred chariots as their steward overseeing the affairs of a town with a thousand households. Whether or not he is benevolent, I cannot say." The counselor continued, "What about Gongxi Hua?" Confucius said: "When Gongxi Hua, with his sash fastened, takes his place at court, he can be put in charge of conversing with the guests of the state. Whether or not he is benevolent, I cannot say."

Rarely could Confucius be persuaded to be categorical in his judgment; he would not say whether a person was virtuous or courageous even when he knew him well. Yet he believed that it was possible to see the truth of a person, however enigmatic or deceptive the person might be. "Observe what a person does," he tells us. "Look into why he does it. And consider in what he feels at home. How then can he hide his character? How then can he hide his character?" A man might perform the duties of a son, but, that, in Confucius' view, "could hardly be called 'being filial.'" "What is difficult to manage," Confucius said, "is the expression on his face." Only the child who "feels at home" in the act of caring for his parents deserves the reputation of "being filial." For his action comes from the heart and is natural.

Does this mean that Confucius believed the inclinations of the heart or human nature to be good? Again, Confucius does not appear to have arrived at any definitive position about human nature or the heart; if he did, he did not state it. The *Analects* says, "It is possible to know about Confucius' cultural accomplishments, but not his views on human nature and Nature's ways." Even so, we can glean from his teachings some of his assumptions. The first of these is that humans are disposed to doing good. Otherwise he would not have said, "As soon as I desire benevolence, it is here." But not to have the strength to fulfill this desire is to let it go to waste, which is the same as not being born with it at all. Thus Confucius attached a corollary to his first assumption. He said: "I have not come across anyone who does not have sufficient strength [to apply himself to benevolence]. There may be such persons, but I have not come across them."

However hopeful these statements appear to be about Confucius' view of human nature, they are only the beginning. For he also tells us in so many different ways that even though our heart wants to do good and has the capacity to do what it wants to do, it does not fulfill its promise. The rush forward is thrown back by a strange resistance, in itself—this, too, is human nature. In fact, this very tension best describes the condition of the heart, and it gives humans a point to their quest and a reason to learn. A skillful teacher plans his lessons accordingly: he brings his understanding of human nature to his instruction. An extraordinary teacher, like Confucius, goes further: he relates human nature to the source—the current to the spring—so that even the resistance in the rush is Nature's way; and he believes that when a lesson is learned and rightfully applied it should not feel onerous or unnatural.

When Confucius organized his teaching into the *Odes*, rites, and music, he must have been reflecting on human nature. He said: "The *Odes* are to stimulate"—to give our mind, heart, and spirit a lift; "the rites are to steady us"—to hold us back lest we become heady or partisan; and "music is the final lesson"—the gathering up of distinct voices and opposing forces in a symphony, and a trope for the perfectibility of human nature. Confucius gave all three components equal weight, yet he had the most to say about the practice of the rites. Either he found it easier to talk about the rites or he felt compelled to make more effort to explain why it was not unnatural to learn and perform something with well-defined structures and rules. Thus he began his teaching with those rites that were intimate and familiar, rites a person would follow out of habit and because of love.

Caring for our parents is one. It is a natural thing to do, and it is what we desire because our parents gave us our earliest memory of feeling warm and safe and assuaged. But it is not easy to reciprocate the love as we remember it. The relationship has changed. We have formed judgments that spare no one, not even our parents; and our parents, too, do not love us in the same way as when we were young and wholly dependent on them. Confucius realized the problems children faced, but still insisted that in giving back what they received, they should not forget what it was like to be utterly loved by someone. He did not make impossible demands on the children, asking only that they remain sensitive to their parents' feelings no matter what the circumstances might be. If they could manage that, he thought, then they would have a chance of being humane.

Confucius wanted the children to succeed because he wagered his hope in the rest of humanity on them. And he began with simple rules. "While your parents are alive," he said, "do not travel to distant places. If you have to travel, you must tell them where you are going to be." In fact, he said, "Give your father and mother no cause for anxiety other than illness." The rules, despite their imperative voice, are hardly exacting. A son who truly loves his parents will want to protect them from fretting about him. He does not need to be told that this is what he ought to do. Yet Confucius formulated it as family rites or rules of propriety (*li*). He wanted the son to have something exact to rely on because he could not risk letting him work out his relationship with his parents all on his own. When asked about "being filial," Confucius replied: "Do not forsake [the rites]. . . . When your parents are alive, observe the rites in serving them; when they die, observe the rites in burying them; observe the rites in sacrificing to them."

The son is fit to observe the rites because he loves his parents. Without love and empathy or any kind of moral impulse, Confucius said, "What can a man do with the rites?" Yet in the absence of measure and control, which only the rites can accord, the same son, even with strong love and honorable intentions, can let things go awry and end up being less than filial. Confucius sketched out a scene in which the parents erred; he showed us how, by complying with the guidelines of propriety, a son might be able to rein in the parents while holding his own and yet not strain the relationship. "In serving your parents," he said,

> be gentle when trying to dissuade them from wrongdoing. If you see that they are not inclined to heed your advice, remain reverent. Do not challenge them. Do not be resentful even if they wear you out and make you wretched.

Confucius does not want us to yield to our parents if they are culpable. At the same time, he discourages any confrontation, big or small. Stay reverent, he says. Which is not a strategy, not a way to gain a higher moral ground, for Confucius is still worried about our parents—that they may lose our respect and thereupon our affection. Do not show contempt, he warns; even when they tax your patience, "Do not be resentful."

The relationship between a child and his parents is a balancing act. This was Confucius' reckoning. The rites enable the child to find the balance, but the object is not appeasement. The truly filial will not betray his own sense of right and wrong even as he tries to steer clear of a conflict. He understands that the rites are meant "to steady him," so that he can hold his own: he holds his own but does not step over the line. Confucius said, "Unless a man acts according to the spirit of the rites, in being respectful, he will tire himself out; in being cautious, he will become timid; in being brave, he will become unruly; and in being forthright, he will become derisive." A son, in the act of being filial, is therefore neither worn out nor timid, neither unruly nor derisive.

But what happens when the filial son leaves his family? Is he any different as "a man of the state"? Can he maintain the strength that has kept him in equilibrium at home? Is he able to apply himself effectively to the problems in the larger world? Confucius sees much promise in the strength one gains as one becomes a filial son. The filial son still has a lot to learn—poetry, music, history, communal and state rituals—if he decides to venture into the world, but he will have possessed an interior, and he will have understood the virtue of taking measured action and measured steps.

"Measured steps" does not refer to steps that follow a rule or square. A good man, Confucius said, "is not slavish to a path others have trodden." This man is not even slavish to the path he himself has trodden, for experience would teach him that every occasion is different: the circumstances change, and they change even as the occasion unfolds. Thus, each time, he has to size up the situation and decide how to make his next move. He marks the line.

When Confucius entered the temple of the Duke of Zhou, we are told, "he asked questions about everything." Confucius may have had a thorough knowledge of the rules and procedures codified for the sacrifice to the first and the grandest of the Lu ancestors, but he still approached the rites as if he was about to perform them for the first time, and he told others, "Asking questions is in itself the correct rite." His precursors, counselors such as Du Xie and Zijiazi, used their knowledge of rituals and of the established norms in practice to instruct their rulers on what might or might not be considered an appropriate action in the political realm. Confucius, however, gave more attention to the nature of the ritual experience, which, he felt, could "take virtue to a higher state" if the skills learned from such an experience had enlivened and heightened awareness. In his conversations with Zizhang, who was eager to advance in the world, he pointed out the practical advantages of having a sharpened perception: it helps "to keep the perilous at bay" and "you will make few mistakes" and "have few regrets." But if a person has a nobler purpose—if he is not just considering his own interests—his awareness may allow him to listen more and observe more, and he may want to get things right "whether he is in the service of the state or in the service of the hereditary family."

But can the pursuit of what is right and what is just be divorced from human feelings and assume a life of its own? Some of Confucius' remarks suggest that he was running that risk. For he was someone who described "keen discernment" as an ability to refrain from reacting too impulsively to "slanders that seep under the skin and grievances that cause pain." And when someone asked him what he thought of the saying "Repay an injury with a good turn," he replied, "What, then, do you repay a good turn with? You repay an injury with what is due. You repay a good turn with a good turn." Confucius also said, "In his relation to the world, the gentleman is neither against or partial to anything, but he is fond of what is right (*yi*)." If these statements give the impression that, in his quest for the moral and the right, Confucius was aiming at something elevated from the self, his conversation with Yan Hui on the subject of benevolence seems to bear it out.

Yan Hui's question was open: "What is benevolence?" The breadth of the question could lead to many answers—the practice of benevolence, its source, examples of such practice. In his response, Confucius chose to explain what was demanded from a person who intended to do good. He told his disciple:

Restrain the self and return to the rites. This is what being benevolent is all about. If you are able to realize it for just one day, then the whole world will gravitate toward benevolence. The act of benevolence rests with the self. How can you depend on other people's strength?

And when Yan Hui asked for something more concrete, Confucius replied:

Do not look if you are not guided by the rites. Do not listen if you are not guided by the rites. Do not speak if you are not guided by the rites. Do not act if you cannot be guided by the rites.

Confucius' explanation of benevolence and its relationship to the rites was often misunderstood. Most readers thought that Confucius was urging the self to yield its inclinations to those rules in the larger order. He seemed to them to be saying that the self had to make a sacrifice if it intended to do good. And Confucius' attempt to be more precise about what he meant by the practice of benevolence could be just as confounding if one had only a rickety knowledge of what he taught regarding the rites. Thus, to understand what he meant by "restrain the self and return to the rites," we would have to look elsewhere.

His disciple Zhonggong also asked him about benevolence. Confucius replied:

When abroad, conduct yourself as if you were receiving an honored guest. When employing the service of your people in your state, deport yourself as if you have been put in charge of a grand sacrifice. Do not impose on others what you do not desire yourself. In this way, you will not incur any resentment whether your work is in the state or in a hereditary family.

In his response to Zhonggong, Confucius did not mention the word *ren* (benevolence). Instead, he gave us something tangible to bring to bear on the idea of the good. He said, "Do not impose on others what you do not desire for yourself." He also gave us examples of ritual practice that could put the idea into effect. On another occasion, he characterized "our ability to make an analogy from what is close at hand"—what we know about ourselves—as "the passage to doing good" and the working principle of benevolence. When Zigong asked whether there is one word that "can be a guide to conduct throughout one's life," Confucius said, "*Shu* (reciprocity)," which he, again, explained as "not to impose on others what you do not desire for yourself." A person should conduct himself in this way, Confucius thought, whether he is abroad or at home, whether he is on a mission or administering a state. Whether he is dealing with officials or the common people, this person should treat everyone with respect. "Respect (*jing*)," with Confucius as its articulator, is not an abstract idea. It is tactile. It fills a person and shows up in his limbs and countenance, and it moves him in such a manner that he looks as if he is "receiving an honored guest" or "participating in a grand sacrifice."

Thus when Confucius told Yan Hui that benevolence was about "restraining the self and returning to the rites," he had in mind someone who has an enlightened and a refined self. The person who is benevolent is aware of what he is capable of doing to others, and to act on this awareness, he relies on his knowledge of ritual experience to hold him to the right measure. He will not look if he is not guided by perspicacity, he will not listen if he is not guided by keenness, he will not speak if he is not guided by a clear voice, and he will not take action if he is not guided by a discerning mind. He conducts himself in a manner that only the rites can cultivate, so that he is not wanton when he is joyful or broken when he is in sorrow; so that he does not give too much when he is happy or take away too much when he is sore. The practice of benevolence, therefore, begins and ends with the self—a person in the act of finding what is humane. Such a person can never be detached from his feelings even when he is in a tight pursuit of what is just and what is right.

The exercise of moral discretion, in Confucius' view, is the toughest and the loneliest of human endeavors; it is not something for the specious, the cowardly, or the lazy. He said:

A partner in learning may not be good enough as a partner if you are on a quest for moral meaning. A partner on a quest for moral meaning may not be good enough as a partner if you are determined to use the rites to help you find a steady frame and an equitable position. A partner who is as determined as you are to use the rites to find a steady frame and an equitable position may not be good enough as a partner if you are in the act of exercising moral discretion.

To act on his discretion for a just end and a moral end, a person must summon those feelings nurtured in the family—feelings of empathy and compassion—and he must let them figure in his judgment without clouding it. A filial son has a better chance of success in the world because he can draw upon his experience at home. And if he succeeds, he can perhaps be called a benevolent man. Confucius said, "A benevolent man is most at home in benevolence." Yet, as we know, the road home is long—full of hurdles and climbs that test the will—and out of tiredness one can always find reasons to stop. A young disciple of Confucius, Zengzi, put it this way: "A gentleman must be big and strong [in spirit and mind], and he must be resolute. His burden is heavy, and his road is long. He takes benevolence as his burden. Is it not heavy? Only with death does his road come to an end. Is it not long?"

Confucius himself liked to talk about benevolence in paradoxes. In fact, it is the only way he knew how to put it into words. Paradoxes seize on the ambiguity inherent in the idea of the good; they give away our feelings about it—our unsureness about it—even when we want it more than anything. Confucius said: "A neighborhood where there is benevolence is most beautiful. How can a man be considered to have knowledge when he has a choice and does not settle on benevolence?" How can he indeed? The rhetorical question Confucius posed must have implied that there were lots of people who knew that a benevolent neighborhood was morally beautiful and yet chose not to reside in it. Why should they resist the choice but for the burden that is fastened to it like a price?

Yet Confucius did not conclude his teaching on a heavy note. He had more lightness than his disciple Zengzi and was more attuned to the aesthetic possibilities of the journey. He knew that, when fully realized, the rightness of an action could seem as timely as a pheasant alighting on a mountain ridge. To drive the point home, he shared with us his spiritual voyage:

At fifteen, I set my heart on learning. At thirty, I found my balance through the rites. At forty, I was free from doubts [about myself]. At fifty, I understood what Heaven intended me to do. At sixty, I was attuned to what I heard. At seventy, I followed what my heart desired without overstepping the line.

Everything Confucius tells us about himself is also about his teaching. There are steps but no regimen because his teaching complements his life—it mirrors a life unfolding, and it is natural.

CHAPTER SEVEN

The Rites of Life and Death

WHEN CIRCUMSTANCES ALLOWED, CONFUCIUS LIVED AN orderly life. Yet no particular principles took control of that life. Each day he let habits steer him through his activities; and he relied on good sense and aesthetic acumen to help him find what was right. This was not always apparent, however, certainly not when Confucius was under public scrutiny and had to perform according to those ritual dictates that governed the political realm. Confucius "drew himself in," the record says, "when he entered the portals of the ruler's court," and he "held his breath when he ascended the grand hall." If Confucius seems unnaturally constrained, it is because either he was using resignation and fear as a disguise, or the writing about him was inadequate—too clumsy to catch him in acts such as these.

More accessible are the accounts of Confucius at home and when he was among friends. When taking his meals, someone observed,

Confucius did not mind if the rice was polished or the meat was finely minced. He did not eat rice that had gone off, nor fish or meat that had spoiled. He did not eat food with a sickly color or a foul odor, nor anything that was overcooked or undercooked. He did not eat food that was not in season nor did he eat except at mealtimes. He did not eat meat that was not properly cut up or meat paired with the wrong sauce.

Even when he was was entitled to better things, Confucius was not an epicure. If he had views about "polished rice" and "minced meat," it was because they were the food he was accustomed to late in his life. The *Classic of Rites* says: "Those over fifty years of age should be able to eat polished rice. Those over sixty should be served meat regularly. Those over seventy should have two tasty dishes [a day]." For: "Without meat, those in their sixties would still feel hungry [after a meal]. Without silk padding, those in their seventies would be cold in their jackets." The family, the local community, and the state, the text says, are all responsible for "looking after the elderly."

But if Confucius was not an epicure, why would he reject meat "not properly cut up" or meat "paired with the wrong sauce"? His later defenders would say that his preferences in food had a ritual overtone—that meat "properly cut up" referred to animals correctly dismembered for the sacrificial offerings. They would set Confucius apart from the cooks and connoisseurs, whose quest for perfection took place mainly in the kitchen. Yet plenty of information on food, wine, and culinary techniques can be gleaned from the early ritual texts—splendid details on how to choose the right dog, pig, or horse for the table and which parts of a wolf, a fox, or a rabbit were not palatable. Such writings give the impression that the priest was working with the cook—not an unlikely relationship except for the fact that the voice of the moralist or the spiritualist was usually absent in these discussions. One example reads: "There is this theory: one should cut elaphure-deer and fish into large slices and river-deer into thin slivers. Wild boar, too, one should cut into large slices, and rabbit into fine slivers." The author of this text, "Regulations in the Home," tells the cook not only whether to slice, dice, julienne, or mince when preparing rabbit or venison, wild boar or fish, but also how to put together flavors and ingredients to create a distinct taste. He says:

> When stewing chicken, add boneless meat sauce (*hai*) and fill the cavity with smartweed. When stewing fish, add fish-roe sauce and stuff the cavity with smartweed. When stewing turtle, [again] add boneless meat sauce and stuff the cavity with smartweed. With dried meat, it is best to have it with frog paste. With meat stew, however, have a rabbit meat sauce as an accompaniment; with cooked elaphure-deer, fish paste; with slivers of fish, mustard sauce; with raw elaphure-deer, boneless meat sauce; and with dried peaches and plums, just salt.

Why should the author of a ritualist text be interested in the work of a cook unless he (and most people in his society) considered culinary art as a ritual form? Perhaps it is for this same reason that Confucius would refuse a meat that should have been sliced instead of diced or a meat that should have been matched with frog paste instead of fish. We may call it a matter of taste, but Confucius would say that matters of taste are the subject of the rites.

When taking his meal, Confucius did not concentrate just on the texture and flavor of the meat. He did not care for "dried meat bought from a shop." And he "would not eat the meat" if it was kept beyond three days after the animal had been slaughtered—which would include even the meat given to him by his lord after a sacrifice. Not to be offered a portion of the sacrificial meat would have worried Confucius, causing him to fret about his relationship with the ruler or the chief counselor, but once the meat was his to take home, he did not feel obliged to eat it if he thought that it was going to make him sick.

Meat was a luxury item with ritual significance. It was intended for the well-heeled, the aged, and the dead. In his old age, Confucius could have had meat every day, but he did not always want it. When in mourning, he abstained from meat and rice. The thought of meat could also make him feel nauseous. When he learned that after his disciple Zilu was killed in Wei, Zilu's enemy turned him into pickled meat sauce (*hai*), Confucius ordered the servants to throw away all the meat sauce in his house.

Sometimes Confucius preferred eating simply, but he did not always have a choice. And when coarse grains and vegetable broth were all that he could afford, "he always made an offering and he always did so reverently." However, even in easy circumstances— when, say, there was plenty of meat—Confucius "tried not to eat more meat than rice;" and it was his habit "not to overeat." However, in the case of wine, "he did not set himself a rigid limit. He simply never drank to the point of becoming addled."

In his everyday habits, Confucius can surprise us. We are not clear, for instance, as to why "he did not converse at meals" or why "he did not talk in bed." Did he consider those occasions not the right time for conversation? But if not then, when could there be a more relaxed moment to share thoughts or ideas? And what about the communal feasts? Do we expect them to be silent affairs aside from the sounds of bells and drums? Some scholars suggested that during such functions, there was a time "for joining in the the chorus of conversations and seeking advice from the elderly" and a time "for eating and drinking," and that the two did not overlap. Eating and sleeping, therefore, could be serious businesses—quiet and solemn and preferably without any outside distractions.

Getting dressed, too, could be exacting for a Chinese of the late Zhou if he had status and some means. Every day he would have to give careful consideration to his attire, and not because he feared that he might commit a fashion blunder. Ritual blasphemy, in his case, would be more hazardous, but functional and aesthetic considerations would also carry some weight. The *Analects* allows us a glimpse of what a gentleman of the late Zhou might have been thinking as he put on his clothes in the morning. There is no doubt that the "gentleman" here refers to Confucius:

The gentleman would not use reddish indigo or iron-grey to trim his robe, nor vermillion and red colors for his casual clothes. In the heat of the summer, he wore an unlined garment of either fine or coarse hemp, but he always topped it with a jacket when he went out. He wore a black dust-gown over lambskin, a white one over fawn-skin, and a yellow one over fox-fur. His informal fur coat was longer than his formal ones but with a shorter right sleeve. When sleeping, he always had a coverlet, which was one and half times the length of his body. He used the thick fur of badgers and foxes as cushions to sit on.

Attire for certain ritual occasions demanded even more attention. Black kidskin jackets and black caps were not worn on condolence calls. Black was an elegant and exalted shade and an auspicious color, which would not agree with feelings associated with mourning. Officials wore black when attending court and state sacrifices. They put on black jackets and pale red tent skirts. The skirt, on such occasions, was made from a single bolt of fabric with multiple pleats. Other types of skirts, however, could not be so lavish: extra material was saved and not bunched up in pleats.

In ritual practice, a perfect balance depended on many variables. Sometimes it was appropriate to be ornate rather than plain, to have more rather than fewer things, to have larger rather than smaller sizes. Other times it was just the reverse. It is not difficult to see why it was correct for an official to wear an extravagant skirt in court functions and simpler ones in other settings. But the calculations behind such choices can often be abstruse. The ceremonial objects of a ruler illustrate the inscrutable side of ritual decorum. A ruler should wear a robe embroidered with dragons, the old text says, and a cap with twelve pendants of jade beads strung on red and green silk; but his jade token should be unadorned and his carriage spare, with only a rush mat on the seat.

Thus when someone asked Confucius for a basic guideline in ritual practice, he replied, "What a big question!" And he was willing to answer it only in this way:

If you are talking about [the material aspects of] the rituals, it is better to err on the side of frugality and paucity rather than on the side of extravagance and excess. If you are talking about the mourning rites, it is better to err on the side of being overly consumed by grief rather than overly meticulous about the formal details.

Because Confucius assumed that missteps were unavoidable on most ritual occasions, his advice pertained only to how best to steer clear of the ones with more harmful consequences. But this hardly delineates a guideline for conduct. Fortunately, the *Analects* provides us enough clues to make out the path he tracked:

> In his own community, Confucius was agreeable and modest, and he gave the appearance that he was too clumsy to speak. In the ancestral temple and at court, though fluent, he did not say more than was necessary.

> At court, when speaking with counselors of lower rank, he was relaxed and affable. When speaking with counselors of high rank, he was frank but respectful. And when the ruler was present, though he was filled with reverence and awe, he carried himself lithely.

> When the ruler summoned him to receive guests of the state, his face took on a solemn expression and his steps a brisk pace. When he bowed to those standing around him, raising his cupped hands to the right and to the left, his robe-skirt swayed up and down without at all being ruffled. When going forward with quickened steps, he was like a bird unfolding its wings. After the guests had left, he always came back to report to the ruler, "The guests are no longer looking back."

> When the ruler's order came to summon him to court, he would set off on foot, without waiting for the carriage to be harnessed.

When the ruler bestowed on him a gift of cooked food, he always tasted it right away after he had adjusted his mat. When his ruler bestowed on him a gift of raw meat, he always cooked it and offered it [to his ancestors] first. When his ruler bestowed on him a gift of a live animal, he always raised it at home. When he was attending the ruler at a meal, after the ruler had made an offering, he would taste the food first [since this was his duty as a counselor], and he would start with rice.

Should the ruler pay him a visit when he was sick, he would lie with his head to the east, and with his robe draped over him and his grand sash placed across his waist and hanging down [the side of the bed].

When [the chief counselor] Jikangzi sent a gift of medicine, [Confucius] bowed his head to the ground and accepted it. But he added, "Not knowing its properties, I dare not taste it."

When asking after someone in another state, he bowed his head to the ground once and then again [as if the person were present] before he saw the messenger off.

Unless the present from a friend was sacrificial meat, in accepting it, he did not bow his head to the ground, even when the present was as sizable as carriage and horses.

When celebrating a drinking festival with people in the local community, he left as soon as those with walking sticks had left.

The stables caught fire. [Having learned about it] upon his return from court, Confucius said, "Did anyone get hurt?" He did not ask about the horses.

When a friend died, and if this person did not have a kinsman who could take his body in [and give him a proper service],

Confucius would say, "I will arrange to have his funeral in my house."

When a guest [from afar] could not find a place to stay, Confucius would say to him, "I have a place for you in my house. [In fact, you are welcome here] when you are living, and should you die while you are staying with me, I can also arrange to have your funeral in my house."

Confucius did not sleep like a corpse. And ordinarily he did not sit in a formal manner, like a guest or someone playing host to a guest.

He did not sit unless his mat was straight.

When climbing into a carriage, he always held his body erect as he clutched the mounting rope in his hand. When inside the carriage, he did not keep looking all around; he did not talk in a loud voice or at rapid speed; and he did not point at this or that.

During periods of purification [just before a sacrifice], he always wore clean undergarments made of cloth.

During periods of purification, he always altered his diet, eating only food prepared with fresh ingredients and clean tastes. [During such time,] he also changed his place of dwelling, [moving from his private bed chamber to a front room in the house, to avoid contact with women].

When Confucius encountered men in mourning clothes or men in ceremonial caps and robes, even though they might be younger than he was, he always rose to his feet; when passing by them, [out of respect,] he always quickened his steps.

Whenever Confucius met a person in mourning clothes, though the person might be a close friend, he always changed his countenance [to assume a grave expression]. Whenever he met a person wearing a ceremonial cap or a person who was blind, though the person might be on familiar terms with him, he always greeted the person with the utmost courtesy. When he passed by a person dressed in funeral attire, he always leaned forward with his hands on the cross-bar of his carriage. The same could be observed when his carriage went past a person carrying official documents.

When a sumptuous meal was brought forth, [out of the respect for the host] he always assumed a serious appearance and rose to his feet.

He also changed his expression when there was a clap of thunder or a fierce wind.

Confucius relied on his awareness of the people around him to get himself anchored in a community or at court, in a temple or on the street. He was not, however, looking for social approval or political dividends; nor was he aiming at any conspicuous end. Confucius put himself in the world of men, allowing himself the experience of being a neighbor, a friend, or a subject, because he wanted to understand what was appropriate and right in human relationships. Thus he could seem "too clumsy to speak" when he was among his kin and men from his own village but could carry himself "lithely" in the presence of a ruler. The agility of his conduct—knowing when to be silent and when to be fluent, how far to stoop to receive a gift and how far to extend himself to help a friend in need—is proof of his mastery of the rites. Yet his subtle moves and deft performance also betray a compassionate heart and a keen knowledge of the human lot.

As for other kinds of phenomena—"a clap of thunder," "a fierce wind," chaos, prodigies, or extreme violence—Confucius "did not speak about them." He did not talk about things he did not understand, and he did not talk about death. He was not fearful of death; nor was he made wretched by anticipating it. He told his followers that "a gentleman should never be surprised to find himself in terrible straits." And when he had to confront the possibility of an unnatural death, first in the town of Kuang and then in the wilds of Chen, he seemed composed, willing to accept his destiny.

When his life was not threatened, Confucius was even less likely to meditate on his mortality or anyone else's. "Everything passes on like the river," he declaimed. "Day and night, it never ceases." Knowing that life was impermanent did not vex him; nor did he let that knowledge become a fixation, as it was for many other moral philosophers, including some of his followers. He said to Zigong, "Death has always been with us since the beginning of time." This was all the solace and counsel he could offer the less illuminated.

Confucius was not obsessed with death, but all aspects of mourning absorbed him: the rites, the emotions, and the truths they tell about the mourners. A Han source tells us:

> When he was in the state of Wei, Confucius happened to witness [the ways of] a son in the funeral procession of his parent. Confucius said to his disciples, "How admirably the man has conducted the mourning rites! Let this be a standard for all of us. So take note of what you have seen." Zigong asked, "What good do you see in his behavior?" Confucius replied, "When he followed [his parent's coffin] to the grave site, he looked as if he was full of yearning, [still unable to let go]. When he came back from the burial, he looked as if he was full of doubt [because he could not tell if the spirit of his parent was at peace]." Zigong added, "Would it not be better, then, for him to hurry home and perform 'the sacrifice of the repose'?" [Ignoring Zigong's comment,] Confucius stressed once again, "All of you, take note of what you have seen. It is not something I could have done as well."

Only a truly filial son would be concerned about his parent as soon as he had buried him. Can the parent get used to being dead? Is he restless underground? Does his spirit still prowl the earthly world? The son is not worried about the trouble the spirit might create for the living, only that the deceased might not be pleased in his new circumstances. And the son knows that the rites cannot assuage all his anxieties, much less those of the dead. Therefore, why should he rush home to perform "the sacrifice of repose"? What distinguished this mourner from other mourners was the depth of his emotion, which was not easy to detect or to understand, but Confucius saw it in the man's longing and in his fretting, and he told those around him never to forget it.

Confucius himself, however, could not have known this kind of anxiety and longing from the death of his own father. He was only three at the time, and his mother, for reasons still obscure, never told him where his father was buried. One early scholar thought that the mother herself did not know where her husband was buried. When her husband "died of old age," this scholar said, she was still a young girl, "and so to avoid being the subject of gossip, she did not take part in his funeral procession and did not know where his grave was." After she died, Confucius "had his mother encoffined in the neighborhood of Wufu Road," and "people who learned about this thought that she was interred there." Later, however, Confucius asked an old matron from his home district where his father was buried. The woman pointed to a spot on Mount Feng. Thereupon Confucius "placed the remains of his parents together in the same site."

A Han dynasty source tells us that after the burial, Confucius tried to pile up a mound to mark the grave, which was contrary to ancient practice. "He said to others, 'I know that ancient graves have no mounds. But since I live a helter-skelter life, I have got to keep track of where my parents are buried.'" This could have encouraged other sons to do the same, to heap up earth and plant trees, to leave some markings on the place that held their parents' remains.

Confucius observed three years of mourning for his mother. When the rites were over, he waited for five days before he took up the zither again, but the sound he made had no melody. He could have been out of practice, yet it is more likely that he was still tugged toward the direction of the dead, and so, to the human ear, his music was a foreign song. Confucius waited for five more days before he took up the *sheng* pipe. Only then he was able to play a tune.

Confucius himself rarely gave rein to his emotions and rarely made a profuse display of joy or sorrow. His behavior at Yan Hui's funeral was an exception. The Han text tells of yet another instance:

> When Confucius went to Wei, he chanced upon the funeral of an innkeeper who had once lodged him at his place. Confucius entered the house and wept in grief. When he emerged, he instructed Zigong to take an outside horse yoked to his carriage and give it [to the bereaved family]. Zigong said, "You never did such a thing at the funeral of any of your disciples. But now you want to present a horse to the innkeeper's family just because he had let you have a place in the past. Is this not a bit much?" Confucius replied, "Just now I went into his house and I wept for him. As it happened, the occasion stirred a sadness in me, and my tears flowed. I should hate it if these tears flowed with nothing [substantial] to follow through [to show my sincerity]. So just do it!"

Confucius did not say what it was in the occasion that "stirred a sadness" in him. The death of the innkeeper? Or what the living had to bear because the innkeeper was now dead? He always "rose to his feet" and "changed his countenance" in the presence of mourners whether they were young or old, and whether he knew them well or not. So was it respect for the dead or sympathy for the survivors that caused his tears to flow? His disciple Zengzi remembered him as having said that mourning for one's parent was the only occasion when a person might apply himself to the utmost. Mourning for a friend or a kinsman is not the same as mourning for one's parent, but one would still want to do what one can. Confucius came upon his landlord's funeral by chance, and for the landlord's family he had only his horse to offer. It was a lavish token but one from the heart.

Even for his dead dog, Confucius insisted on a proper burial. He put Zigong in charge of the task, saying,

> I have heard that it is best not to throw away old and frayed bed-curtains because one can use them to bury horses; that it is best

not to throw away old and frayed carriage canopies because one can use them to bury dogs. I am poor and have no carriage canopy. So use my mat when you put the dog into his grave. Be sure not to let his head get stuck in the mud.

For all the consideration Confucius gave to mourning and burial, it was life that gripped him. He was astonished that every living thing had the will to carry on despite the hostilities and ill fortune that lay ahead. Of the pine and the cypress, he said, "Only when the cold season comes is the point brought home that they are the last to lose their green." Confucius' own time came in 479 BC, on the eighteenth day of the fourth month in the sixteenth year of Duke Ai's reign. The last person to see him was Zigong.

Leaning on a stick, Confucius was pacing by the gate. [When Zigong finally arrived,] he said, "Si, what took you so long to get here?" He then sighed and sang this song: "Mount Tai is crumbling. The pillars are being destroyed. The philosophers are in decline." Tears flowed down from his eyes [as he sang]. He then turned to Zigong and said, "The world has long been without a moral way. Therefore, no one is able to appreciate me. People of the Xia dynasty encoffined the dead at the top of the eastern steps. People of the Zhou performed the same ceremony on top of the western steps. People of the Shang performed the ceremony between the two pillars. Last night I dreamt that I was sitting between two pillars. Since I am a man of Shang, I shall die soon." Seven days later, Confucius died.

Gongxi Chi was put in charge of the funeral. This disciple possessed an impressive knowledge of the ritual world, of its history, its varied implements and elaborate rules, and even the emblematic meanings vested in the fans, banners, curtains, and canopies that were on display. He could explain why on certain ceremonial occasions one kind of material was used and not another and why an object had to be of a special length or shape. Yet Gongxi Chi was a self-effacing man. He never thought of ranking himself with the likes of Yan Hui or Zigong. He was fond of rituals but professed only modest ambitions. He told his teacher that if he had a chance of realizing his capacity, he would want only to be in a position to assist a minor official in the line of protocol. Confucius, however, saw a slightly higher promise in him, that of a gracious host and a skillful communicator in state affairs, and a reliable authority on all ritual matters. For the funeral of his teacher, we are told,

> Gongxi Chi adorned the curtains that sheltered the coffin from above and on all four sides; he constructed square-shaped fans to give the coffin more shade; he installed silk ropes on both sides of the catafalque [to stop the coffin from slipping off]. In these things, he followed the practice of the Zhou. He designed banners with tooth edges. In this, he followed the practice of the Shang. He hung long streamers on tall poles wrapped in plain silk. In this, he followed the practice of the Xia.

We can only surmise what objects accompanied Confucius to his afterlife. They were probably things that were close to him and things he used every day and was accustomed to having around: texts, writing brushes, bells, drums, zithers, pipes, and stone chimes; curtains, cushions, and armrests; bamboo baskets, wooden bowls, and earthenware.

Grave objects were made by special artisans, men who were aware of the delicate line between life and death. Confucius had said:

> To see the dead person to his grave with the thought that he is unmistakably dead is inhuman and not something one should do. To see the dead to his grave with the thought that he is still alive is unwise and also not something one should do. For these reasons, grave objects should be bamboo vessels that [have no woven borders and so] cannot be of use; earthenwares [that have not been baked and so] cannot hold soup; wooden containers, unfit to be decorated with carved designs; zithers, strung but not evenly;

pipes that are complete but not in tune; and stone chimes without their stands. The things are called *mingqi,* implements that serve the spirits (*shenming*).

In Confucius' view, "the makers of grave objects understood the principles of the funeral rites." It would be a "tragedy," he said, to bury the dead with "the actual implements of the living" and with "wooden figures that had the likeness of human forms," for this would bring the danger of their "leading to the interment of the living with the dead." He preferred clay carriages and straw figures because they resembled the genuine articles only in spirit.

During the mourning period for Confucius, the disciples wore headbands and waistbands made of hemp when they were outside of their homes. But they could not agree on what mourning clothes to wear, if any at all, because they were not sure of the nature of their relationship to Confucius. Zigong insisted that it was one of father and son, since Confucius himself had mourned Yan Hui and Zilu like a father mourning the death of his sons. Not everyone went along with his reasoning. The disciples also clashed on other issues, even on the question of whether Confucius' coffin should be hard-wearing or not. It is possible that the friction was exaggerated, but whoever made up the scenes must have wanted them to underscore the competition and the conflict among Confucius' followers after he died. Mencius, who was a second-generation disciple of Confucius' grandson and so a more reliable source, tells this story:

> One day Zixia, Zizhang, and Ziyou wanted to serve You Ruo as they had served Confucius because of his resemblance to the sage. They tried to force Zengzi to join them, but Zengzi said, "That will not do. Washed by the Yellow River and the Han River, bleached by the autumn sun, so immaculate was he that his whiteness could not be surpressed."

Zigong, too, had stayed away from those who gathered around You Ruo. Again Mencius says:

When Confucius died and the three-year mourning period had elapsed, his disciples packed their bags and prepared to return to their families. They went in and bowed to Zigong [because he was their senior]. Facing one another, they wept until they lost their voice before setting out on their journey home. [After seeing them off,] Zigong came back and built a hut in the burial grounds. He remained there on his own for another three years before returning home.

With Yan Hui and Zilu dead, Zigong was the one who had been with Confucius the longest and stood by him the longest. Thus when someone spoke evil of his teacher, Zigong said: "He is simply wasting his time. Great men by other people's measures are like the hills— one can still climb them. Confucius is like the sun and the moon—he is unsurmountable. Even when people want to estrange themselves from the sun and the moon, what harm would it do to either? This only goes to show that they have overestimated themselves."

To take Confucius down from his height, some tried another strategy: they worked on Zigong's vanity. One said to him, "You are just being modest, aren't you? How can Confucius be superior to you?" Zigong, however, was unmoved. In his riposte, he put Confucius right back in the sky. "My teacher cannot be equaled, just as the sky cannot be scaled," he said.

> Were the Master to become the head of a state or of a hereditary family, he would be like the man described in the saying, "He only has to help them stand on their own, and they will stand on their own; he only has to steer them [in the right direction], and they will forge ahead; he only has to set them at ease, and they will gravitate toward him; he only has to mobilize them, and they will work in harmony." He was honored when he was alive and mourned when he died. How can he be equaled?

Here it was Zigong who was boastful. Confucius might have been as tall as the firmament, but he could not have made good the magic Zigong said he could in an earthly kingdom like Lu. His record in politics did not support Zigong's claim, and even if he had risen to a position of authority, the world in the last years of the Spring and Autumn period had already swung too far from the path for magic—any kind of magic—to work.

After Confucius died, the ruler of Lu delivered a eulogy:

> Merciful Heaven is not kind! You left me not one learned elder to lend me support. You forsook me in the dark, alone on my throne. So alone am I that I feel as if I were suffering an affliction. Alas, Father Confucius, [since you are gone] I have no one as a measure.

The royal accolade did not impress Zigong. "When Confucius was alive," Zigong said, "[our ruler] was unwilling to put his talents to use. Now that Confucius is dead, he sings his praise." In Zigong's judgment, the gestures and the oration were "a violation of the rites."

What, then, should one say about Confucius to mourn him? What can one say so that it rings true? And what of that truth is worth remembering? Zigong tried a quieter tribute sometime later, after a counselor at court had announced that Zigong was more competent and more accomplished than his teacher:

> Let us take the outer walls as an analogy. My walls are shoulder high, so that it is possible to peer over them and see the beauty of the house. But the Master's walls are twenty or thirty feet high, so that, unless one gains admittance through the gate, one cannot see the magnificence of the ancestral temples or the splendor of the official buildings. Since only a few had gone through the gate, is it any wonder that this counselor should have spoken as he did?

What would Confucius say about himself? What truth would he tell and how would he like people to remember him?

I was poor and from a lowly station. That is why I am skillful in many menial things.

I could not prove myself in office. That is why I acquired many skills.

Do I possess knowledge? No, I do not. A rustic put a question to me and my mind was a complete blank. I kept knocking at the two sides [of the question] until I got everything out.

I work as hard as anyone, but I have not yet had any success in conducting myself as a gentleman.

To serve high officials when abroad, and my elders when at home; in arranging funerals, not to dare to spare my efforts; and to be able to hold my drink—these are trifles that give me no trouble.

Joy is to be found in eating coarse rice, drinking water, and using one's arm for a pillow. Wealth and rank attained the wrong way have as much to do with me as the passing cloud.

If it is proper to seek wealth, I would be willing to be a guard holding a whip at the marketplace. If it is not, I will pursue something that I like.

[I am] the sort of man who forgets to eat when he tries to solve a problem that has been driving him to distraction, who is so full of joy that he forgets his worries and who does not notice the onset of old age.

How dare I claim to be a sage or benevolent man? Perhaps it might be said of me that I learn without flagging and teach without growing weary.

I have never refused to teach anyone who approached me on his own with a bundle of dried meat [as a gift].

I would not give a person a boost or a start if he does not know the frustration of trying to solve a difficult problem or the frenzy one would get into when trying to put an idea into words.

After I have shown a student one corner [of a square], if he does not come back with the other three, I will not repeat what I have done.

I am a fortunate man. When I make a mistake, others are sure to notice it.

Grant me a few more years so that when I reach the age of fifty, I may try to understand the principle of change and I shall steer clear of making serious mistakes.

Is it not a pleasure, having learned something, to try it out when it is timely? Is it not a joy to have friends coming from afar? Is it not gentlemanly not to feel upset when no one takes notice of [your learning or your accomplishment]?

Would I not rather die in the arms of a few good friends than in the arms of retainers? And even if I could not have a minister's burial, it was not as if I was dying by the wayside.

From the beginning of their history, the subtlest of Chinese have worked to perfect the art of retreat—from high to low, from pomp to modesty, from grandeur to the familiar, from the visible to the indiscernible—in living and in dying. This is cultivation. This is even good form. Confucius was a genius at the art, as is evident from a story told about him in the early sources. Once, on his travels,

Confucius got separated from his disciples. So he stood alone by the east gate of the city wall. A man of Zheng, who had seen him there, later remarked to Zigong, "There is a man by the east gate. He has the forehead of the sage ruler Yao, the neck of the supreme arbiter Gao Yao, the shoulders of the prime minister Zichan, and is just three inches shorter than the great emperor Yu from the waist down. Yet he looks confused and miserable, like a dog that has lost his way home." Later, when Zigong found Confucius, he repeated exactly what this man had told him. Confucius smiled and said, "I can't really accept what this man suggested about my shape and build. But what he said about me looking like a stray dog is true. I can't argue with that."

Even when feeling tired and dejected, Confucius retreated to the lowly and found "a ready measure of [his] significance." Yet "nestling" in "the lowly" did not make him diminished or depressed; on the contrary, it allowed him to rise above his troubles. This is the elegance of the art of retreat—he who pursues the art must, in his secret heart, desire to stay ahead and to travel upward. When Confucius told Zigong that no one understood him and that he was "thinking of giving up speech," Zigong protested, saying, "What would there be for us to transmit if you give up speech?" To which Confucius replied: "What does Heaven ever say? Yet there are the four seasons going around and there are the hundred things coming into being. What does Heaven ever say?" Here the retreat to silence is a cut above cultivation or any art of life. By giving up speech, Confucius confers upon himself a power equal to the forces of Nature. Yet even at such a moment, he would feel the heaviness of his own failure, and he would be careworn. This was the paradox of Confucius.

CHAPTER EIGHT

Defenders

B Y HOISTING HIM UP TO A CELESTIAL HEIGHT, DISCIPLES of Confucius put him at risk. Who on earth could be his spiritual heir? they asked. Who would qualify? For a while, You Ruo played the part. He was a younger disciple and had been active in Lu politics. A scattering of men followed him after they had buried Confucius, and they called him master, but You Ruo hardly earned the title or the right to be Confucius' heir. He merely bore a resemblance to his teacher, and so the likes of Zixia, Zizhang, and Ziyou must have been clinging to the shade of Confucius when they decided to serve You Ruo.

There were reports that, besides You Ruo, other disciples also carved out schools for themselves, but no one knew what became of them. A hundred years after Confucius' death, the philosopher Mencius reflected on the problems of transmission—how effortless it had been for the geniuses of the past and how difficult for the men of his time:

From [the sage emperors] Yao and Shun to [the founder of the Shang dynasty,] King Tang, over five hundred years elapsed. Men like Yu and Gao Yao knew Shun personally, but others like King Tang knew him only by repute. From King Tang to King Wen, another five hundred years elapsed. Men like Yi Yin and Lai Zhu knew King Tang personally, but others like King Wen only knew him by repute. From King Wen to Confucius, it was again five hundred years. Men such as Tai Gong Wang and Sanyi Sheng knew King Wen personally, but others like Confucius knew him only by repute. From Confucius to the present, it has only been a hundred years. In time, we are not so distant from this sage. In space, we live so close to his home. Yet, if there is no one to succeed him, there is no one to succeed him.

Did Mencius really believe that there was no one to succeed Confucius? Since this statement ends the work that bears his name, the *Book of Mencius,* could he or the editors of the book be putting his name forward as a candidate for this hallowed position? After all, it was Mencius who lived "so close to [Confucius'] home," just thirty kilometers away in Zou, a district that had once belonged to a neighboring state but by Mencius' time had come under the jurisdiction of Lu. It was also Mencius who said: "The influence of the gentleman and the petty man runs out in five generations. I have not had the good fortune to have been a disciple of Confucius, but I have come under his beneficence privately through various people." Mencius wanted others to know the special relationship he had with Confucius. He was not a direct disciple, he admits, but he had access to Confucius through private transmission before the span of five generations expired, which in Chinese reckoning added up to about a hundred and fifty years.

Just who were the "various people" who allowed Mencius an intimate knowledge of Confucius? One group of historians said that those people were disciples of Confucius' grandson Zisi. Another group claimed that Mencius' teacher was Zisi himself, who in turn had studied with Confucius' disciple Zengzi. If this were true, it would draw Mencius even closer to Confucius, but as several scholars have pointed out, even if Zisi had been born in 482, the year his father died, and had lived to the age of eighty-two, he clearly could not have taught Mencius, who, as we know, was a man of the fourth century BC. Still, many early sources associated Mencius with Zisi: one of them "sings," and the other "harmonizes," says one critic. Thus if Mencius and Zisi did make music together, the performance could not have been contemporaneous.

Given his relationship to Confucius' grandson Zisi, was Mencius truly privy to an insider's knowledge of Confucius? Certain details in the *Book of Mencius* seem to point that way. For instance, Mencius said: "When Confucius held office in Lu, the people of Lu were in the habit of fighting over the catch in a hunt [to use it in a sacrifice]. Confucius also joined in the fight." This is a real scoop, but it is curious that Mencius should have disclosed such information about a man he would passionately defend against any whiff of criticism. Should he not have been concerned about just how easy it would be for rivals to turn this description of Confucius into a farce? Mencius was not a blunderer or a thoughtless man, which is the reason why his use of the knowledge he had regarding Confucius is particularly interesting.

Although he never wanted to admit it, Mencius was disputatious and a debater, and he encouraged his own disciples to parley with him, to treat him like an opponent. On the whole, he did not enjoy the dialectic tension in these sessions, but conversations forced him to think more clearly—not about eternal principles, which he did not believe existed, but about what is right, what is timely, and what is constant and sustained in the world of flux. Examples from Confucius' life, he decided, could often drive the point home, and so he put to use all the facts and reports that reached him through disciples of Zisi and other people. Some of the details about Confucius could be jarring, yet Mencius found them to be effective in persuasion. Thus when his disciple Wan Zhang insisted that the regional rulers "were no different from robbers" because they took from their subjects things to which they had no right, he recounted Confucius' behavior at the hunt while the latter was an official of Lu. Confucius "joined in the fight over the catch," because it was the custom at the time and the people of Lu thought the scuffle "propitious behavior" before a sacrifice; therefore, Mencius said, "to insist that the act of taking something that does not belong to you is robbery is to push the question of rightness to an extreme."

Still, Mencius did not consider rightness just as a variable of time and place, of history and custom. Being a moral philosopher, he could not be satisfied with having only contingent truths. He wanted truths to be stable and reliant but not so as to let him become inflexible. Again, he was able to find suitable examples from Confucius' life to illustrate his point. He said:

> Poverty should not be the reason why you take office, but there are times when a man takes office because he is hard up. To have someone look after your parents should not be the reason to get married, but there are times when a man takes a wife so that there is someone to care for his parents. A man who takes office because he is poor should choose a low office instead of a high one, an office with a small salary instead of one with a large salary.

And what might be a "suitable position" to choose? "A gatekeeper or a night watchman," Mencius suggested. He said:

> Confucius was once a minor official in charge of the granaries. He said, "All I have to do is to keep accurate accounts." He was once a minor official in charge of the livestock in the field. He said, "All I have to do is to raise the sheep and cattle to be fat and healthy."

It is wrong to take office because you need to make a living, but you might be forced to do so if you are destitute. And should this happen, Mencius says, settle for a position of slight consequences and follow the example of Confucius: Do not "talk about lofty things"; perform only the charge of your office.

Mencius knew full well that his teachings would lose ground and credibility if he began to make exceptions in matters of right and wrong. But this was his way of searching for what was fair and compassionate when charting a difficult course, and he often looked to

Confucius as his guide. Confucius, he declared, "did not carry himself to extreme ends; and he was the sage who acted in a timely way." There were other types of sage, he explained: those whose characters were so "immaculate" that "they would only serve the right prince and govern the right people"; those who were so "politically responsible" that they would "serve any prince" and "govern any people"; and those who were so "amiable and open-minded" that they "were not ashamed to serve a prince with a tarnished name" and did not "scorn the offer of a modest post." But Confucius was different from them. He knew when to jump into action and when to retreat; he even knew how fast or slowly to retreat. Mencius said, "When Confucius left the state of Qi, he started after emptying the rice from the steamer, but when he left Lu, he said, 'I proceeded as slowly as possible.'" "This," Mencius explained, "is the way to leave the state of one's mother and father."

Timeliness need not be driven by moral urgency. Most people who act in a timely way are simply alert and observant. Confucius, however, calculated his action by the exigency of his circumstances and by moral necessity. He left Qi at the right moment because he was perceptive, but it was the difference in the speed with which he left one place and then another that distinguished him as "the sage who acted in a timely way." Mencius would say that the moral is in these details. And as he tried to glean the moral from all the bits of knowledge he had about Confucius, he also helped to bring Confucius to life.

Even though Mencius thought Confucius bigger and subtler than all the other philosophers he knew, he did not latch on to him. He adapted Confucius' teachings freely and proposed ideas of his own, the boldest of which concerns human nature. And even there, he wagered his big theory on one small example. "Every person has a heart which is sensitive to the suffering of others," Mencius said.

> The reason I say that every person has such a heart is this. Suppose a man—any man—suddenly sees a young child on the verge of falling into a well. He will, for sure, feel alarmed, his heart

aching. [That he should feel this way] is not because he wants to be on intimate terms with the child's parents; not because he seeks praise from the neighbors and friends in his village; and [certainly] not because he dislikes the child's crying. From this we can see that whoever is without a heart of compassion is not human.

Mencius believed that all humans are born with a moral impulse; therefore, the sight of a young child about to plunge to his death horrifies us and afflicts us with pain. The horror—the pain—is an unthinking, an unmeditated, response: an impulse from the heart. Those who do not feel it are not human, declared Mencius; and it is not the fault of their inborn nature if they resemble animals, because, "without exception, everyone is endowed with a heart of compassion." To be human is to be born with a potential to commiserate. If the potential is absent, a man has only himself to blame: he must have let it dissipate. Mencius thought that perhaps Confucius "was referring to the heart's potential" when he said, "Hold on to it and it will exist. Let it go and it will vanish. One does not know when it comes or goes, where it is going or coming from."

We have no way of verifying whether Confucius said this or not. If he did, did he have the heart's moral potential in mind? Did Confucius, in fact, believe, as Mencius claimed he did, that the heart, by nature, had the power to commiserate? Zigong told us that Confucius was not interested in talking about human nature and the nature of things. But as we know, he must have assumed that humans wanted to be good and could become good if they tried hard enough. Otherwise, his teachings of rites and music would have no point. "What can a man do with rites or with music," he asked, "if he has no humanity?" Still, Confucius was not given to speculation. He had a hunch about our nature, which was likely to be optimistic, and his teaching relied on the upbeat to propel itself forward.

Mencius, too, began on a bright note, but unlike Confucius, he could get carried away by the promise in it. As a result, what he said may sound lyrical or far-fetched or both. He said of the Emperor Shun:

When Shun dwelled in the depths of the mountains, he lived among trees and stones, and had as companions deer and pigs. The difference between him and the uncouth man of the mountains was slight. But when he heard a single good word, witnessed a single good deed, it was like water causing a breach in the dykes of the Yangtse or the Yellow River. It swells up and overflows, and nothing could hold it back.

Mencius was a storyteller and a hyperbolist. His tale of Shun gets taller and better—more harrowing and touching—as Shun grows older. We learn that despite his passionate longing for the good, Shun could never find it in his family. His parents and brother were brutes. They loathed him in spite of his love for them, and they wanted nothing more than to see him dead. And as Shun toiled in the field under "an autumnal sky," he "wept and wailed, calling upon Heaven for mercy," but Heaven was distant and silent. Mencius' disciple Wan Zhang asked, "Why did Shun weep and wail?" He was yearning for the love of his parents and he was anguished, Mencius replied. Wan Zhang continued: "'If your parents love you, you must feel joyful, but you should not forget [to look after them]. If your parents despise you, you must not resent them even when they make you wretched and wear you out.' Are you saying that Shun was resentful toward his parents?"

Wan Zhang probably had in mind Confucius, who said: "In serving your parents, try to dissuade your parents from doing wrong in the gentlest way. If you see your advice being ignored, do not defy them but remain reverent. You must not resent them even when they wear you out." In his response, Mencius scoffed at the thought that Shun could be resentful toward his parents. An ordinary man would have said, "I have worked hard in tilling the fields and in discharging my duty as a son. If my parents do not love me, what is that to me?" But Shun would have asked, "What is wrong with me?" Other men would have been content with "beautiful women," "wealth," or "high positions," Mencius tells us, but "none of these things could have delivered Shun from the anxiety which the pleasure of his parents alone could relieve. . . . Even at the age of fifty, Shun yearned for his parents."

The story of Shun was an old one, enigmatic and full of gaps in the early classics. Would Confucius have pursued it in the same way? Would he have wanted to do such a thing? Would he have wanted to create a supreme model of a filial son, thus running the risk of being asked, as Mencius was, whether Shun, as an emperor, would stop the authorities from apprehending his father if his father had killed a man? Would Shun as a filial son protect his father from the law? Mencius gave his response: "How could Shun interfere with the law?" How could he stop the judge "from exercising the authority he had received"? "But," he continued, "Shun looked upon casting aside the empire as no more than discarding a worn shoe. He would have secretly carried the old man on his back and fled to the edge of the sea and lived there happily, never giving a thought to the empire."

Confucius would not have gone as far as Mencius. He was cautious about singling out anyone—in mythology or in history—as the perfect example of a virtue, and he would have been reluctant to elevate filiality above all other human duties and hold it as absolute. Duty to the family should have more import than other kinds of obligation, and so, in Confucius' view, father and son should not inform on each other when either is in trouble with the law. These were the moral conditions Confucius imposed on the father and the son. Their conflict with the law, however, remained their problem, and he left it to them to find "the rightness therein." Thus, if the father had committed a crime and someone else notified the authorities and had him arrested, Confucius would not have wanted the son to carry his father on his back and flee to the edge of the world. For by running away, what could the son have learned? In Mencius' imagination, Shun would have taken this step had he found himself in the same predicament. By choosing his parent over his empire, Shun would have been "the supreme example of filiality." But was his action moral?

Mencius' own disciples asked him similar questions. Although his answers never fully satisfied them or even himself, Mencius could not let Shun give up being a son to his parents no matter how much of a menace the parents might be to society and to him. But Mencius was not inflexible. He "disliked forced arguments" and was not inclined to push any principle to an extreme. Shun was the exception because his life provided the right material (lowly birth, dark family history, heightened sensibilities) from which Mencius' most cherished beliefs could find their expression. Mencius said:

> Shun rose from the fields [at the foot of the Mount Li]; Fu Yue was raised to office from the piles of boards and planks; Jiao Ge from the heaps of fish and salt; Guan Zhong from the hands of the prison guards; Sun Shuao [from his hut] by the sea; and Boli Xi from [the hurly-burly of] the marketplace. Thus when Heaven is about to place a great responsibility on a man, it always tests his resolution, exhausts his frame, starves his body, and frustrates his effort so as to shake him from his mental lassitude, toughen his nature, and make good his deficiencies.

But the burden Shun carried was greater than most. Besides having an insensate father, a cruel stepmother, and a scheming half brother, he had a tendency to gather the force of the negatives back into himself, and he would turn it into an occasion for self-examination and self-reproach. In this way, Mencius tells us, Shun became a man of infinite strength and a son of supreme filiality. But Shun was an ideal in spite of his human attributes and his all-too-human circumstances. Mencius himself never tried to find the likes of Shun in human history or in his own world. In the Mencian configuration of things, Shun was kept on sacred ground: even Confucius stood at a safe distance.

In his judgment of human character, particularly the character of people he knew personally, Mencius could be very lenient. His contemporaries were shocked to learn that he "socialized" and "treated with courtesy" a man other people deemed "unfilial." The man, Kuang Zhang, was not allowed to be near his father, let alone take care of him, because father and son "had taxed each other on a moral issue." Mencius did not tell us what issue could have caused so permanent a breach, implying only that the father had done something wrong and that the son might have been too direct in reproving him. Mencius said: "It is for friends to demand goodness from each other. For father and son to do so seriously undermines the love between them." Was this the source of Kuang Zhang's estrangement from his father? And was this the reason why Mencius was so charitable toward him? Moreover, because Kuang Zhang could not attend to his own father, he "sent his wife and children away" and "would not let them look after him." Mencius asked, "Do you think that Kuang Zhang does not want to be a husband to his wife and a father to his children?" This man chose a life of aloneness and privation in order to let his offense be more bearable. "That's Master Zhang for you!" Mencius said, conveying at once his sympathy and his admiration for a friend.

Mencius was kind to men, such as Kuang Zhang, who were willing to confront the most demanding and intractable of human circumstances—men who tried their best but still fell short of doing the right thing. He was drawn to them and even to their imperfections. In this, he followed Confucius. And like Confucius, he was contemptuous of the glib man and exasperated with the painfully scrupulous. Of the glib, especially of the glib "goody man," Mencius said: "If you want to censure him, you cannot find any evidence of his wrongdoing, and if you want to attack him, you cannot find a clear target. He is in tune with the prevalent custom and blends in with the sordid world." And this explained why Confucius regarded such a man as "an enemy of virtue."

With the painfully scrupulous, Mencius had more fun. Like Confucius, he preferred them over the glib but could not resist parodying them. Of all the famous prigs, there was one who, in order to keep his life and himself pristine, wore only the sandals he had made himself and the hemp and silk his wife had cultivated. He came from "an old family," Mencius tells us, and his elder brother had a hefty income, but he considered the income and his brother's house "ill-gotten," and so he lived apart from him and his mother.

One day he went there for a visit and found that someone had given his brother a live goose. He knitted his brow and said, "What good is this honking creature?" Another day his mother killed the goose and cooked it for him, and he ate it. His brother, who had just come home, said to him, "This is the meat of that honking creature." He rushed out and *wua!*—out came his meal of goose.

"This man ate what his wife cooked him but not what his mother cooked him," observed Mencius, "and he lived somewhere else but not in his brother's house." But did he know whether a gentleman or a bandit had built his house, whether a gentleman or a bandit had grown the millet he ate? "Pushed to its limit," Mencius said, "his way of life would only be possible for an earthworm which eats the dry earth above and drinks the Yellow Spring below."

Mencius liked flexibility in behavior, fluidity in thought, and a naturalness of effort, and water was a favorite metaphor. Not water "collected in the gutter" but "water from an ample source," water that "comes tumbling down, day and night without ceasing, going forward only after it has filled all the hollows." "Anything that has an ample source is like this," he said. It is "what Confucius saw in water when he exclaimed, 'Water! Oh, water.'" But a downpour, uncontrolled and unresisted, can cause a deluge. This, too, became a metaphor for Mencius. He said: "In the time of Yao, water ran contrary to its natural course, thereby inundating the entire central kingdom; and reptiles made their home there, depriving the people of a settled life. . . . The *Classic of Documents* says, 'The deluge was a warning to us.'" A warning about the consequences of excess, explained Mencius. Thus, just as Emperor Shun put Yu in charge of controlling the flood, the Duke of Zhou took upon himself the responsibility of reining in the cataract of violence and death, and Confucius, too, sought ways to check the surge in instances of gross misdeeds. Yu "dug channels in the ground" and "guided flood water into the sea." The Duke of Zhou helped King Wu execute a punitive war against tyranny, thus restoring order to the world. Confucius possessed the knowledge and skills of a historian, and so he set out to compose a chronicle of his state. The judgment he pronounced on the men and women of the past was enough "to strike terror into the hearts of all the rabble-rousers and unfilial children."

Mencius tells us that he wished to follow in the footsteps of these three men. Since he did not have the technical competence of Yu or the political prowess of the Duke of Zhou, he could have emulated only Confucius. But was he his true heir? Mencius was a moral philosopher, not a historian. He lacked a historian's dispassion and acumen, and he was contentious—more so than Confucius. He perceived rivals and opposition all around him. Their theories, he said, threatened "to overcrowd and override the path of morality," and he took it upon himself to engage his enemies through disputation. "I am not fond of disputation," Mencius claimed, "but I have no alternative." His targets were mainly the followers of Yang Zhu and Mo Di. Mencius said of Yang and Mo:

> Yang Zhu advocated doing things only to serve yourself, which amounted to denying the existence of [everyone else, including] the ruler; Mo Di argued the importance of loving everyone equally, which amounted to negating [all distinctions in human relationships, including] the father.

"Without the concept of a ruler and the concept of a father, we are simply beasts," Mencius argued. Yet nearly all teachings and all forms of rhetoric during his time were "derivatives of the Yang School or of the Mo School." Their words "filled every corner under Heaven," like a deluge, and so Mencius "was apprehensive," fearful of what might become of humans if "the ways of Yang and Mo are not stopped and the way of Confucius is not brought to light."

Contrary to what Mencius would like his audience to believe, the teachings of Yang Zhu and of Mo Di were not hollow or deceptive. Yang Zhu proclaimed that he "would not pluck a single hair from his body even when it can benefit the world." What may seem like a position of extreme selfishness was, in fact, a loud affirmation of the self—that no one person should sacrifice himself just because the state, the family, or the future generation demands it for its own good. Mo Di was the opposite of Yang Zhu. He had boundless love for everyone but no love for himself. Thus, he would travel the world, sometimes for ten days and ten nights without sleep or rest, "until there was no down left on his calf and no hair on his shin," to offer his assistance to the beleaguered and the desperate.

Mencius' problems with the followers Yang Zhu and Mo Di were not based entirely on spiritual or moral grounds. Like Mencius, most of these men were professionals. They competed for political recognition, for the same students, and sometimes for the same jobs. They all needed employment and an income, but few would admit that they were working solely for their own interests. Mencius referred to himself and those on similar quests as "custodians of the way of the former kings." He argued that they earned their keep honorably because by upholding morality they would benefit the next generation of men who aspired to learning.

Mencius' defense of his profession hints at the problems others might have had with men who considered "being filial to their parents at home and respectful to elders when abroad" as services rendered to society and mankind. Someone said to Mencius: "It is the intention of the carpenter and the carriage maker to make a living. When a gentleman pursues the moral way, is it also his intention to make a living?" To demand payment for trying to live morally, as the followers of Confucius had, could and did make the whole Confucian project vulnerable to ridicule and reproof, and of all the critics, Mo Di was the most savage. In an essay called "Against Confucians," Mo Di says:

> Confucians corrupt men with their elaborate and showy rites and music and deceive parents with lengthy mournings and hypocritical grief. . . . They are greedy for food and drink and too lazy to work. . . . They behave like beggars, stuff away food like he-goats, and walk around like castrated pigs. . . . If they can get enough to eat and drink and get themselves put in complete charge of a

few funerals, they are satisfied. What wealth they possess comes from other families, and what favors they enjoy are the products of other men's fields. When there is a death in a rich family, they are overwhelmed with joy, saying, "This is our chance for food and clothing."

The source of Mo Di's invective was self-righteousness, not professional jealousy. However, one can hardly blame him for being so hostile. Here was a man who asked neither appreciation nor a fee for his efforts to save the world, while the Confucians around him were making a profit out of other people's grief. Others might have been grateful for the services Confucians performed, but to Mo Di, their doings were the work of exploiters and freeloaders.

Mencius was not a contemporary and so could not have been the object of Mo Di's rancor, but people of Mencius' time, too, questioned whether it was right for him "to travel with a retinue of hundreds of followers in scores of chariots, and to live off one feudal lord after another." In response, Mencius stressed that he made a proper living because he did "good work" but his work was different from that of the farmer or that of the craftsman. Of this difference, he said: "There are those who use their minds, and there are those who use their muscles. The former do the ruling; the latter are ruled. Those who do the ruling are supported by those who are ruled." Mencius pointed to Yao, Shun, and Yu as examples of rulers who put their minds to work and succeeded in setting the affairs of the people in order. These rulers could accomplish great things because they had big worries about the state of their empire and the future of human existence, and they were anxious about what might happen to either should they fail to fulfill their responsibilities as rulers. Their anxiety, Mencius said, was different from that of a farmer who "frets about his plot of a hundred *mu* not being cultivated."

Mencius did not presume to place himself in the same league as these august figures, but he made it clear that he, too, was someone who would not be content spending his life fretting about the rice plants. Thus he aligned himself with the rulers. He worked with them and lived off them, and he felt justified about the considerable income his profession could bring in, which was much more than what physical labor could realize. He said, "The fact that things are unequal is their natural condition. Some are worth twice or five times, ten or a hundred times, even a thousand or ten thousand times more than others. To insist that all things are equal is to create chaos in the world." But to be in the company of rulers and to benefit from their generosity had its own toll, and it could also leave a poor impression.

Few among his contemporaries would have disagreed with what Mencius said about the inequality of things or his argument that even teachers and philosophers needed some means of livelihood; yet many would find fault with him anyway. Why, then, did he not inspire trust? What virtues did he lack? A comparison with Confucius is helpful. Both men relied on the rich and powerful for material support. Contemporaries of Confucius seemed to accept how he made his living, yet acquaintances of Mencius described him as someone who "lived off one feudal lord after another." Confucius traveled with three or four disciples and nearly died of starvation in the wilds of Chen or Cai. Mencius traveled with as many as a hundred men and scores of carriages and seemed to be accustomed to wearing silk and dining on bear paws and grain-fed mutton and beef. Just how much emolument did Mencius ask from a ruler for a long engagement or shorter one? What was his fee? And what was the price exacted from him once he accepted a job? How pliable did he have to be at the beginning, so that the ruler would feel comfortable having him around? How compliant did he become if he wanted to extend his stay? And under what circumstances would he pick up and leave?

From the conversations we have of Mencius with the rulers who hired him, it appears that he gave as much as he took. By Mencius' own account, in the six or seven years he resided in the state of Qi, his earnings were a hundred thousand *zhong* or a hundred and thirty thousand *dan* of grain, which translates to around five hundred tons or sixty thousand bushels of grain per year. He arrived at Qi around 319 BC, and once he was settled, the ruler who hired him, King

Xuan, began working on him to get him to go along with his plan to invade another state. King Xuan called his undertaking a punitive war against a country where the deceased ruler had arranged to have a counselor, not his own son, succeed him. This, King Xuan argued, was a highly irregular practice and could have serious moral consequences. Mencius must have agreed with him. He consented first to the invasion and then to a military occupation after the conquest, hoping, of course, that his ruler might bring succor to the people there. It was not until he learned that the army of Qi "had practiced tyranny" over the people they had subdued, "killing the old and binding the young, destroying the ancestral temples and appropriating the valuable vessels," that Mencius decided to leave.

As Mencius was going, it took him three nights to get to the next town, just three kilometers away. "But even so," he said, "it did not take long enough. I had hoped against hope that the king would change his ways. I was sure that if he did, he would call me back." The king, of course, made no attempt to change his ways or to send after Mencius. But even when his hopes were dashed, Mencius never ceased to believe that the king was "capable of doing good." He said: "If only the king would change his ways. That is what I hope for every day. I am not like those petty men who, when their advice is rejected by the prince, would become irate and take on a sour countenance, and, when they leave, would travel all day until they have exhausted all their energy before they would stop somewhere for the night."

The enigma of Mencius was that he knew, from the beginning, the truth about his ruler. The ruler, too, was candid about himself. He told Mencius plainly that he was fond of women and wealth, and of a warrior's valor; that he was shallow and did not have the makings of a true king. Mencius did not listen to him or to his own better judgment. Instead, he concentrated on the particles of good he observed in the king, and out of them he created a lie. The lie helped him to keep his hope alive. And just like Shun, who yearned for his parents all his life, Mencius yearned for his ruler, not for his affection but for a sign—any sign—that he wanted to change for the better. But such labor wears one down, and the work is risky. In the case of Mencius, it was his giving in a little and flattering a little in the act of moral persuasion that led some to think that he was weak and cocky, shifty and self-righteous.

Mencius had many critics while he was alive and in the two centuries after he died. The most forceful and astute among them was Xunzi, who was also a follower of Confucius but lived a century after Mencius. Xunzi accused Mencius and Mencius' teacher Zisi of "deflecting" the teachings of Confucius, and of creating something "aberrant," "obscure," and "esoteric," so that one was left with "no model" to pursue, "no disquisition" to think through, and "no explanations" to lend light to those in the dark. Xunzi did not imply that Mencius had done this intentionally. Some critics had another point of view. They suggested that Mencius was being deliberately abstruse and slippery, which was his character; that even as a teacher, he would reach far back into the past to find as his perfect examples men like Yao and Shun, who were so shrouded in mystery and mystique that one could neither emulate nor contest his judgments.

Xunzi, however, preferred men closer to his own time as models of conduct, and teachings that rulers and counselors could readily adapt to the demands of the occasion. He also preferred to reflect on the mind's potentials rather than the heart's. If the mind's potentials are cultivated, he said, they can allow us a more precise measure of right and wrong. That measure, in his view, is a deeper and more reliable source of human compassion than the stirring of the heart. Later Confucians would notice the disparity between Xunzi and Mencius, and they would take sides. But their writings in this respect were the stuff of polemics.

Xunzi did not dwell on his differences with Mencius. He thought of himself as a later disciple of Confucius, so he spent a large part of his time expounding what Confucius had taught, and in the process he also tried to compose the idea of Confucius. To this idea, he would add the idea of the Duke of Zhou and contrive the concept of a "great Confucian." The Duke of Zhou, he says, was born into power and knew how to utilize power, but it was his half brother, Wu, who was the king of Zhou and ruler of China. The Duke of Zhou had a chance, though, to become the sovereign when King Wu died unexpectedly, leaving behind his child-son to succeed him. Xunzi writes:

> The Duke of Zhou [stepped in at this point and] acted as a shield for [the young] King Cheng. Dreading the prospect of a general revolt against the Zhou rule, he succeeded King Wu [and acted on behalf of the young king] in order to insure political continuity in the world. He assumed the role of the Son of Heaven, and he heard judicial cases. [All in all,] he seemed so at ease that it looked as if he had clinched the position. Yet people in the empire did not regard him as greedy [for the throne]. When he had his brother Guanshu killed [after Guanshu had staged a rebellion in the east], people in the empire did not consider him cruel. When he had acquired complete control of the world and established seventy-one fiefs, fifty-three of which were for members of his own clan, people in the empire did not consider him partial.

The Duke of Zhou was great, Xunzi thought, not just because he consolidated the Zhou rule and mapped out for the future Zhou kings a larger and stronger geopolitical space, but, more important, because throughout his tenure as the young king's regent, no one felt that he was "greedy," "cruel," or "partial."

Confucius, on the other hand, was not born into power. What power he had, he acquired through his own merit, and the highest he rose was to a middle-level position in a state government. Yet as soon as he received his position as the minister of crime of Lu, Xunzi says, "a certain Shenyou did not dare to pump his sheep with water" before taking them to the market to sell; "a certain Gongshen drove his wife out" because of her wanton behavior; "a certain Shenhui headed for the border and ran" because he had been living an extravagant life; and "traders of horses and cattle" no longer tried to cheat their buyers "with inflated prices." Confucius also possessed greatness, Xunzi observed, because from only a subordinate position, he was able "to reform social customs."

Xunzi was interested in the idea of power—not the power of brute force or the power vested in status or claimed through wealth, but power that reflects Nature's strength and Heaven's virtue. Heaven and earth "do not speak," yet "we feel safe in the knowledge" that one is "high" and the other is "solid," he says. "The four seasons do not speak, yet everyone can expect that they will arrive in the right order. The reason they are constant is that they do all they can." The same can be said about "the gentleman who has perfected his virtue," observes Xunzi. "Though he is silent, people understand him. Though he bestows no favor, people gravitate toward him. Though he shows no anger, people find him awe-inspiring."

Xunzi thought that Confucius and the Duke of Zhou both had this power within them. Youngsters from Confucius' neighborhood "knew to divide the catch in their nets so that those with parents were given a larger share." Criminals and miscreants in his state knew to reform themselves while he was in office. The power that the Duke of Zhou possessed resembled that of Nature even more closely. His actions at times might seem irregular, yet his people trusted him in the same way that they trusted the four seasons; they knew that things "had always been in order" and that he "had never overstepped the line."

Mencius, too, was interested in this kind of power, but he did not try to give a careful and rational explanation of its mystique. Nor was he able to bring himself to reconcile violence with a ruler's moral sway. He said:

> If a ruler of a state is drawn to benevolence, he will have no match in the empire. When he marched to the south, the northern barbarians complained; when he marched to the east, the western barbarians complained. They all said, "Why does he not come to us first?"

But if records in history suggested that there was physical resistance and bloodshed in a conquest distinguished by moral efficacy, Mencius was prepared to dispute them, no matter how hallowed the records might be. Of the chapter in the *Classic of Documents* in which there was a description of the final battle King Wu's army fought against the people of the Shang, Mencius said that he could accept only "two or three strips of the bamboo text." "A benevolent man [like King Wu,]" he said, "has no match in the empire. How could it be that 'the blood spilled was enough to carry the staves along with it,' when the most benevolent man waged a war against the most cruel?"

Xunzi, too, hyperbolized the virtue of men like King Wen and King Wu. He writes, "Those who are close by will sing his praise and rejoice in him, whereas those who are far away will stumble and fall over one another in their rush to be near him." But he also explains why the world would want to submit to such a man: "If this person could gain an empire by committing one unjust act or by executing one innocent man, he would refuse to do it. The fact that in dealing with people he takes justice and trust to this degree is what gets relayed to the entire world, which responds to him in a single approving voice."

Xunzi wrote passionately on the subject of justice, for what he feared most was its termination in the absence of reason. His idea of the end of the world was not a deluge of dangerous men with preposterous theories but opacity and darkness, followed by chaos. Off and on and for long periods of time, Xunzi had taught in the famed Jixia Academy in the state of Qi. He was used to having intellectual opponents around him and did think of some of these men as mad and menacing, but he would never flatter them, as Mencius had, by saying that their theories were so dangerous and potent that they could turn men into beasts. Xunzi had more trust in the human intellect. In fact, he began his moral philosophy with the assumption that there was no upside to our inborn nature; but he believed that, with learning and thought, the guidance of the rites and good teachers, and steady, conscious effort, we can acquire an understanding so keen that it will take us to the right judgment even in the most trying circumstances. It was also his trait as a philosopher to consider difficult and delicate moral questions by way of paradoxes. On the subject of equality, for instance, he says, "Equality is possible only when we recognize that all things are unequal." To bestow equal power and equal status on all, he warns, is a prescription for disaster because every man will then think that he is better than the next person and so deserves more than what he already has. Discontent will lead to quarreling, he says, and "quarreling to disorder, and disorder to exhaustion."

Xunzi took the same approach in his attempt to understand human desires. Just as being unequal is the natural state of things, he says, desiring more than what is appropriate is the condition of our inborn nature. But it would be wrong to think that by doing away with desires a person can solve the problem of his nature, for having no desires is no different from "being dead." Xunzi writes:

> A man's nature is what he receives from Heaven. Emotions are the substance of his nature, and desires are the responses of his emotions. And it is his emotions that have made it impossible for him not to believe that his desires can be satisfied; thus [as long as they have the upper hand] he will not try to refrain from satisfying his desires. Thus when he decides that his desires can be satisfied and that he will try to guide them to this end, it must be due to his perception and awareness.

Perception and awareness can save a man from himself. They also granted Xunzi a certain distance from what he taught, allowing his ideas to come into their own. As a result, he avoided the kind of predicaments Mencius would sometimes find himself in.

Mencius was a philosopher of the heart. His heart was sensitive not only to the suffering of others but also to criticisms and slights; and he did not take defeats well. When he failed to reform a king, he would feel that the kingdom was doomed. Xunzi was different. He, too, had his share of sparring with the rulers of his time, and politically he was more experienced than Mencius. Yet in reading his essays, one cannot tell what might be his private feelings about the powerful men he knew or his frustrations as a hired hand in a regional court. Xunzi kept his teachings apart from his heart. This, however, does not mean that his ideas were cool and remote. For even when an idea was abstract, he would begin shaping it into something palpable. In formulating the concept of fairness, or "public rightness," for instance, he let it grow out of a long description of the dispositions of a gentleman:

> Though poor and hard pressed, a gentleman has large ambitions. Though rich and eminent, he is respectful in his manner. Though at ease, his spirit does not grow indolent. Though weary, he does not have a withered look. He does not take away too much in anger nor give too much in joy.... Not to take away too much in anger nor give too much in joy is to let the kingly model hold back [the extreme behavior] of private feelings. The *Classic of Documents* tells us, "Do not go by what you like. Follow the way of the king. Do not go by what you dislike, follow the road of the king." This says that the gentleman is able to let his sense of public rightness rein in his private desires [lest they become rampant].

The kingly model—the kingly way—is what is right and what is fair; it is an abstract idea but one that is inseparable from the man who does not "take away too much in anger nor give away too much in joy." As with most of Xunzi's ideas, it was distilled from Xunzi's experiences, though he was careful not to disclose what they were like, certainly not in his formal writings.

Xunzi lived to be nearly a hundred years old and experienced the last decades of the Warring States period, when violence was so out of control that the offenders no longer offered apologies. He traveled widely and was a witness to many incidents of the awful and the unbearable. The most agonizing chapter in the history of the Warring States unfolded during his lifetime and in his home state of Zhao. According to the account in Sima Qian's history, in a campaign against Zhao in 260 BC, the Qin army buried alive the thousands of Zhao soldiers they held in captivity, and we know that Xunzi happened to be home when this took place.

Violent history and analogies based on violence are staples in Xunzi's writings. They were meant to shake the men of his time from their mental idleness. But even we feel a jolt when we read what he says about the physical experience of extremity: "If the naked blade is about to strike your chest, you will not notice the fleeting arrows. If the lance is about to strike your head, you will not notice your ten fingers being cut off." "One cannot attribute any of this to inattention," Xunzi explains. It is all "a matter of priority." All that a person can feel when the blade strikes his chest or the lance strikes his head is the "pain and agony," and the "urgency and gravity of the situation."

What Xunzi describes was a crisis without recourse. Writing about it was his way of urging his contemporaries to reform their government and to improve themselves before it was too late. The violence in his analogy was a device, and Xunzi would apply it often, like therapy, to anyone, but most of all to the power brokers of his time. To one such man, a prime minister of Qi who aspired to follow the great kings of the past but whose conduct showed no such promise, Xunzi said, "For you [to harbor such ambitions] is analogous to lying down flat on one's face and trying to lick the sky or trying to rescue a man who has hanged himself by pulling at his feet."

Xunzi shocks while Mencius soothes, but both were in the business of moral persuasion. Xunzi spent the the first half of his professional life mainly as a teacher. But in 255, when Xunzi was around the age of fifty-five, the prime minister of Chu, a certain Lord Chunshen, offered him the position of magistrate of Lanling. Xunzi was dismissed after ten years, and so he went home to Zhao. Another few years would elapse before Lord Chunshen had a change of heart. He sent an envoy to Xunzi asking him to come back to his old job. Xunzi responded with a formal refusal, and his letter did not begin with "I have been hoping against hope that you might change your ways." Instead, it reads, "'Even a leper pities a king.'" "These words might seem disrespectful," he continues. "Still, we have to consider them carefully." The saying, he explains, refers to those rulers who died unnaturally from "being roughed up and murdered":

Though a leper endures ulceration, swelling, and disease, this is better than, as in earlier times, being strangled with a tassel [like King Kang of Chu] or being shot in the rump with an arrow [like Duke Zhuang of Qi], or, as in recent times, having one's tendons drawn [like King Min of Qi] or being starved to death [like King Wuling of Zhao]. Surely a ruler who dies from being roughed up and murdered endures more mental anguish and physical pain than a leper. From this, we see why "even a leper pities a king."

Xunzi closes his letter with a poem:

> *The blind, he deemed sharp of vision,*
> *the deaf, keen of hearing.*
> *Right, he sees as wrong,*
> *auspicious, as inauspicious.*
> *Heavens above, what do I have common with him?*

Lord Chunshen realized that the poem was intended for him, but he was not one to hold a grudge. He sent for Xunzi a second time, and the philosopher acquiesced. Two years after Xunzi resumed his post in Lanling, Lord Chunshen was killed in an ambush for his involvement in a succession dispute; and so his death was not unlike the death of those kings that even a leper would pity. After Lord Chunshen was murdered, Xunzi was relieved of his duties again. He lived for at least another twenty years.

Confucius and Xunzi did not have parallel lives, but their careers followed similar tracks. Both found government employment in their fifties but were pushed out of their jobs after a few years. Both were then invited back. However, Xunzi would live for some twenty years after returning to his job, Confucius only five after he came home to Lu. From what we know about the temperament of the two men, we cannot be sure that they would have gotten on well had their paths crossed. Yet in spirit and in thought one is the father and the other his son. Both were clear-eyed about the world. They were not disposed to vagueness or indecision. And they would always maintain an emotional distance from matters that needed adjudication, arbitration, or just a sensible voice. Thus Confucius said to Zizhang that a man of "keen discernment" would not let anger or pain rush him into action. And he told Ran Qiu that he would never stoop to the level of Duke Ai and his counselor and go along with their policies in war and taxation; he would never fool himself into thinking that a compromise would be better for everyone in the end.

Mencius was to be more tactful. This partly explains why, throughout China's long history, most rulers were fond of him. His voice was gentler and less taxing on their conscience, and these rulers knew that they could bend his ideas to suit them. Mencius, of course, had not expected his philosophy to be complicitous. Given its intellectual provenance, which would include the instructions of Confucius and Zisi, it did not seem possible that his teaching could be aligned with the interests of those at the top. After all, it was Zisi who asked his own prince, "How can you presume to be friends with me" when "in point of virtue you should be the one serving me?"

Toward the end of his life when he was growing weary of all that was irreparable and irreconcilable in human affairs, Mencius, too, sought a form of retreat—into his family, his teaching, and personal cultivation. But it was not a clean break with politics and the powerful. For he could never say what Zisi had said to his superior, and he could never tell a prince or a prime minister, "Even a leper pities a king." It is not that Mencius was incapable of judgment, but that his heart got in the way. And on account of this heart, he could never climb as high as Confucius and declaim as Confucius did, in splendid arrogance, that "he was thinking of giving up speech" because "what does heaven ever say."

Even though Mencius felt uneasy about the time he spent with kings, his relationship with them would become cozier and more agreeable after he died. His ideas would earn him a permanent place, second only to that of Confucius, in the state-sponsored Confucian temple. More important, they would guarantee him a favored status in state doctrines and a bright spot in the heart of the emperors of China, whether Chinese, Mongol, or Manchu. Moreover, these ideas did not endear themselves just to the emperor and the state. Conservatives and reformers, loyalists and dissenters, scholars and merchants—they all claimed Mencius as one of theirs. They all liked his theory on human nature: it gave them encouragement and a reason to be optimistic. One eminent scholar of the last century called it "the correct and positive assumption in Confucian thought."

This assumption and other aspects of Mencius' teachings gained an extra boost during the Confucian revival of the Song dynasty, especially in the eleventh and twelfth centuries. The principals of that movement were particularly taken with his starting point and with his emphasis on self-examination as the way to cultivate one's moral potentials. Out of these ideas and what they learned from the *Analects* and the early classics, the Song Confucians created a vibrant philosophy powerful enough to face the challenge of Buddhist teachings and sturdy enough to undergo change and revision with the shifts and swings in human sentiments and political ethos. Their philosophy could have been their own, but like Confucius they insisted that they were not creators but transmitters—that they were committed to the cultural tradition of Yao, Shun, Yu, King Wen and King Wu, the Duke of Zhou, Confucius, and Mencius. And because Mencius' vision supported their philosophical preferences, it was his reading of Confucius and of the classics—his book and his thought—that won him intellectual prominence in the academy and special attention in the curriculum.

Successors of the Song dynasty thinkers would go further to make Mencius a fixture in the government examinations, which reinforced even more his relationship with the state. What is odd is that by the time the constitutional reformers of the late nineteenth century came along, they would find fault with absolute monarchy but deep inspiration in the teachings of Mencius. Because of his sympathy for the destitute, they would regard Mencius as a champion of "people's rights," and his ideas as a precursor of the democratic spirit. They would forget that he never questioned the legitimacy of imperial rule.

In fact, no gentlemen in Mencius' world could have acquired their virtue in the absence of an autocrat. For what would have become of Shun without his heartless father, or thousands of good counselors without their despots? The modern reformers were not inclined to pursue these questions, preferring instead to concentrate mainly on what Mencius said about the plight of the poor and what kings could do to ease their condition. They never asked why Mencius for two thousand years had been the pick of the throne, why no rulers suspected his political theories of being subversive, and why no rabble-rousers in China's imperial history cited Mencius as their prophet. Even at the height of a fierce struggle in 1898 between the Empress Dowager Cixi and the constitutional reformers, Mencius managed to please both sides.

Xunzi had a different fate in his posthumous life. He was first given a supporting role in the Confucian pantheon. By the time of the Confucian revival in the Song, he was on his way out. The Song Confucians found "no trace of a sage or of a worthy" in him because Xunzi considered "human nature unseemly and repulsive." The thrust of the Song critique was, therefore: What is the point of talking about his teachings, when he did not understand human nature? These thinkers realized, of course, that to go along with what Xunzi said about human nature would undermine the foundation of their own moral philosophy.

Toward the end of the Song, in the thirteenth century, there were even suggestions of driving Xunzi out of the Confucian temple, "not letting him enjoy the sacrificial offerings," which was the same as killing him in his afterlife and erasing him from the Confucian spiritual lineage. The act was not carried out until two dynasties later, at the beginning of the sixteenth century, when a Ming emperor ordered a reorganization of the Confucian temple. Xunzi had a brief redress in the eighteenth century under the Qing. The scholars of that period were on an exhaustive search for knowledge and understanding. They were interested in all the Warring States philosophers, not just Mencius, and while on their pursuit, they discovered a like mind in Xunzi: in his attention to learning, in his trust of the intellect, and in his love for the six arts, particularly the rites; they also liked the rigor of his argument. However, by the end of the nineteenth century, the political agenda would once again dictate the scholars' perception of Xunzi. Some of the smartest and most progressive minds of that era would accuse Xunzi of being a defender of absolute rule; they would again point to his theory on human nature as lacking a moral directive; and they would drag him out just as a foil to Mencius, who was their favorite Confucian.

On a recent trip to China, I visited Mencius' temple in Shandong province. A Chinese emperor from the twelfth century had it built in Mencius' hometown in Zou. Next to the temple stands the compound created for the families of Mencius' descendents. This was a smaller space when it was first constructed in the Song, but under a Manchu emperor five hundred years later, it was enlarged and enriched to its present splendor, with exquisite gardens and elegant courtyards, magnificent reception halls and a well-stocked library, and over eighty rooms of living area on a ten-acre plot. Even the heirs of Mencius had it good.

There was also a shrine to Xunzi in Shandong, about eighty miles southeast of Mencius' home in Zou. A friend showed me photos she took of this shrine during a recent visit. Neglected and unkempt, the structure stands alone, with no peddlers and no self-appointed guides in sight. Yet even as an image on paper, it projects an unbending, tough-minded spirit, not at all unlike the way I imagine him now.

If Confucius were alive, he would not find fault with the present state of Mencius' grounds, and he would not be upset about Xunzi's fate. In fact, he would see traces of himself in the afterlife of each. But he would point out which of the two had understood the demands of authentic morality. Like Xunzi, Confucius perceived the world to be an unsettling place, under the threat of tyrants who could choose to do whatever they liked with the life and dignity of any human being. It would not be enough, then, just to try to talk the tyrants into reforming themselves. The philosopher has to do more, Confucius would say. He has to be tougher with these men. But how far to go? This, Confucius would leave to the philosopher, but he would ask him to steady his stride as he ventured forth, and he would tell him, "Do not forget the first whiff of life and the knowledge in your heart."

Epilogue

THE TEMPLE TO CONFUCIUS IN QUFU IS ANOTHER STORY. I made my journey to this ancient capital of Lu at the most perfect time. I was coming to the end of writing this book, and it was early winter. The visitors were few—a busload of Canadians, a handful of Chinese, myself, and a friend. There was a fog, thick as clouds, and the local people seemed depressed. In slack season, there was little to do in this tourist town, except for tending the leeks and scallions, the winter wheat and sweet potato plants, in the surrounding fields. Yet the fog and the chill provided the right climate for me to reflect on Confucius. They forced me to see through the clouds of my own making of him. As I walked on the stone path leading to his shrine, I asked myself: What do I see? What does he say? What does he look like?

The Confucius I found that day was the Confucius on his travels in the records of the *Analects,* Confucius paired with Yan Hui in Zhuangzi's head and heart, and Confucius in the final chapter, the final paragraph, of Sima Qian's chronicle. There was, however, one more Confucius that stood out. This Confucius appeared in a source a few centuries after Sima Qian's account. The author was a spiritual kin of Zhuangzi, and in his story, Confucius is again set off by his

222 ■ ANNPING CHIN

disciples. The foil, in this case, is the gentle, elusive Yan Hui. Yan Hui in this scene celebrates a "free of care" kind of "rejoicing in Heaven and knowing destiny." He arrives at it through "inner cultivation"— by "realizing that life's vicissitudes are not something that a man can have control over" and so "should not cause him anguish or distress." Confucius, however, tells Yan Hui about another kind, a "full of care" kind, of "rejoicing in Heaven and knowing destiny." He says:

> Not long ago when I edited the *Odes* and the *Documents*, and corrected rites and music, my aim was to restore order to the world and bequeath this order to the generations to come. It was not merely to cultivate myself or to bring order to my own state of Lu. Yet the power brokers of Lu daily usurped the authority of their superiors; and we are steadily losing our humanity and our measure of rightness. Our moral nature and our feelings have thinned out. If this way does not work in this one state and in this single age, what hope do we have for the world and for the generations to come? It was then that I realized the *Odes* and *Documents*, rites and music, are of no help in saving the world from chaos. Yet I don't know of any other way to improve what I tried to do. This is the reason why a person who rejoices in heaven and knows destiny is careworn. Still, I have found it.

What Confucius found was "a rejoicing in everything, knowing everything, caring for everything, and doing everything."

A mile away from Confucius' temple lies his burial ground. In the forest of ancient cypresses and silvery junipers, one finds what one is looking for. On the mound, turfs of stubborn grass—"the beautiful uncut hair of graves"—and beneath the soil, the spirit that feeds the eager, the hopeful, and the weary who can still delight in human form and fate.

Notes

PROLOGUE

page

1   *"when I reach the age of fifty . . ."*   *Analects* 7:17. My reading follows the commentary in the *Lunyu zhengyi*, p. 144.

1   *their strength gave out*   *Analects* 6:12.

3   *"I am old enough . . ."*   *Analects* 15:26

5   *"I transmit but do not create . . ."*   *Analects* 7:1.

INTRODUCTION

page

10   *Students could be expelled*   See Chin, *Four Sisters of Hofei,* p. 103.

11   *"to declare him safely dead"*   See Ho, "To Protect and Preserve," in *The Chinese Cultural Revolution as History*, p. 92.

11   *Confucius and Lin Biao*   See Spence, *The Search for Modern China,* pp. 616, 634–36; also Ho, in *Chinese Cultural Revolution* "To Protect and Preserve," p. 92.

12   *Confucian Institutes and Confucianism in China today*   See French, "Another Chinese Export Is All the Rage," *New York Times,* January 11, 2006; Robertson and Liu, "Can the Sage Save China?" *Newsweek,* March 20, 2006.

12   *"always used correct pronunciations"*   *Analects* 7:18. I have followed Liu Baonan's reading of this passage in *Lunyu zhengyi*, pp. 144–45.

13 *the common gentlemen (shi) and the junzi*   See Cho-yun Hsu, "The Spring and Autumn Period," in *The Cambridge History of Ancient China*, pp. 583–84.

16 *land tenure and industries*   Ibid., pp. 576–78; Hsu, *Ancient China in Transition*, pp. 119–30.

16 *roads and merchants*   See Hsu in *Cambridge History of Ancient China*, pp. 580–82.

17 *content to live in "a shabby neighborhood"*   *Analects* 6:11.

18 *"my mind was a complete blank . . ."*   *Analects* 9:8.

19 *"like home"*   See *Analects* 4:1–2.

19 *Cheng Yi and Zhu Xi on the concept of* ren   See, for example, Zhu Xi's "Treatise on *Ren*" (*Renshuo*) in *Zhu Wengong wenji* (Literary works of Zhu Xi), 67:21–22, and Zhu Xi's commentary to *Analects* 1:2 in *Sishu zhang ju jizhu* (Commentaries on the Four Books), p. 48.

20 *Kang Youwei and Tan Sitong on the concept of* ren   See Hao Chang's illuminating discussion on this subject in *Liang Ch'i-ch'ao and Intellectual Transition in China, 1890–1907*, pp. 45–47, 67–70.

20 *a recent conference on Confucian thought*   See the proceedings of the International Conference on Mencian Thought and Contemporary Values, held in Zoucheng, Shandong, April 2006.

Chapter One: Leaving Home
page

24 *Confucius' ancestry*   See Sima Qian, *Shiji* 47:1905; *Kongzi jiayu*, pp. 522–25; Guo Keyu, *Luguo shi*, pp. 259–60. Robert Eno in his recent essay challenges the traditional historiography regarding Confucius' ancestry. He believes that Confucius' mother was originally from the state of Zhulou, a small non-Chinese state that was later absorbed by Lu, and that through the influence of his maternal family Confucius was associated with a culture outside of the Zhou tradition. See Eno, "The Background of the Kong Family of Lu and the Origins of Ruism," in *Early China* 28 (2003).

24 *common gentlemen (shi)*   See Hsu, "Spring and Autumn Period," in *Cambridge History of Ancient China*, pp. 583–86. For a comprehensive discussion of the common gentleman, see also Liu Zehua, *Xianqin shiren yu shehui*, especially pp. 1–101.

25 *the couple "made love in the fields (yehe)"*   In his reading of *yehe*, the

Confucian scholar Qian Mu understood it to mean "divine conception" (*gentian ersheng*). See Qian's *Kongzi zhuan,* p. 4.

25   *"The couple prayed . . ."*   *Shiji* 47:1905.

25   *he "grew to a height of well over six feet"*   See *Shiji* 47:1909. According to Sima Qian, Confucius' height was nine *chi* and six *cun.* The Zhou measurement of a *chi* is about three-quarters of a foot.

25   *"skilled in many menial things"*   *Analects* 9:6.

25   *"could not prove himself in office"*   *Analects* 9:7.

26   *disciples as apprentices*   See Qiu Xigui's discussion of the Chinese idea of "disciples" (*tu*) during the Spring and Autumn and the Warring States periods in *Gudai wenshi yanjiu xintan,* pp. 400–408. See also Liu Zehua on the relationship of teacher to disciple in *Xianqin shiren yu shehui,* pp. 51–58.

26   *"The men of Qi . . ."*   *Analects* 18:4.

26   *"Confucius was the minister of crime . . ."* and *"Those who did not understand him . . ."*   *Mencius* 6B:6.

27   *"They chose eighty pretty girls . . ."* and *"There will be a sacrifice . . ."* *Shiji* 47:1918.

29   *entries in the* Spring and Autumn Annals *for 498 BC*   See *Chunqiu Zuozhuan zhu,* Duke Ding, 12th year, Yang ed., pp. 1585–87.

30   *"When Confucius was in the service . . .*   See *Chunqiu Gongyangzhuan zhushu,* Duke Ding, 10th year. A wall of one hundred *zhi* is over ten feet high and three thousand feet long.

30   *Confucius as the one who tried to destroy the Three Families*   See *Kongzi jiayu* p. 11. See also *Shiji* 47:1916.

31   *"If I cannot practice a proper way here . . ."*   *Analects* 5:7.

32   *"This man must have had some purpose . . ."*   *Analects* 17:5.

32   *"Has it not also been said . . ."*   *Analects* 17:7.

33   *"Would you call a man . . ."*   *Analects* 17:1

33   *"the bandit"*   *Chunqiu Zuozhuan zhu,* Duke Ding, 8th year, p. 1563.

33   *Nan Kuai*   Ibid., Duke Shao, 12th and 14th years, pp. 1335–36, 1364.

34   *Nan Kuai and Yang Hu*   The Qing dynasty scholar Gao Shiqi has a chapter on the family retainers in his work on the *Zuo Commentary, Zuozhuan jishi benmo,* pp. 115–25. See also the *Luguo shi,* pp. 126–32.

34   *Yang Hu's political demise in 502*   See *Chunqiu Zuozhuan zhu,* Duke Ding, 8th year, pp. 1568–70.

35 *"The people of Lu feared him . . ."* Gao Shiqi, *Zuozhuan jishi benmo*, pp. 124–25.

36 *The district of Yun and the conflicts with Qi* For the history of Yun, see *Chunqiu Zuozhuan zhu*, Duke Zhao, 26th and 27th years, pp. 1469–70, 1481. Regarding the tension between Lu and Qi, see Duke Ding, 6th, 7th, and 8th years, pp. 1555–64.

36 *Qi refused to give Yang Hu assistance* Ibid., Duke Ding, 9th year, pp. 1572–74.

36 *Confucius "knows the rites . . ."* Ibid., Duke Ding, 10th year, pp. 1577–78.

36 *history of the "people of Lai"* Ibid., Duke Xiang, 6th year, pp. 947–48. See also Eno's theory on Confucius' relationship to the people of Lai in "Background of the Kong Family of Lu."

37 *meeting at Xiagu* See *Chunqiu Zuozhuan zhu*, Duke Ding, 10th year, pp. 1578–79.

38 *another version of this account* *Chunqiu Guliangzhuan*, Duke Ding, 10th year, 19:116–26.

38 *Sima Qian's account* *Shiji* 47:1915–1916.

39 *The* Zuo Commentary *as the most reliable source and Confucius as "chief counselor"* See Jiang Yong and Quan Zuwang's discussion in *Chunqiu Zhouzhuan zhu*, Yang Bojun's collected commentaries on the *Zuo zhuan*, pp. 1577–78.

39 *the revolt of another retainer* This other retainer is Hou Fan. Ibid., 1581–83.

40 *Jihuanzi's regrets* See, for instance, *Shiji* 47:1918.

CHAPTER TWO: FAMILIES AND POLITICS
page

41 *"If it is the hereditary counselors who are in charge . . ."* *Analects* 16:2.

41 *Those who were born with knowledge* See the *Analects* 16:9; *The Book of Zhuangzi*, chapter 10 (revised from Watson's translation in Zhuangzi, *The Complete Works of Chuang Tzu*, p. 108). See also the Zuo Commentary about people born with knowledge, who, in early China, were also referred to as *shengren*, or sages: *Chunqiu Zuozhuan zhu*, Duke Xiang, 22nd year, p. 1065.

42 *"When the moral way prevails . . ."* *Analects* 16:2.

42 *"For more than forty years . . ."* *Shiji* 4:134.

43 *the crisis in early Zhou* See the "Prince Shi" (Junshi) chapter in the *Classic of Doctrine* (*Shangshu*): Sun Xingyan, ed., *Shangshu jinguwen zhushu*, pp. 446–47. The Warring States thinker Xunzi also gave a clear and concise description of the crisis the Zhou court faced when King Wu suddenly died, leaving behind a young child as his successor: *Xunzi jijie* (ed. Wang Xianqian, pp. 73–74). See also Edward L. Shaughnessy's "Western Zhou History," in *Cambridge History of Ancient China,*" pp. 307–17.

43 *The feng jian enfeoffment system* See Shaughnessy, "Western Zhou History," in *Cambridge History of Ancient China,* pp. 317–22. See also Li Feng's learned study of the geopolitical structure of the Western Zhou, *Landscape and Power in Early China,* pp. 58–82.

43 *display of archery* See Liu Yu, "Xi Zhou jinwen zhong de sheli" ("Archery rituals as described in the bronze inscriptions of the Western Zhou").

44 *institutional reforms* See Li Feng, "Succession and Promotion," and Shaughnessy, "Western Zhou History," in *Cambridge History of Ancient China,* pp. 323–28.

44 *relationship of the Zhou king to the aristocrats* See Li Feng, *Landscape and Power,* pp. 121–34.

45 *the end of the Western Zhou* See *Shiji* 4:147–49; Shaughnessy, "Western Zhou History," in *Cambridge History of Ancient China,* pp. 342–51; Li Feng, *Landscape and Power,* pp. 193–221.

46 *"During the time of King Ping . . ."* *Shiji* 4:149.

46 *"I must be slipping!"* *Analects* 7:5.

47 *"The Zhou represents the apogee . . ."* *Analects* 3:14. In his recent work *Chinese Society in the Age of Confucius (1000–250 BC)*, the archaeologist Lothar von Falkenhausen argues that the early Zhou rites were close in spirit and practice to the rites of the previous, Shang, dynasty; that two major reforms, around 860 BC and 650 BC, gave the Zhou rites their distinct shape and character. Thus according to Falkenhausen, the rites that Confucius tried to restore were not the rites of the early Zhou kings but the rites of the late Western Zhou and of the mid–Spring and Autumn period, that is to say, rites that were much closer to Confucius' own time. I appreciate this archaeological perspective, but until there are further studies, I am not yet ready to modify my judgment on the question of the origins of the Zhou rites and Zhou culture.

47 *counselors who made kings great* See *Shangshu,* "Junshi" chapter: pp. 451–55.

47 *his action was of a practical kind* See *Mencius* 2B:9; *Xunzi,* chapter 8 (*Xunzi jijie,* pp. 73–74); Gong Zizhen, *Chunqiu jueshi bidawen,* no. 3, in *Gong Zizhen quanji,* pp. 58–59.

47 *"A person in a ruling position . . ."* *Analects* 18:10.

48 *the Duke of Zhou and Confucius* In a highly original essay, "Yuandao" (On the Dao), the Qing scholar Zhang Xuecheng suggests that it was Confucius who first formulated a set of teachings from what the Duke of Zhou said and did. See *Wenshi tongyi,* vol. 1, 2:3–7. See also David Nivison's illuminating essay on Zhang's disquisition on the Dao in *The Life and Thought of Chang Hsüeh-ch'eng,* pp. 140–50.

48 *creation of the Three Families* See both the *Zuo Commentary* and the *Gongyang Commentary,* Zhuang, 32nd year; Min, 1st and 2nd years; Xi, 1st year (*Chunqiu Zuozhuan zhu,* pp. 250–63; *Chunqiu Gongyangzhuan zhushu,* pp. 184–206). Hsu Cho-yun refers to the creation of the hereditary families as "secondary feudalization." See his discussion in *Cambridge History of Ancient China,* pp. 570–72.

49 *youngest brother* The youngest brother, Qingfu, also had a long affair with his sister-in-law—the deceased ruler Duke Zhuang's wife. Qingfu's death was a poignant chapter in the history of the *Zuo Commentary.* See *Chunqiu Zuozhuan zhu,* pp. 262–63.

49 *division of the state army* Ibid., Duke Xiang, 11th year, pp. 984–87.

50 *"Their wealth is greater . . ."* *Analects* 11:17. See also Liu Baonan's gloss on the subject of taxation in the history of Lu (*Lunyu zhengyi,* pp. 246–47).

50 *"They have eight rows . . ."* *Analects* 3:1.

50 *"a terrible oath"* *Zuo Commentary,* Duke Xiang, 11th year (*Chunqiu Zuozhuan zhu,* pp. 986–87).

50 *reorganize the armies once more* Ibid., Duke Zhao, 5th year, pp. 1261–62.

51 *changes in feudal states* See Hsu's discussion of the changes in state administration during the Spring and Autumn period, in *Cambridge History of Ancient China,* pp. 572–75.

51 *Jiwuzi and Shusun Bao* *Zuo Commentary,* Duke Xiang 11th year (*Chunqiu Zuozhuan zhu,* p. 987).

52 *Shusun Bao and Niu* Ibid., Duke Zhao, 4th year, pp. 1256–57.

53 *Shusun Bao's death*   Ibid., pp. 1258–59.

53 *"As soon as Zhaozi took on his duties . . ."*   Ibid., Duke Zhao, 5th year, p. 1263.

54 *"It was terribly difficult . . ."*   Ibid., p. 1263. The counselor Zhou Ren is also mentioned in the *Zuo Commentary*, Duke Yin, 6th year, and *Analects* 16:1.

55 *"My lord, on behalf of our ruler . . ."*   Ibid., Duke Zhao, 4th year (*Chunqiu Zuozhuan zhu*, p. 1259).

56 *Du Xie "left Lu . . ."*   Ibid., p. 1262.

56 *Zichan of Zheng*   Ibid., Duke Xiang, 30th year, pp. 1175–82.

56 *"He was respectful . . ."; "without swerving from the track."*   *Analects* 5:16, 2:2.

57 *Zigong*   Ibid., 4:29.

57 *"What would be the next best? . . ."*   Ibid., 13:20.

58 *Jipingzi*   See *Chunqiu Zuozhuan zhu*, Duke Zhao, 12th and 25th years, pp. 1335–38, 1456.

58 *series of petty incidents*   Ibid., Zhao, 25th year, pp. 1456–57, 1460–63. Some scholars have even suggested that it was at the height of this upheaval that Confucius took his first trip abroad and had several conversations with the ruler of Qi. It is unlikely that this happened. Confucius was thirty-four at the time. He was an unknown in the political world of the Spring and Autumn period and so could not have had an audience with the ruler of Qi. Those scholars who put him in Qi around 517 probably did so in order to suggest that conditions in Lu were so distressful that Confucius decided to explore his options elsewhere. See Sima Qian's biography of Confucius in *Shiji* 47:1910–11. See also Qian Mu's discussion in *Kongzi zhuan*, pp. 14–17, and Shirakawa Shizuka's disagreement with this theory in *Kōshi den*, pp. 28–34.

59 *"These small-minded men . . ."*   *Chunqiu Zuozhuan zhu*, Duke Zhao, 25th year, pp. 1462–63.

59 *"He has been making political decisions . . ."*   Ibid., pp. 1463–64.

60 *"other people pressured you . . ."*   Ibid., pp. 1464–65.

61 *"Heaven does not bestow . . ."*   Ibid., p. 1465.

61 *"I am not clever . . ."*   Ibid., pp. 1456–66.

61 *Zhaozi*   Ibid., p. 1466.

62 *the ruler of Wei*   Ibid., Duke Xiang, 14th and 16th years, pp. 1010–14, 1112.

CHAPTER THREE: COMPANIONS
page

63　*Fan Li*　See *Shiji* 41:1739–53; 129:3256–58. See also *Chunqiu Zuozhuan zhu*, Duke Ai, 11th year, pp. 1664–65.

64　*"There is something hopeless . . ."*　*Analects* 15:17.

64　*"not to speak to . . ."*　*Analects* 15:8.

65　*"Rotten wood . . ."*　*Analects* 5:10. Revised from Huang's translation, p. 74.

65　*"Rulers of the Xia dynasty . . ."*　*Analects* 3:21. See also Liu Baonan's collected commentaries (*Lunyu zhengyi*, p. 64) regarding what most scholars said about Confucius' response to Zaiwo.

65　*Liu Baonan's reading*　See *Lunyu zhengyi*, pp. 64–66.

66　*Duke Ai "was incompetent . . ."*　Ibid., p. 66.

66　*Confucius and Zaiwo on the mourning rituals*　*Analects* 17:21.

67　*"Zaiwo asked, 'If a truly humane man . . .'"*　*Analects* 6:26.

68　*"to make an analogy . . ."*　*Analects* 6:30.

68　*"go and take a look . . ."*　*Analects* 6:26.

68　*In two instances*　They are mentioned in *Analects* 17:5, 17:7. In the first instance, Confucius was thinking of serving the chief steward of the Jisun family of Lu. In the second instance, he nearly said yes to the invitation of the chief steward of the Zhao family from the state of Jin.

69　*"Zigong was affable . . ."*　*Analects* 11:13.

69　*"What do you think of me? . . ."*　*Analects* 5:4.

70　*"A gentleman is not a vessel . . ."*　*Analects* 2:12. See Zhu Xi, *Sishu zhang ju jizhu* (p. 76), and Fingarette, *Confucius—the Secular as Sacred* (pp. 71–79), for interpretations that suggest Confucius did not want to wound Zigong with what he had said.

70　*Zigong's strengths*　See *Analects* 1:3, 14:29, 11:19.

70　*Zigong's administrative talents*　This was Liu Baonan's interpretation. See *Lunyu zhengyi*, Liu's reading of *Analects* 5:4.

70　*"The stuff is not different from . . ."* *Analects* 12:8 (Lau's translation, pp. 113–14).

71　*"Hui is almost there . . ."*　*Analects* 11:19.

71　*"Who is the better man . . ."*　*Analects* 5:9.

72　*"What do you think of the expression . . ."*　*Analects* 1:15.

72　*Confucius' observations of Yan Hui*　*Analects* 11:4, 9:20, 2:9.

73 "*living in a shabby neighborhood . . .*" *Analects* 6:11.

73 "*When Shun dwelled . . .*" *Mencius* 7A:16 (Lau's translation, pp. 184–85).

73 "*Heaving a sigh . . .*" *Analects* 9:11.

74 "*I thought you were dead . . .*" *Analects* 11:23.

74 "*If not for Hui . . .*" *Analects* 11:10. See also 11:9.

74 "*Yan Hui never displaced his anger . . .*" *Analects* 6:3.

75 "*When you walk, I walk . . .*" *Zhuangzi jishi*, "Tian Zifang," p. 308.

76 "*I have gone through life . . .*" Ibid., pp. 308–9.

76 *Yan Hui's burial* *Analects* 11:8, 11:11.

77 *ritual rules for former ministers* See Liu Baonan's gloss in *Lunyu zhengyi*, p.184.

77 "*By pretending I had retainers . . .*" *Analects*, 9:12.

77 guoren *and* yeren See Hsu in *Cambridge History of Ancient China*, pp. 548–49, 572–73.

78 *description of Zilu* See Sima Qian, *Shiji*, 67:2191. See also *Xunzi*, 27:334.

78 *the brave man from Bian* The man's name was Bian Zhuangzi. See *Shiji* 70:2302; *Analects* 14:12; *Hanshi waizhuan* 10:9b.

78 *A person may have these attributes . . .* See *Analects* 17:8.

78 "*Only the two of us . . .*" *Analects* 7:11 (revised from Lau's translation, p. 87).

79 "*just a bundle of dried meat . . .*" *Analects* 7:7.

79 "*I would guide the men of the field . . .*" *Analects* 11:1.

80 "*He had the fire of two . . .*" *Analects* 11:22.

80 "*May I then ask about death?*" *Analects* 11:12.

80 "*What is Zilu's lute doing in my room?*" *Analects* 11:15.

80 *Zilu's character* *Analects* 9:27, 12:12.

80 "*there are people . . .*" *Analects* 11:25.

81 *Zilu would not "die a natural death."* *Analects* 11:13.

81 "*Lady Bo, having finished her dinner . . .*" *Chunqiu Zuozhuan zhu*, Duke Ai, 15th year, pp. 1694–95 (slightly revised from Watson's translation, *The Tso Chuan: Selections from China's Oldest Narrative History*, p. 198).

82 *Zilu's death* *Chunqiu Zuozhuan zhu*, Duke Ai, 15th year, pp. 1695–96. See also *Liji shijie*, p. 61.

82 "*The Master was not on the side of the son.*" *Analects* 7:15. The displaced heir apparent was called Kuai Kui. His son was called Che.

82 *followers who traveled with Confucius*   See Liu Baonan's discussion in *Lunyu zhengyi*, pp. 237–38.

82 *Ran Qiu and the Jisuns*   See *Chunqiu Zuozhuan zhu*, Duke Ai, 11th year, pp. 1658–59.

82 *Ran Qiu and Zilu*   *Analects* 11:22, 6:8, 11:18, 13:3, 14:12, 11:3.

83 *"Zhonggong could be given a seat . . ."*   *Analects* 6:1.

83 *"a bull born of plough cattle . . ."*   *Analects* 6:6 (slightly revised from Lau's translation, p. 82).

83 *the mystery of Zhonggong*   See *Xunzi*, "Contra Twelve Philosophers" (*Fei shierzi*) in *Xunzi jijie*, pp. 60–66. In this essay, Xunzi expressed contempt for several of Confucius' disciples; he also mentioned one person that he felt was Confucius' true heir. This man's name shared the character *gong* with "Zhonggong," which has led many scholars to conclude that he was indeed Zhonggong. And among the recently excavated texts, there is one in the Shanghai Museum collection that is entitled *Zhonggong*. The discovery created a lot of excitement within the scholarly community. The text, however, did not add much to what was recorded in *Analects* 13:2 and the *Kongzi jiayu*. Zhonggong asked Confucius about government but did not divulge anything about himself. See *Shanghai bowuguan cang Zhanguo Chu zhushu*, vol. 3, pp. 261–83.

CHAPTER FOUR: WANDERINGS
page

85 *Sima Qian's account of Confucius' travels*   See Sima Qian, *Shiji* 47:1919–35.

86 *Zhuangzi's account*   This account of Confucius' travels was repeated four times in the *Zhuangzi*, in "The Turning of Heaven" (*tianyun*), "The Mountain Tree" (*shanmu*), "Giving Away a Throne" (*rangwang*), and "The Old Fisherman" (*yufu*). See Watson's translation in Zhuangzi, *Complete Works of the Chuang Tzu*, pp. 159, 214–15, 318–19, 348. Here I have followed Shirakawa Shizuka, who felt that the itinerary sketched out in the *Zhuangzi* made the most sense. See his argument in *Kōshi den*, pp. 47–48.

86 *in She, a district under the jurisdiction of Chu*   See *Analects* 13:16, 13:18.

86 *in Wei before returning home to Lu*   See *Analects* 9:15.

87 *"Let the ruler be a ruler . . ."* *Analects* 12:11.

87 *"I am too old . . ."* *Analects* 12:11.

87 *"The two governments of . . ."* *Analects* 13:7.

87 *Kangshu and the Duke of Zhou* The earliest account of their relationship is found in "Announcement to the Prince Kang" (*Kanggao*) in the *Book of Documents* (*Shangshu*). See James Legge's translation, *The Shu King (Shujing)*, pp. 380–98.

87 *"Among the children of King Wen . . ."* *Chunqiu Zuozhuan zhu*, Duke Ding, 6th year, p. 1556.

88 *"With one great change, the state of Qi . . ."* *Analects* 6:24.

89 *good counselors of Wei* See *Analects* 14:19, 15:7, 15:8, 14:18.

89 *"If you had a beautiful piece of jade . . ."* *Analects* 9:3 (slightly revised from Lau's translation, p. 98). Here I have followed Qian Mu's reading. See Qian's *Kongzi zhuan*, pp. 39–40.

89 *travel to Jin* The *Analects* mentions that when Bi Xi, a retainer from a hereditary family in the state of Jin, asked Confucius to join him, Confucius considered accepting the invitation (see 17:7). Later scholars, however, disagreed as to when this took place, whether it was in the winter of 497 or the summer of 490. See *Lunyu zhengyi*, pp. 371–72, and Qian Mu, *Xianqin zhuzi xinian*, pp. 39–40. I have followed Qian Mu.

90 *"If I have done anything wrong . . ."* *Analects* 6:28.

90 *"The wife of Duke Ling . . ."* Sima Qian, *Shiji* 47:1920–21.

91 *"Wang Sunjia once said to Confucius . . ."* *Analects* 3:13. See Qian Mu's discussion of Confucius' response to Wang Sunjia in *Kongzi zhuan*, pp. 45–47.

92 *for "a gentleman to lose his position . . ."* *Mencius* 3B:3. See *Mengzi zhengyi*, pp. 247–51.

92 *"Why are you so restless? . . ."* *Analects* 14:32.

92 *"Why do you worry about him not having an office? . . ."* *Analects* 3:24.

93 *Qu Boyu* See *Analects* 14:25. See also *Shiji* 47:1920.

93 *"Qu Boyu has been going along for sixty years . . ."* *Zhuangzi*, "Zeyang." See Watson's translation, p. 288.

93 *who played host to Confucius in Wei* *Mencius* 5A:8. See *Mengzi zhengyi*, 388–89 (Lau's translation, p. 147).

94 *Mi Zixia* Ibid. See also *Hanfeizi jijie*, chapter 12, "Shuinan," pp. 65–66 (Watson's translation in *Basic Writings of Mo Tzu, Hsün Tzu, and Han Fei Tzu*, pp. 78–79).

95   *indiscretions of Duke Ling and his wife Nanzi*   See *Chunqiu Zuozhuan zhu,* Duke Ding, 14th year, p. 1597. See also the notes to chapter 3 of the present book regarding the succession problem and Zilu's death.

95   *Duke Ling as a randy swine*   See Watson's translation of the *Zhuangzi* (Zhuangzi, *Complete Works of Chuang Tzu*), p. 289.

96   *"Duke Ling of Wei asked Confucius . . ."*   *Analects* 15:1. See also Qian Mu's reading of the sentence *mingri zhuxing.* Although the words suggest that Confucius left the next day, Qian Mu felt that it was not possible for Confucius to pack up and go so swiftly, after he had resided in Wei for so long. In Qian's view, after this conversation with Duke Ling, Confucius must have "decided to leave Wei." See *Kongzi zhuan,* p. 51.

96   *"Duke Ling and his wife . . ."*   Sima Qian, *Shiji* 47:1920–21.

96   *"A woman's tongue . . ."*   Ibid., p. 1918.

97   *"Since there are no gods . . ."*   *Chunqiu Zuozhuan zhu,* Duke Xiang, 14th year, p. 1013. Duke Ling's grandfather was Duke Ding. His father was Duke Xian. As soon as Duke Ding died, his wife, Ding Jiang, observed that the heir apparent "expressed no sorrow," and predicted that this man, Duke Xian, "was going to be the ruin of the state of Wei." See *Chunqiu Zuozhuan zhu,* Duke Cheng, 14th year, p. 870.

98   *"When a man chooses to forgo . . ."*   *Kongzi jiayu,* chapter 43, "Quli Zixia wen," p. 112–13.

98   *"Don't look wan and sallow."*   Ibid.

98   *"There is no female intelligence superior to that . . ."*   Ibid.

99   *"her female intelligence is like that of a man"*   *Guoyu* (Sayings of the states), in the "Luyu" (Sayings of the state of Lu) section, p. 211. There is yet another version of this story in the *Liji* (*Classic of Rites*). See *Liji shijie,* chapter 4, "Tangong xia," p. 128.

99   *Confucius' forebears*   See *Kongzi jiayu,* chapter 39; "Benxing jie," p. 93; *Shiji* 38:1623; *Chunqiu Zuozhuan zhu,* Duke Zhao, 7th year, 1294–96.

100   *"Confucius was not happy . . ."*   *Mencius* 5A:8.

100   *"They tried to chop down a tree . . ."*   This was repeated several times in the *Zhuangzi.* See Watson's translation, pp. 159, 214, 318, 348.

100   *"Heaven has given me this power . . ."*   *Analects* 7:23.

100   *"Confucius came to Song . . ."*   *Shiji* 47:1921. In another section of his general history of China, Sima Qian retold the story of Confucius and Huan Tui. It is interesting that his narrative there followed that of Men-

cius (see *Shiji* 38:1630). If the ambush never materialized, Confucius' statement in the *Analects* regarding Huan Tui can still make sense: his disciples asked him to be prepared for a surprise Huan Tui might try to stage, and Confucius responded, "What can Huan Tui do to me!"

101 *Huan Tui* See *Chunqiu Zuozhuan zhu,* Duke Ding, 10th year, p. 1582. According to the *Zuozhuan,* Huan Tui became so powerful in Song that by 481 BC the ruler of Song regretted the fact that he had "spoiled Huan" for so long. Thus he tried to get rid of Huan, who in response staged a rebellion and failed. After that, Huan Tui lived as an exile first in Wei and then in Qi. See *Chunqiu Zuozhuan zhu,* Duke Ai, 14th year, pp. 1686–88.

101 *Huan Tui and Yang Hu* It is Shirakawa Shizuka who writes that because the counselor of Jin, Zhao Jianzi, had helped both Yang Hu and Huan Tui's brother, Sima Niu, when they were in a tight spot, Yang and Huan must have known each other (see *Kōshi den,* pp. 49–52). To understand Zhao Jianzi's relationship to these men, see *Chunqiu Zuozhuan zhu,* Duke Ding, 9th and 10th years, pp. 1573–74, 1582–83; Duke Ai, 2nd and 14th years, pp. 1612–13, 1688.

102 *Kuang* Scholars disagreed about the location of Kuang, whether it was in Song, Wei, or Zheng. By placing Kuang in Zheng, I have followed the editor of the *Lunyu zhengyi* (pp. 176–77) and the editor of the *Chunqiu Zuozhuan zhu* (Duke Ding, 6th year, pp. 1556–57). On the question of when Confucius was in Kuang, see Qian Mu's discussion in *Kongzi zhuan,* pp. 40–43, and the discussion in *Lunyu zhengyi,* pp. 176–77.

103 *Confucius and Yan Ke* *Shiji* 47:1919.

103 *"Confucius was in a tight situation . . ."* *Analects* 9:5.

104 *"Because Confucius looked like . . ."* See *Hanshi waizhuan* 6:21.

104 *Sima Qian's scenario* *Shiji* 47:1919.

104 *Ning Wuzi* For the dates of Ning Wuzi, see *Lunyu zhengyi,* p. 176.

105 *"When I was in a rut . . ."* *Analects* 11:2.

105 *"The reason why Confucius was in straits . . ."* *Mencius* 7B:18.

105 *"It must have been the temples of . . ."* *Chunqiu Zuozhuan zhu,* Duke Ai, 3rd year, p. 1622.

105 *"the state of Wu sent an expedition against Chen . . ."* Ibid., Duke Ai, 6th year, p. 1632.

105 *"In Chen, when the provisions . . ."* *Analects* 15:2.

106 *"There are plenty of people . . ."* Xunzi jijie, chapter 28, "Youzuo," pp. 345–46.

106 *"Confucius was in trouble . . ."* Zhuangzi, chapter 20 (slightly revised from Watson's translation in Zhuangzi, *Complete Works of Chuang Tzu*, p. 217).

107 *"Confucius could not go anywhere. . . ."* Shiji 47:1930–32.

108 *The men of Chen and Cai* See Quan Zuwang's argument as to why the officers of Chen and Cai could not have worked together to try to stop Confucius from going to Chu in *Jingshi wendabian* (Critical responses to questions in the classics and in history), quoted in *Lunyu zhengyi*, p. 332.

109 *Yan Hui* See *Zhuangzi*, chapter 21, and my discussion in chapter 3 of the present book about Yan Hui's relationship to Confucius.

109 *Yan Hui living on millet and water* Analects 6:11.

110 *"What is considered good government?"* Analects 13:16.

110 *returned to She* For the history of She and its relationship to the states of Cai and Chu, see *Chunqiu Zuozhuan zhu*, Duke Ai, 2nd and 4th years, pp. 1618, 1625–28. See also Qian Mu's discussion of the history of She in his *Kongzi zhuan* (Life of Confucius), pp. 54–55, and in his *Xianqin zhuzi xinian*, pp. 55–56.

110 *"Right here, in my native place . . ."* Analects 13:18.

111 *"Someone making an irrevocable statement . . ."* Cheng Yaotian, "Talking about Public Spirit" (*Shugong*) in *Lunxue xiaoji* (Informal notes on the topic of learning), found in his collected works, *Tongyi lu* (On understanding the art of things), 1:53a.

111 *"When everyone else acts . . ."* Ibid.

112 *Cheng on the meaning of "uprightness lies therein"* Ibid., 1:53b–54a.

112 *Conflicting reports on Upright Gong* See *Hanfeizi jijie*, chapter 49, "Wugu" (The five vermin), pp. 344–45 (Watson's translation in *Basic Writings of Mo Tzu, Hsün Tzu, and Han Fei Tzu*, pp. 105–6). See also *Lüshi chunqiu xinjiaozheng*,(Newly edited commentary on *Mr. Lü's Spring and Autumn Annals*), 11 *juan*, "Dangwu," pp. 110–11.

113 *"Let's go home . . ."* Analects 5:22.

113 *"'Not being able to be within the reach of . . .'"* Mencius 7B:37. See also *Analects* 13:21.

113 *"As Jie Yu went past Confucius' door . . ."* Analects 18:5.

114 *"In times like the present . . ."* Qian Mu, *Zhuangzi zuanjian*, chapter

4, "Renjianshi" (In the world of men), p. 38. See Qian Mu's interpretation of these lines in the *Zhuangzi zuanjian*. He said that *miyang* was either brambles growing on the Chu plain or land so overgrown with wild vegetation that a traveler could lose his way in it.

114 *"Confucius went past them . . ."* Analects 18:6. My translation follows the readings suggested in the *Lunyu zhengyi*, pp. 391–91. The commentary also points out that the two names, Changju and Jieni, mean literally "tall men with their feet covered in mud." So they could have been the nicknames Zilu used when he told Confucius about his encounter with these two recluses.

115 *"The old man said, 'You look like someone . . .'"* Analects 18:7.

117 *"But I am different from all these men . . ."* Analects 18:8.

117 *"The man said, 'This playing is fraught . . .'"* Analects 14:39. My reading follows the commentaries in the *Lunyu zhengyi*, pp. 325–26.

118 *"A dragon drinks from the clear water . . ."* Lü chunqiu xin jiaozheng (Newly edited commentary on *Mr. Lü's Spring and Autumn Annals*), 19 *juan*, "Junan" (The difficulties of recommending someone), p. 252.

CHAPTER FIVE: RETURN
page

119 *Zigong and Ran Qiu* See Sima Qian, *Shiji* 47:1927–28; *Chunqiu Zuozhuan zhu*, Duke Ai, 7th and 8th years, pp. 1641, 1649.

119 *Kong Yu's family troubles* Chunqiu Zuozhuan zhu, Duke Ai, 11th year, pp. 1665–67.

120 *"[Kong Yu] was quick . . ."* Analects 5:15.

120 *"How dare I act . . ."* Chunqiu Zuozhuan zhu, Duke Ai, 11th year, p. 1667.

120 *"To attack the wrongful act . . ."* Analects 12:21.

120 *"Men in government . . ."* Chunqiu Zuozhuan zhu, Duke Zhao, 5th year, p. 1163.

121 *"Confucius returned home."* Ibid., Duke Ai, 11th year, p. 1667.

121 *"The number of soldiers and chariots . . ."* Ibid., pp. 1657–58.

121 *Ran Qiu put himself in charge* Ibid., pp. 1658–59.

122 *"The Qi army was coming at us . . ."* Ibid., pp. 1659–60.

122 *"I learned it from Confucius."* Shiji 47:1934.

122 *Zigong's political career* Chunqiu Zuozhuan zhu, Duke Ai, 7th, 11th, 12th years, pp. 1641, 1663, 1671.

123   *Zigong and the chief counselor of Wu*   Ibid., Duke Ai, 7th year, pp. 1640–41.

123   *Confucius was their "state's elder"*   Ibid., Duke Ai, 11th year, p. 1668.

124   *"The gentleman gauges his action . . ."*   Ibid.

125   *The* Zuo Commentary *on the land tax*   Ibid., Duke Xuan. 15th year, p. 766.

126   *Another commentary on the land tax*   Chunqiu Guliangzhuan zhu, Duke Xuan, 15th year, 12:15a–b.

126   *"The land tax was administered."*   Chunqiu Zuozhuan zhu, Duke Ai, 12th year, p. 1669.

126   *"The wealth of the Jisun family . . ."*   Analects 11:17.

126   *locust plagues*   Chunqiu Zuozhuan zhu, Duke Ai, 12th and 13th years, pp. 1669, 1674.

127   *"Chih [Gongxi Hua] went off to Qi . . ."*   Analects 6:4.

127   *Jikangzi intended to "set out offerings . . ."*   Analects 3:6.

127   *capable of serving "on the supervisory staff . . ."*   Analects 11:24.

128   *Chen Heng creating a succession crisis*   Chunqiu Zuozhuan zhu, Duke Ai, 14th year, pp. 1682–86.

128   *"On the sixth day of the sixth month, Chen Heng . . ."*   Ibid., Duke Ai, 15th year, p. 1689.

129   *Confucius actually went to see the Jisuns*   Analects 14:21. As for my understanding of Duke Ai in this situation, I have followed the commentary in the *Lunyu zhengyi*, pp. 317–18.

130   *Confucius and Jikangzi*   See *Analects* 6:8, 12:17, 12:18, 12:19.

130   *"How do we know that the generations to come . . ."*   Analects 9:33 (Lau's translation, p. 146).

131   *"Zizhang asked, 'What is keen discernment?' . . ."*   Analects 12:6.

131   *"Zizhang asked, 'Is it possible to know ten generations hence?' . . ."*   Analects 2:23.

131   *"Zizhang asked, 'How would you characterize . . .'"*   Analects 11:20.

131   *"Zizhang asked, 'What must an educated man . . .'"*   Analects 12:20.

132   *"Zizhang asked, 'How does one take virtue . . .'"*   Analects 12:10.

132   *"To get on in the world . . ."*   Analects 15:6.

132   *"Use your ears well . . ."*   Analects 2:18.

132   *Zizhang*   Analects 19:16, 19:15.

133   *Ran Qiu, who liked "to gloss . . ."*   Analects 16:1.

133   *Zizhang "wrote down on his sash"*   Analects 15:6.

133 *Zixia and Zizhang*   Analects 19:3.

134 *"Do not make friends . . ."*   Analects 1:8.

134 *"Love all . . ."*   Analects 1:6.

134 *Zizhang "overshoots the mark," while Zixia "falls short"*   Analects 11:16.

134 *what Zixia could teach his own students*   Analects 19:12.

135 *Zixia on learning*   Analects 19:12.

135 *"In leveling ground . . ."*   Analects 9:19.

135 *"gather up in a thick pile"*   Analects 19:6.

135 *"There must be a lot to see . . ."*   Analects 19:4.

135 *"Ask scores of them . . ."*   Analects 19:6.

135 *"If a person merely learns and does not think . . ."*   Analects 2:16.

135 *"Artisans live in their shops . . ."*   Analects 19:7.

136 *"when he was singing in the company . . ."*   Analects 7:32.

136 *Zixia "excelled in his knowledge . . ."*   Analects 11:3.

136 *Zixia as the precursor of the interpretative traditions*   The earliest examples of word-by-word and sentence-by-sentence reading are found in the Gongyang and the Guliang commentaries of the *Spring and Autumn Annals* (the Chunqiu). And scholars of both the Gongyang and Guliang traditions—Dai Hong of the Eastern Han dynasty, and Xu Yan and Yang Shixun of the Tang dynasty, for instance—pointed to Zixia as their "first teacher." See *Chunqiu Gongyangzhuan zhushu,* p. 1, and *Chunqiu Guliangzhuan,* p. 1.

136 *"What is the meaning of these lines . . ."*   Analects 3:8.

136 *Confucius and Zigong discuss an ode*   Analects 1:15.

137 *someone who "liked to ask questions about everything"*   Analects 3:15.

137 *the bride is "elegant and slender . . ."*   Book of Poetry, Ode 57 (revised from Waley's translation, *The Book of Songs,* pp. 48–49).

138 *"can give the spirit exhortation . . ."*   Analects 17:9.

138 *"Unless you learn the Odes . . ."*   Analects 16:13.

138 *"unless you apply yourself . . ."*   Analects, 17:10.

138 *Zixia and the* Odes   Among the early commentaries on the *Odes, or Book of Poetry,* the Mao Commentary was the most influential. The work is distinguished by its moralistic interpretation, and many scholars associated the Mao tradition of reading with Zixia. See *Hanshu, Yiwenzhi* 30:1708 and Legge, trans., *The Chinese Classics,* vol. 4, *The She King* (Shijing), pp. 30–31.

139 *"Were there affairs of the state . . ."*   Analects 13:14.

139 *"To make the old feel at home . . ."*   *Analects* 5:26.

139 *Conversation with four disciples*   *Analects* 11:26.

140 *Wang Yangming's understanding of Confucius and Zeng Dian*   See *Wang Yangming quanshu,* 1:12 (p. 12).

140 *"Zhi, the Grand Musician, left for Qi . . ."*   *Analects* 18:9.

CHAPTER SIX: TEACHING

page

142 *"When he approached the steps . . ."*   *Analects* 15:42.

143 *"Even when walking in the company . . ."*   *Analects* 7:22.

144 *"From whom does Confucius not learn? . . ."*   *Analects* 19:22.

144 *"If a student does not come back . . ."*   *Analects* 7:8.

144 *"I have never refused to teach . . ."*   *Analects* 7:7.

144 *"the frustration of trying to solve . . ."*   *Analects* 7:8.

144 *Yan Hui as a student*   See *Analects* 11:4, 2:9, 9:20, 11:7, 9:11.

145 *"When encountering matters . . ."*   *Analects* 15:36.

145 *Dong Zhongshu on the military commander of Chu*   See *Dong Zhongshu Chunqiu fanlu yizheng,* chapter 3, "Zhulin" (Bamboo forest), pp. 51–55. The original story of Zifan, the military commander of Chu, appears in the *Zuo Commentary* (*Chunqiu Zuozhuan zhu,* Duke Xuan, 15th year, pp. 760–62). However, being a Gongyang scholar, Dong Zhongshu, in his retelling of the story, followed the version that appeared in the Gongyang Commentary on the *Spring and Autumn Annals.* See *Chunqiu Gongyangzhuan zhushu,* Duke Xuan, 15th year.

146 *"When slanders that seep . . ."*   *Analects* 12:6.

147 hui, xun, *and* jiao   See Xu Shen, *Shuowen jiezi* 3A:10a, 3B:41a (pp. 91, 128).

147 *Confucius on the usage of* jiao   *Analects* 13:29; 13:30; 20:2.

147 *"Exalt the good . . ."*   *Analects* 2:20.

148 *"When I tried to enlighten you . . ."*   *Analects* 2:17.

148 *Confucius himself "loathed purple . . ."*   *Analects* 17:18.

148 *Confucius instructed in four categories*   *Analects* 7:25.

148 *enrich him and pull him in*   See *Analects* 9:11.

149 *"One day, my father . . ."*   *Analects* 16:13.

149 *a transmitter, not an innovator*   See *Analects* 7:1.

149 *"Follow the calendar of the Xia . . ."*   *Analects* 15:11.

150 *"put to the test"*   *Analects* 15:25. In this passage, Confucius says that he never praised or condemned someone arbitrarily—if he praised someone, that person most certainly had been "put to the test."

150 *"You stand to benefit . . ."*   *Analects* 16:4.

150 *"A gentleman cherishes a true friendship . . ."*   *Analects* 2:15.

150 *"A gentleman is agreeable . . ."*   *Analects* 13:23.

151 *"The gentleman is easy to serve . . ."*   *Analects* 13:25 (revised from Lau's translation, pp. 122–23.

151 *petty men "understand profit"*   *Analects* 4:16.

151 *The music of Zheng was lewd*   See the commentary in *Lunyu zhengyi* on *Analects* 15:11 (pp. 339–40).

151 *"Watercress grows here and there . . ."*   *Shijing*, Ode 1, "Fishhawk" (Owen's translation in *An Anthology of Chinese Literature*, pp. 30–31).

152 *"There is joy yet no wantonness . . ."*   *Analects* 3:20.

152 *Shun's succession and his love for virtue*   *Mencius* 7A:16.

152 *"When the nine movements came to a close . . ."*   Sun Xingyan, ed., *Shangshu jinguwen zhushu*, p. 130. The full description of this performance is found in *Shangshu jinguwen* (*Book of Documents*), "Gaoyaomo," part 3 (pp. 123–33).

152 *"I never dreamt that the joys of music . . ."*   *Analects* 7:14.

153 *"When Confucius had just arrived at the outer gate . . ."*   Liu Xiang, *Shuo Yuan jiaozheng*, 19:33 (p. 499).

153 *"Confucius said of the* shao *music . . ."*   *Analects* 3:25 (Lau's translation, p. 71).

154 *"We are able to know this much about music . . ."*   *Analects* 3:23.

154 *The severely scrupulous, the politically responsible, and Confucius*   See *Mencius* 2A:9, 5B:1.

155 *Mencius on "the village goody man"*   *Mencius* 7B:37.

155 *Confucius on "the village goody man"*   Ibid.

155 *Sima Qian on Shaozheng Mao*   *Shiji* 47:1917.

156 *Xunzi on Shaozheng Mao*   *Xunzi jijie*, chapter 28, "Youzuo," pp. 341–42.

157 *Deng Xi "maintained ambiguous assertions . . ."*   *Liezi*, chapter 6, "Liming" (Endeavor and destiny). See Lieh-tzu, *The Book of Lieh-tzu* (Graham's translation), p. 127.

157 *Confucius on Zichan*   *Analects* 5:16, 14:9.

157 *"Sichuan of Zheng had Deng Xi killed . . ."*   *Chunqiu Zuozhuan zhu*, Duke Ding, 9th year, pp. 1571–72. The sentence "When you think of

someone, you even love the tree he once sat under" refers to Ode 16 of the *Book of Poetry*. According to tradition, this poem, entitled "Sweet Pear-Tree" (*Gantang*), was composed by the people of the south in memory of the Duke of Shao, brother of the Duke of Zhou, and it begins in this way: "Young and tender is this sweet pear-tree; / Do not lop it or knock it, / For the Lord of Shao took shelter under it." See *The Book of Songs* (Waley's translation), p. 16.

158 *accounts of Dengxi's action*   Both of the third-century BC accounts come from the *Lüshi chunqiu xinjiaozheng* 18:3 (pp. 224–25).

159 *"Shaozheng Mao lived in Lu . . ."*   Wang Chong, *Lun heng*, "Jiang-duan," p. 164.

160 *"Do I possess knowledge?"*   *Analects* 9:8 (revised from Lau, p. 97).

160 *Confucius stayed away from four things*   *Analects* 9:4.

160 *"Even though the law treated this man . . ."*   *Analects* 5:1.

162 *Confucius always exercised great caution*   *Analects* 7:13.

162 *Confucius assessing Zilu, Ran Qiu, and Gongxi Hua*   *Analects* 5:8.

162 *"Observe what a person does . . ."*   *Analects* 2:10.

162 *"What is difficult to manage . . ."*   *Analects* 2:8.

163 *"It is possible to know about Confucius' . . ."*   *Analects* 5:13.

163 *"As soon as I desire benevolence . . ."*   *Analects* 7:30.

163 *"I have not come across anyone . . ."*   *Analects* 4:6.

163 *"The* Odes *are to stimulate . . ."*   *Analects* 8:8.

164 *"While your parents are alive, . . ."*   *Analects*, 4:19.

164 *"Give your father and mother . . ."*   *Analects* 2:6.

165 *"being filial"*   *Analects* 2:5.

165 *rites without love and empathy*   See *Analects* 3:3.

165 *"In serving your parents, be gentle . . ."*   *Analects* 4:18.

165 *"Unless a man acts according . . ."*   *Analects* 8:2 (revised from Lau's translation, p. 92).

166 *A good man "is not slavish . . ."*   *Analects* 11:20.

166 *"Asking questions is in itself the correct rite."*   *Analects* 3:15.

166 *ritual experience could "take virtue to a higher state"*   *Analects* 12:10.

166 *the practical ends of ritual practice*   *Analects* 2:18.

167 *the pursuit of what is morally right*   *Analects* 12:6, 14:34, 4:10.

167 *"Restrain the self . . ."*   *Analects* 12:1.

168 *a common misreading of "restrain the self and return to the rites"*   See, for instance, Cheng Yi and Zhu Xi's reading in *Sishu zhangju jizhu*,

12:1 (pp. 131–32). See also Liu Baonan's critique of the Cheng-Zhu reading in *Lunyu zhengyi*, p. 262.

168 *"When abroad, conduct yourself . . ."* *Analects* 12:2.

168 *"our ability to make an analogy . . ."* *Analects* 6:30.

169 *"A partner in learning . . ."* *Analects* 9:30.

170 *"A benevolent man is most at home . . ."* *Analects* 4:2.

170 *"A gentleman must be big and strong . . ."* *Analects* 8:7 (revised from Lau's translation, p. 93).

170 *"A neighborhood where there is benevolence . . ."* *Analects* 4:1.

170 *as timely as a pheasant alighting on a mountain ridge* *Analects* 10:27.

171 *"At fifteen, I set my heart on learning. . . ."* *Analects* 2:4.

CHAPTER SEVEN: THE RITES OF LIFE AND DEATH

page

172 *Confucius "drew himself in . . ."* *Analects* 10:4.

173 *"Confucius did not mind if the rice . . ."* *Analects* 10:8.

173 *"Those over fifty years of age . . ."* See *Liji shijie*, chapter 12, "Neize" (Regulations in the home), pp. 381–82.

174 *"When stewing chicken . . ."* Ibid., p. 375.

174 *Confucius did not care for "dried meat bought from a shop"* *Analects* 10:8.

174 *Confucius "would not eat meat" kept beyond three days* *Analects* 10:9.

175 *abstaining from meat and rice during mourning* *Analects* 17:21.

175 *Confucius' reaction to Zilu's fate* *Liji shijie*, chapter 3, p. 61.

175 *"he always made an offering . . ."* *Analects* 10:11.

175 *"he did not set himself a rigid limit. . . ."* *Analects* 10:8 (revised from Lau's translation, p. 103).

175 *why Confucius did not talk at meals and in bed* See the commentary on *Analects* 10:10 in *Lunyu zhengyi*, p. 224.

176 *"The gentleman would not use reddish indigo . . ."* *Analects* 10:6.

176 *to dress in black or not to dress in black* See *Analects* 10:6 and *Liji shijie*, chapter 3, p. 99, and chapter 10, p. 316.

176 *skirts* See *Analects* 10:6.

176 *ornate rather than plain* See *Liji shijie*, p. 316.

177 *"If you are talking about . . ."* *Analects* 3:4.

177 *"In his own community . . ."* *Analects* 10:1.

177 *"At court, when speaking . . ."* *Analects* 10:2.

177 *"When the ruler summoned him . . ."* *Analects* 10:3.

177 *"When the ruler's order . . ."* *Analects*, 10:20.

178 *"When the ruler bestowed on him . . ."* *Analects* 10:18. My translation follows the commentary in *Lunyu zhengyi*, pp. 229–30.

178 *"Should the ruler pay him a visit . . ."* *Analects* 10:19 (slightly revised from Lau's translation, p. 104). See the discussion in *Lunyu zhengyi*, pp. 230–231, regarding what the ritual texts considered to be the correct spatial orientation of a subject to his ruler when the ruler came to pay him a visit.

178 *"When [the chief counselor] Jikangzi sent a gift . . ."* *Analects* 10:16 (slightly revised from Lau's translation, p. 104).

178 *"When asking after someone . . ."* *Analects* 10:15.

178 *"Unless the present from a friend . . ."* *Analects*, 10:23.

178 *"When celebrating a drinking festival . . ."* *Analects* 10:13.

178 *"The stables caught fire. . . ."* *Analects* 10:17.

178 *"When a friend died . . ."* *Analects* 10:22.

179 *"When a guest [from afar] could not find a place to stay . . ."* *Liji shijie*, chapter 3, p. 102.

179 *"Confucius did not sleep like a corpse. . . ."* *Analects* 10:18.

179 *"He did not sit unless . . ."* *Analects* 10:12.

179 *"When climbing into a carriage . . ."* *Analects* 10:26. The translation was based on my reading of the commentaries in the *Lunyu zhengyi*, pp. 204–5.

179 *"During periods of purification . . ."* *Analects* 10:7. The translation was based on my reading of the commentaries in the *Lunyu zhengyi*, pp. 219–20.

179 *"When Confucius encountered men in mourning clothes . . ."* *Analects* 9:10. The commentaries in the *Lunyu zhengyi*, pp. 232–33, added a great deal to my understanding of this passage.

179 *"Whenever Confucius met a person in mourning clothes . . ."* *Analects* 10:25.

180 *When a sumptuous meal . . .* *Analects* 10:25.

180 *things Confucius "did not speak about"* *Analects* 7:21.

180 *"a gentleman should never be surprised . . ."* *Analects* 15:2.

181 *"Everything passes on like the river. . . ."* *Analects* 9:17.

181 *"Death has always been with us . . ."* *Analects* 12:7.

181 *"When he was in the state of Wei . . ."* *Liji shijie*, chapter 3, p. 78.

182 *the burial place of Confucius' father and mother* See Sima Qian's *Shiji*

suoyin quoted in the notes to the Zhonghua edition (1959) of the *Shiji*, p. 1907. See also *Liji shijie*, p. 62.

182 *Confucius tried to pile up a mound*   See *Liji shijie*, p. 60. In his *Life of Confucius*, Qian Mu argued that Confucius' mother did not know where her husband was buried because the ancients did not mark their graves. See *Kongzi zhuan*, p. 6.

182 *playing the zither at the end of the mourning period*   See *Liji shijie*, chapter 3, p. 69.

183 *"When Confucius went to Wei . . ."*   Ibid., pp. 77–78.

183 *mourning for one's parent*   See *Analects* 19:17.

183 *"I have heard that it is best not to . . ."*   *Liji shijie*, chapter 4, p. 152.

184 *of the pine and the cypress*   *Analects* 9:28.

184 *"Leaning on a stick . . ."*   *Shiji* 47:1944.

184 *Gongxi Chi*   Gongxi Chi is also Gongxi Hua. See *Analects* 11:26 and 5:8.

185 *"Gongxi Chi adorned the curtains . . ."*   *Liji shijie*, chapter 3, p. 81. See also Chu Hsi, *Chu Hsi's Family Rituals*, pp. 110–12, for Patricia Ebrey's description of a catafalque. This was a later (and a simpler) version of the one described in the *Liji* (*Classic of Rites*). In the same book, Ebrey includes illustrations of a funeral procession from an eighteenth-century ritual text; see pp. 118–19.

185 *"To see the dead person to his grave . . ."*   *Liji shijie*, chapter 3, p. 92.

186 *Confucius on grave objects*   See *Liji shijie*, chapter 4, p. 124; *Mencius* 1A:4.

186 *disagreement over funerary rites for Confucius*   See *Liji shijie*, chapter 3, pp. 82, 80–81, 93.

186 *"One day Zixia, Zizhang, and Ziyou . . ."*   *Mencius* 3A:4 (revised from Lau's translation, p. 103).

187 *"When Confucius died . . ."*   Ibid.

187 *Zigong said: "He is simply wasting his time. . . ."*   *Analects* 19:24.

187 *"My teacher cannot be equaled . . ."* *Analects* 19:25.

188 *"Merciful Heaven is not kind! . . ."*   *Chunqiu Zuozhuan zhu*, Duke Ai, 16th year, p. 1697. This is also quoted in the *Shiji* (47:1945).

188 *"When Confucius was alive . . ."*   *Chunqiu Zuozhuan zhu*, Duke Ai, 16th year, p. 1698.

188 *"Let us take the outer walls . . ."*   *Analects* 19:23 (slightly revised from Lau's translation, p. 156).

189 *"I was poor and from a lowly station . . ."* *Analects* 9:6.

189 *"I could not prove myself in office."* *Analects* 9:7.

189 *"Do I possess knowledge?"* *Analects* 9:8 (slightly revised from Lau's translation, p. 97).

189 *"I work as hard as anyone . . ."* *Analects* 7:33.

189 *"To serve high officials . . ."* *Analects* 9:16 (slightly revised from Lau's translation, p. 98).

189 *"Joy is to be found . . ."* *Analects* 7:16.

189 *"If it is proper to seek wealth . . ."* *Analects* 7:12.

189 *"[I am] the sort of man . . ."* *Analects* 7:19 (Lau's translation, p. 88).

189 *"How dare I claim . . ."* *Analects* 7:34 (Lau's translation, p. 90).

190 *"I have never refused to teach . . ."* *Analects* 7:7.

190 *"I would not give a person a boost . . ."* *Analects* 7:8.

190 *"After I have shown a student . . ."* *Analects* 7:8.

190 *"I am a fortunate man. . . ."* *Analects* 7:31 (Lau's translation, p. 90).

190 *"Grant me a few more years . . ."* *Analects* 7:17.

190 *"Is it not a pleasure, . . ."* *Analects* 1:1.

190 *"Would I not rather die in the arms of a few good friends . . ."* *Analects* 9:12.

190 *"Confucius got separated from his disciples . . ."* *Shiji* 47:1921–22.

191 *"a ready measure of [his] significance"* A. R. Ammons, "Still," *Selected Poems*, p. 129.

191 *no one understood him* *Analects* 14:35.

191 *"thinking of giving up speech"* *Analects* 17:19.

CHAPTER EIGHT: DEFENDERS

page

192 *You Ruo played the part* You Ruo appears at the very beginning of the *Analects*, which suggests that he was an editor and that he played a considerable role in the transmission of Confucius' teachings. See *Analects* 1:2, 1:12, 1:13. See also what Mencius said about You Ruo in *Mencius* 3A:4 (*Mengzi zhengyi*, pp. 231–32) and Qian Mu's discussion in *Kongzi zhuan*, pp. 85–91.

192 *disparate schools after Confucius' death* See *Xunzi jijie*, chapter 6, pp. 59–66; *Hanfeizi jijie*, chapter 50, p. 351. The recently excavated texts can also throw light on this question. See Liang Tao, "Zisi Ziyi Biaoji Fangji sixiang shitan."

192 *"From [the sage emperors] Yao and Shun . . ."* *Mencius* 7B:38.

193 *"The influence of the gentleman and the petty man . . ."* *Mencius* 4B:22.

193 *Mencius' relationship to Zisi* See *Mengzi zhengyi*, pp. 4–5; *Mengzi shizhu*, pp. 1–2. In the past 150 years, there have been some scholars who argued that Zisi's teacher was Ziyou, not Zengzi. See Liang Tao, *Zhanguo shiqide shanrang sichao yu datong xiaokangshuo*.

194 *"When Confucius held office in Lu . . ." Mencius* 5B:4

195 *"to insist that the act of taking something . . ."* Ibid. See the commentary in *Mengzi zhengyi*, pp. 413–14.

195 *"Poverty should not be the reason . . ."* *Mencius* 5B:5.

195 *"Confucius was once a minor official . . ."* Ibid.

196 *"When Confucius left the state of Qi . . ."* *Mencius* 5B:1.

196 *"Every person has a heart . . ."* *Mencius* 2A:6.

197 *"Hold on to it and it will exist. . . ."* See *Mencius* 6A:8.

197 *"What can a man do . . ."* *Analects* 3:3.

198 *"When Shun dwelled in the depths . . ."* *Mencius* 7A:16 (revised from Lau's translation, p. 184).

198 *"In serving your parents . . ."* *Analects* 4:18.

198 *"none of these things . . ."* *Mencius* 5A:1 (revised from Lau's translation, pp. 138–39).

199 *"How could Shun interfere with the law? . . ."* *Mencius* 7A:35 (revised from Lau's translation, p. 190).

199 *"the supreme example of filiality"* *Mencius* 5A:1.

200 *"Shun rose from the fields . . ."* *Mencius* 6B:15 (revised from Lau's translation, p. 181).

201 *"It is for friends to demand goodness . . ."* *Mencius* 4B:30 (Lau, p. 135).

201 *the glib man* *Mencius* 7B:37; *Analects* 17:13.

202 *the prig, his mother, and older brother* *Mencius*, 3B:10.

202 *water as a metaphor* See *Mencius* 4B:18, 7A:24. See also *Analects* 9:17.

202 *deluge as a metaphor* *Mencius* 3B:9.

203 *"I am not fond of disputation . . ."* Ibid.

203 *"Yang Zhu advocated . . ."* Ibid.

203 *Yang Zhu and Mo Di* See the "Yang Zhu" chapter in the *Liezi* (Liehtzu, *The Book of Lieh-tzu*, trans. Graham, pp. 135–57). See also Zhuangzi's very perceptive critique of Mo Di in the "Tianxia" chapter of the *Zhuangzi* (Zhuangzi, *The Complete Works of Chuang Tzu*, trans. Watson, pp. 364–67).

204   *"custodians of the way of the former kings"*   Mencius 3B:4.

204   *"It is the intention of the carpenter . . ."*   Ibid.

204   *"Confucians corrupt men . . ."*   *Mozi*, section 39, "Fei Ru," in Watson, trans., *Basic Writings of Mo Tzu, Hsün Tzu, and Han Fei Tzu*, p. 127.

205   *"to travel with a retinue . . ."*   Mencius 3B:4.

205   *"There are those who use their minds . . ."*   Mencius 3A:4 (Lau's translation, pp. 101–3).

206   *"The fact that things are unequal . . ."*   Ibid. (revised from Lau's translation, p. 104).

206   *"lived off one feudal lord after another"*   Mencius 3B:4.

206   *bear paws, mutton, and beef*   Mencius 6A:7, 6A:10.

206   *a hundred thousand* zhong   Mencius 2B:10. To reconfigure the ancient measure of *zhong* into the modern measure of *dan*, I followed Jiao Xun's commentary. (See *Mengzi zhengyi*, pp. 298–99). I then converted the measure of grain in *dan* into tons.

206   *Mencius and King Xuan of Qi*   See *Mencius* 2B:8, 1B:10, 1B:11, 2B:9, 2B:12. In 5A:6, Mencius explains why hereditary succession was the correct way for the three dynasties. See also Liang Tao's illuminating essay on the idea of *shanrang* (handing over the throne to someone outside of the family) during the Warring States period. And to understand the relationship of Mencius and King Xuan, see Chin, "Shigui houshi wanggui" (Is a *shi* nobler than a king?).

208   *Xunzi's critique of Mencius*   See *Xunzi jijie*, chapter 6, p. 59.

208   *Mencius was being deliberately abstruse*   See the collected commentaries on chapter 6 of the *Xunzi jijie*, p. 59.

209   *"The Duke of Zhou . . . acted as a shield . . ."*   *Xunzi jijie*, chapter 8, "Ruxiao," pp. 73–74.

209   *Xunzi on the Duke of Zhou and Confucius*   Ibid., pp. 75–77.

210   *Heaven and earth "do not speak" and "the gentleman who has perfected his virtue"*   Ibid., chapter 3, "Bugou," pp. 28–30.

210   *the power of Confucius and the Duke of Zhou*   Ibid., pp. 73–76.

210   *"If a ruler of a state is drawn to benevolence . . ."*   Mencius 7B:4 (Lau's translation, pp. 194–95).

211   *"A benevolent man [like King Wu] . . ."*   Mencius 7B:3 (slightly revised from Lau's translation, p. 194).

211   *"If this person could gain an empire . . ."*   Xunzi jijie, pp. 76–77. This idea is also expressed in the Guodian excavated text *Zundeyi*.

212 *"Equality is possible only when we . . ."* Xunzi jijie, chapter 9, "Wangzhi," p. 96 (revised from Watson's translation in *Basic Writings*, p. 36).

212 *having no desires is no different from "being dead"* Xunzi jijie, chapter 22, "Zhengming," p. 283.

212 *"A man's nature is what he receives . . ."* Ibid., p. 284.

213 *"Though poor and hard pressed, a gentleman . . ."* Ibid., chapter 2, "Xiushen," pp. 21–22.

213 *Qin's campaign against Zhao* See *Shiji* 73:2334–37; 5:213. In the *Shiji*, Sima Qian says that over 400,000 soldiers from the state of Zhao died in the war against the Qin. He must have exaggerated the figure to emphasize just how violent this episode had been.

214 *"If the naked blade is about to strike your chest . . ."* Xunzi jijie, chapter 16, "Qiangguo," p. 204 (Knoblock's translation, *Xunzi*, vol. 2, p. 249).

214 *"For you [to harbor such ambitions] is . . ."* Ibid. (revised from Knoblock's translation, vol. 2, p. 244).

215 *"Though a leper endures ulceration . . ."* Zhangguo ce, 17 juan, "Chuce" (revised from Knoblock's translation in vol. 1 of *Xunzi*, p. 27).

216 *"How can you presume to be friends with me . . ."* Mencius 5B:7.

216 *into his family, his teaching, and personal cultivation* See *Mencius* 7A:20.

217 *"the correct and positive assumption in Confucian thought"* See Qian Mu, *Zhongguo xueshu sixiangshi luncong* 2:241, quoted in Huang Chin-shing, "Xunzi: Kongmiao congcide quexizhe" ("Xunzi: The Confucian temple's absentee"), p. 16.

218 *Song critique of Xunzi* Huang, pp. 6–7.

218 *driving Xunzi out of the Confucian temple* Ibid., p. 9.

218 *interest in Xunzi during the Qing* Ibid., pp. 10–11.

EPILOGUE

page
222 *"Not long ago . . ."* Liezi zhu, in *Xinbian zhuzi jicheng*, vol. 4, pp. 39–40.

222 *"the beautiful uncut hair of graves"* Walt Whitman, "Song of Myself," *Leaves of Grass* (Penguin, 2005), p. 33.

A Note on the Sources

In writing this book, I took advantage of the Chinese scholarship of the past three centuries—a scholarship so rigorous that it insists on "tracking every piece of evidence" (*kaozheng*) as the point of research and the path to understanding. When handling the early sources on Confucius, these *kaozheng* scholars explored not only the essential concepts in Confucius' moral thought—virtue, courage, fairness, rightness, benevolence—but also topics like weights and measures, weapons and war drums, ritual wares and funerary attire, musical instruments and temple beams, service tax and land tax, the logistics of communal life, and every historical person, place, and event. Such details can prompt new questions. For instance, we learn from the *Analects* that after a meeting with Confucius, a border warden told the few disciples of Confucius who happened to be around that "Heaven is about to use your master as the wooden tongue for a bronze bell." Scholars who studied this passage asked: Who could have been this warden? Whose border was he guarding? How important was his position? Why did Confucius come to this border? Was he thinking of crossing it? What did the border guard mean by what he said? Why would Heaven use Confucius "as the wooden tongue of a bronze bell?" How was such a bell ordinarily used in Confucius' time, and who would use it? What about a bell with a bronze tongue; did that serve a different purpose?

The cumulative discussions of questions such as these about each fragment of a record make up most of my secondary sources. Without this exegetical tradition, I could not have gone very far in my reading of the *Analects* (*Lunyu*) and the *Zuo Commentary* (*Zuo zhuan*), the two books most critical to my own work.

Bibliography

Ammons, A. R. *Selected Poems*. Ithaca: Cornell University Press, 1968.

Ban Gu (班固). *Hanshu* (漢書) (History of the former Han). Vol. 6. Beijing: Zhonghua shuju, 1962.

The Book of Songs. Translated by Arthur Waley. Edited, with additional translations, by Joseph Allen. New York: Grove Press, 1996.

Brooks, E. Bruce, and A. Taeko Brooks. *The Original Analects: Sayings of Confucius and His Successors, 0479–0249*. New York: Columbia University Press, 1998.

The Cambridge History of Ancient China: From the Origins of Civilization to 221 B.C. Edited by Michael Loewe and Edward L. Shaughnessy. Cambridge: Cambridge University Press, 1999.

Chang, Hao. *Liang Ch'i-ch'ao and Intellectual Transition in China, 1890–1907*. Cambridge, MA: Harvard University Press, 1971.

Cheng Yaotian (程瑤田). *Tongyi lu* (通藝錄) (On understanding the art of things). Yangzhou: Jiangsu guangling guji, 1991.

Chin, Annping (金安平). "*Chengzhi wenzhi* in the light of the *Shangshu*." In *Guodian Chujian guoji xueshu taolunhui lunwenji* (the conference volume of the International Conference on the Guodian Bamboo Manuscripts from the Ancient State of Chu). Wuhan: Hubei renmin chuban she, 2000.

———. *Four Sisters of Hofei: A History*. New York: Scribner, 2002.

———. "Shigui houshi wanggui: Mengzi yu Qi Xuan Wang de duihua" (士貴或是王貴: 孟子与齊宣王的對話) (Is a *shi* nobler than a king: Conversations between Mencius and King Xuan of Qi). *Zhonguo ruxue* 2 (2006).

———. "Teaching Three Disciples: Confucius in His Later Years." In *Early China* (forthcoming).

Chu Hsi. *Chu Hsi's Family Rituals*. Translated by Patricia Buckley Ebrey. Princeton: Princeton University Press, 1991.

Chunqiu Gongyangzhuan zhushu (春秋公羊傳注疏) (The Gongyang Commentary on the *Spring and Autumn Annals*). Annotated by He Xiu (何休). Sibu beiyao (四部備要) (SPPY) ed. Shanghai: Zhonghua paiyin ben, 1933.

Chunqiu Guliangzhuan (春秋穀梁傳) (The Guliang Commentary on the *Spring and Autumn Annals*). Annotated by Fan Ning (范甯). Sibu beiyao (四部備要) (SPPY) ed. Shanghai: Zhonghua shuju, 1930.

Chunqiu Zuozhuan zhu (春秋左傳注) (the *Spring and Autumn Annals* with the *Zuo Commentary*). Edited by Yang Bojun (楊伯峻). 4 vols. Beijing: Zhonghua Shuju, 1990.

Creel, Herrlee Glessner. *Confucius and the Chinese Way*. New York: Harper & Row, 1960.

Dong Zhongshu (董仲舒), *Chunqiu fanlu yizheng* (春秋繁露義證) (Luxuriant gems of the *Spring and Autumn Annals* with annotations). Edited by Su Yu (蘇輿). Beijing: Zhonghua shuju, 2002.

Eno, Robert. "The Background of the Kong Family of Lu and the Origins of Ruism." *Early China* 28 (2003): 1–41.

Falkenhausen, Lothar von. *Chinese Society in the Age of Confucius (1000–250 BC): The Archaeological Evidence*. Los Angeles: Cotsen Institute of Archaeology, UCLA, 2006.

Fang Xuanchen (方炫琛). "Zuozhuan renwu minghao yanjiu" (左傳人物名號研究) (A study of the alternative names in the *Zuo Commentary*). PhD dissertation, National Zhengzhi University, Taiwan, 1983.

Fingarette, Herbert. *Confucius—the Secular as Sacred*. New York: Harper & Row, Torchbook ed., 1972.

French, Howard. "Another Chinese Export Is All the Rage: China's Language." *New York Times*, January 11, 2006.

Gao Shiqi (高士奇). *Zuozhuan jishi benmo* (左傳紀事本末) (The ins and outs of the events recorded in the *Zuo Commentary*). 3 vols. Beijing: Zhonghua shuju, 1979.

Gong Zizhen (龔自珍). *Gong Zizhen quanji* (龔自珍全集) (Complete works of Gong Zizhen). Shanghai: Shanghai Guji chubanshe, 1975.

Graham, A. C. *Disputers of the Tao*. La Salle, IL: Open Court, 1989.

Gu Derong (顧德融) and Zhu Shunlong (朱順龍). *Chunqiu shi* (春秋史) (History of the Spring and Autumn period). Shanghai: Renmin chubanshe, 2001.

Guo Keyu (郭克煜). *Luguo shi* (魯國史) (History of Lu). Beijing: Renmin chubanshe, 1994.

Guodian chumu zhujian (郭店楚墓竹簡) (The Guodian Chu bamboo manuscripts). Edited by Jingmen Shi Bowuguan. Beijing: Wenwu chubanshe, 1998.

Guoyu (國語) (Sayings of the states). 2 vols. Shanghai: Guji chubanshe, 1978.

Hanfeizi jijie (韓非子集解) (Collected commentaries on *Hanfeizi*). Edited by Wang Xianshen (王先慎). In *Xinbian zhuzi jicheng* (新編諸子集成) (New edition of the works of the early philosophers), vol. 5. Taipei: Shijie shuju, 1974.

Hanshi waizhuan (韓詩外傳) (The outer chapters of Han Ying's commentary on the *Book of Poetry*). In *Jifu congshu* (畿輔叢書) 94:6–8. Taipei: Yiwen yinshuguan, 1966.

Ho, Dahpon David. "To Protect and Preserve: Resisting the 'Destroy the Four Olds' Campaign, 1966–1967." In *The Chinese Cultural Revolution as History*. Edited by Joseph W. Esherick, Paul G. Pickowicz, and Andrew G. Walder. Stanford: Stanford University Press, 2006.

Hsu, Cho-yun. *Ancient China in Transition: An Analysis of Social Mobility, 722–222 B.C.* Stanford: Stanford University Press, 1965.

Huang, Chichung, trans. *The Analects of Confucius*. New York: Oxford University Press, 1997.

Huang Chin-shing (黃進興). "Xunzi: Kongmiao congcide quexizhe" (孔廟從祀缺席者) (Xunzi: The Confucian temple's absentee). In *Sifenxilun xueji*. Vol. 1. Edited by Liu Cuirong. Taipei: Yunchen wenhua gongsi, 2006.

Kongzi jiayu (孔子家語) (Recorded conversations from the private collections of the Kong family). Commentary by Wang Su (王肅). In *Xinbian zhuzi jicheng* (新編諸子集成) (New edition of the works of the early philosophers), vol. 2. Taipei: Shijie shuju, 1974.

Lau, D.C., trans. *Confucius: The Analects (Lun yü)*. Harmondsworth, UK: Penguin Books, 1979.

———. *Mencius.* Harmondsworth, UK: Penguin Books, 1970.

Legge, James, trans. *The Chinese Classics.* Vol. 1, *Confucian Analects; The Great Learning; The Doctrine of the Mean.* Vol. 2, *The Works of Mencius.* Vol. 3, *The Shu King* (*Shujing*). Vol. 4, *The She King* (*Shijing*). Oxford: Clarendon, 1893–95. Reprint. Hong Kong: Hong Kong University Press, 1960.

Leys, Simon, trans. *The Analects of Confucius.* New York: W. W. Norton, 1997.

Li Feng. "'Feudalism' and Western Zhou China: A Criticism." *Harvard Journal of Asiatic Studies* 63:1 (June 2003).

———. *Landscape and Power in Early China.* Cambridge: Cambridge University Press, 2006.

Liang Tao (梁濤). "Zhanguo shiqide shanrang sichao yu datong xiaokangshuo" (戰國時期的禪讓思潮与 "大同," "小康" 說), in *Zhongguo ruxui* 1 (2005).

———. "Zisi Ziyi Biaoji Fangji sixiang shitan" (子思〈緇衣〉,〈表記〉,〈坊記〉思想試探). *Mengzi sixiang de dangdai jiazhi guoji xueshu yantaohui* (孟子思想的當代價值國際學術討論會) (Proceedings of the International Conference on Mencian Thought and Contemporary Values), held in Zoucheng, Shandong, April 2006.

Lieh-tzu. *The Book of Lieh-tzu.* Translated by A. C. Graham. New York: Columbia University Press, 1990.

Liezi zhu (列子) (Commentary on the *Liezi*). Edited, with commentary, by Zhang Zhan (張湛). In *Xinbian zhuzi jicheng* (新編諸子集成) (New edition of the works of the early philosophers), vol. 4. Taipei: Shijie shuju, 1974.

Liji shijie (禮記釋解) (The *Book of Rites* with modern Chinese explication). Edited by Wang Wenjin (王文錦). 2 vols. Beijing: Zhonghua shuju, 2001.

Liji Zheng zhu (禮記鄭注) (The *Book of Rites* with Zheng Xuan's commentary). Edited, with commentary, by Zheng Xuan (鄭玄). Sibu beiyao (SPPY) ed. Shanghai: Zhonghua shuju, 1936.

Liu Xiang (劉向). *Shuo Yuan jiaozheng* (說苑校證) (*The World of Stories* with annotations), collated by Xiang Zonglu (向宗魯). Beijing: Zhonghua shuju, 2000.

Liu Yu. "Xi Zhou jinwen zhong de sheli" (西周金文中的射禮) (Archery rituals as described in the bronze inscriptions of the Western Zhou). *Kaogu* 231:12 (1986).

Liu Zehua (劉澤華). *Xianqin shiren yu shehui* (先秦士人与社會) (The *shi* and their society before the Qin dynasty). Tianjin: Tianjin renmin chubanshe, 2004.

Lü Simian (呂思勉). *Xianqin shi* (先秦史) (History before the Qin dynasty). Hong Kong: Taiping shuju, 1962.

Lunyu jishi (論語集釋) (Collected glosses on the *Analects*). Edited by Cheng Shude (程樹德). 4 vols. Beijing: Zhonghua shuju, 1990.

Lunyu zhengyi (論語正義) (Collected commentaries on the *Analects*). Edited, with commentary, by Liu Baonan (劉寶楠). In *Xinbian zhuzi jicheng* (新編諸子集成) (New edition of the works of the early philosophers), vol. 1. Taipei: Shijie shuju, 1974.

Lüshi chunqiu xinjiaozheng (呂氏春秋新校正) (Newly edited commentary on *Mr. Lü's Spring and Autumn Annals*). Collated by Bi Yuan (畢沅), with commentary by Gao You (高誘). In *Xinbian zhuzi jicheng* (新編諸子集成) (New edition of the works of the early philosophers), vol. 7. Taipei: Shijie shuju, 1974.

———. *Mengzi shizhu* (孟子釋注) (Modern Chinese translation of the *Mencius* with annotations). Edited, with commentary, by Yang Bojun (楊伯峻). 2 vols. Beijing: Zhonghua shuju, 1960.

Mengzi zhengyi (孟子正義) (Collected commentaries on the *Mencius*). Edited, with commentary, by Jiao Xun (焦循). In *Xinbian zhuzi jicheng* (新編諸子集成) (New edition of the works of the early philosophers), vol. 1. Taipei: Shijie shuju, 1974.

Morohashi Tetsuji (諸橋轍次). *Nyoze gamon Kōshi den* (如是我聞孔子傳) (Thus I have heard about the life of Confucius). Tokyo: Daihōrinkaku, 1969.

Nivison, David S. *The Life and Thought of Chang Hsüeh-ch'eng (Zhang Xuecheng)*. Stanford: Stanford University Press, 1966.

Owen, Stephen, ed. and trans. *An Anthology of Chinese Literature: Beginnings to 1911*. New York: W. W. Norton, 1996.

Pines, Yuri. *Foundations of Confucian Thought: Intellectual Life in the Chun-qiu Period, 722–453 B.C.E.* Honolulu: University of Hawaii Press, 2002.

Plato. *Gorgias.* Translated by Walter Hamilton. Harmondsworth, UK: Penguin Books, 1960.

Qian Mu (錢穆). *Kongzi zhuan* (孔子傳) (Life of Confucius). Beijing: Sanlian shudian, 2002.

———. *Xianqin zhuzi xinian* (先秦諸子繫年) (A study of the dates of events in the lives of the pre-Qin philosophers). Beijing: Shangwu Yinshuguan, 2001.

———. *Zhuangzi zuanjian* (莊子纂箋) (Commentary on the *Zhuangzi*). Taipei: Dongda tushu, 1985.

Qiu Xigui (裘錫圭). *Gudai wenshi yanjiu xintan* (古代文史研究新探) (New inquiries into the study of early Chinese literature and history). Nanjing: Jiangsu guji chubanshe, 1992.

Robertson, Benjamin, and Melinda Liu. "Can the Sage Save China?" *Newsweek*, March 20, 2006.

Schaberg, David. *A Patterned Past: Form and Thought in Early Chinese Historiography*. Cambridge, MA: Harvard University Asia Center, dist. by Harvard University Press, 2001.

Schwartz, Benjamin I. *The World of Thought in Ancient China*. Cambridge, MA: Belknap Press of Harvard University Press, 1985.

Shanghai bowuguan cang Zhanguo Chu zhushu (上海博物館藏戰國楚竹書) (The Shanghai Museum collection of the Warring States Chu bamboo manuscripts). Edited by Ma Chengyuan (馬承源). 5 vols. Shanghai: Shanghai guji chubanshe, 2001–5.

Shirakawa Shizuka (白川靜). *Kōshi den* (孔子傳) (Life of Confucius). Tokyo: Chuō Kōronsha, 1991.

Sima Qian (司馬遷). *Shiji* (史記) (Records of the Grand Historian [with collected annotations]). 10 vols. Beijing: Zhonghua shuju, 1959.

Spence, Jonathan. *The Search for Modern China*. New York: W. W. Norton, 1990.

Sun Xingyan (孫星衍), ed. *Shangshu jinguwen zhushu* (尚書今古文注疏) (Commentary on the *Book of Documents*). Beijing: Zhonghua shuju, 1986.

Waley, Arthur, trans. *The Analects of Confucius.* London: Allen & Unwin, 1938.

Wang Chong (王充). *Lunheng* (論衡) (Disquisitions weighed in the balance). In *Xinbian zhuzi jicheng* (新編諸子集成) (New edition of the works of the early philosophers), vol. 7. Taipei: Shijie shuju, 1974.

Wang Yangming (王陽明). *Wang Yangming quanshu* (王陽明全書) (Complete works of Wang Yangming). Vol. 1. Taipei: Zhengzhong shuju, n.d.

Watson, Burton, trans. *Basic Writings of Mo Tzu (*Mozi*), Hsün Tzu (*Xunzi*), and Han Fei Tzu.* New York: Columbia University Press, 1967.

———. *Tso Chuan: Selections from China's Oldest Narrative History.* New York: Columbia University Press, 1989.

Whitman, Walt. *Leaves of Grass.* New York: Penguin Books, 2005.

Xu Shen (許慎). *Shuowen jiezi* (說文解字) (Etymological dictionary). With annotations by Duan Yucai (段玉裁). Taipei: Shuming chuban gongsi, 1990.

Xunzi. *Xunzi: A Translation and Study of the Complete Works.* Translated by John Knoblock. 3 vols. Stanford: Stanford University Press, 1988–94.

Xunzi jijie (荀子集解) (Collected commentaries on the *Xunzi*). Edited by Wang Xianqian (王先謙) and based on commentary by Yang Jing (楊倞). In *Xinbian zhuzi jicheng* (新編諸子集成) (New edition of the works of the early philosophers), vol. 2. Taipei: Shijie shuju, 1974.

Yang Kuan (楊寬). *Zhanguo shi* (戰國史) (History of the Warring States period). Shanghai: Renmin chubanche, 1955.

Zhang Xuecheng (章學誠). *Wenshi tongyi* (文史通義) (General principles of literature and history), vol. 1. Taipei: Guangwen shuju, 1967.

Zhongguo lishi ditu, vol. 1. Edited by Chang Ch'i-yun, Ch'eng Kuang-yü, and Hsü Shen-mo. Taipei: Zhongguo wenhua chubanbu, 1980.

Zhongguo lishi dituji, vol. 1. Edited by Tan Qixiang. Beijing: Zhongguo ditu chubanshe, 1982.

Zhu Xi (朱熹). *Sishu zhangju jizhu* (四書章句集注) (Commentaries on the Four Books). Beijing: Zhonghua shuju, 1986.

———. *Zhu Wengong wenji* (朱文公文集) (Literary works of Zhu Xi). 2 vols. Taipei: Taiwan Shangwu yinshu, 1980.

Zhuangzi. *The Complete Works of Chuang Tzu* (Zhuangzi). Translated by Burton Watson. New York: Columbia University Press, 1968.

Zhuangzi jishi (莊子集釋) (Collected commentaries on the *Zhuangzi*). Edited by Wang Xianqian (王先謙). In *Xinbian zhuzi jicheng* (新編諸子集成) (New edition of the works of the early philosophers), vol. 4. Taipei: Shijie shuju, 1974.

Index

"Against Confucius" (Mo Di), 204–05

Ai, Duke, 65–66, 123, 128–29, 216

Analects (Lunyu)
on Chen Heng and succession crisis in the state of Qi, 129
on Confucius and musicians, 142
on Confucius and rites, 177–80
on Confucius' avoidance of certain things, 160
on Confucius' need for employment, 92
Confucius on disciples, 105, 140
Confucius on Duke of Zhou, 46
Confucius on governments of Wei and Lu, 87
Confucius on hereditary counselors, 42
Confucius on Jisun family, 50
Confucius on Kong Yu, 120
Confucius on Qu Boyu, 93
Confucius on Zilu as a disciple, 31, 106
Confucius' travels recorded in, 85, 86, 87, 90, 91, 95–96, 100, 101, 103, 110, 114–16, 117, 221
on Confucius' view of human nature, 163
conversations between Zaiwo and Confucius recorded in, 64–67
departure of Confucius from Lu recorded in, 26
on Duke Ling and Confucius in the state of Wei, 95–96
on Jie Yu and Confucius in the state of Chu, 113
lack of information about Confucius' parents in, 99
Lin Biao and, 11
men who withdrew from society described in, 116–17
on musicians of the state of Lu, 140–41, 142
on pronunciation used by Confucius, 12
on rites connected with clothing, 175–76
as source for life of Confucius, 3–4, 5, 217
teachings of Confucius reflected in, 21
teaching (*xun*) not mentioned in, 147
Upright Gong incident described in, 110
on Yan Hui as a disciple, 73–74
on Zaiwo and Zigong as disciples, 64–65
on Zhonggong as a disciple, 83
on Zigong as a disciple, 69, 70
on Zilu as a disciple, 80, 114–16
on Zixia as a disciple, 136
Zizhang as a disciple and, 132, 133, 146–47

benevolence (*ren*), 19–20, 21, 167–70

Bi (city), 30, 39

Bian district in state of Lu, 78

Bigan, Prince, 107
Book of Mencius, 100, 193. *See also* Mencius
Book of Odes
    Confucius as a teacher and, 149,
      163–64
    Confucius' favorite poem in, 151–52
    conversation between Confucius and
      Yan Hui on, 222
    conversation between Confucius and
      Zigong on, 72, 136, 138
    conversation between Confucius and
      Zixia on, 136, 137–38
Book of Zhuangzi, 95, 100. *See also*
    Zhuangzi
Bo Yi, 107
Bo Yu (son of Confucius), 25, 40, 141,
    149–50
Buddhism, 217
burial rites, 182–84

Cai (state), Confucius' travels in, 86,
    105–09
Cao (state), 101
Chen (state), Confucius' travels in, 86,
    100, 105–09, 113, 130
Cheng, King, 42, 43, 48
Cheng (city), 30
Cheng Yaotian, 111–12
Cheng Yi, 19–20
Chen Heng, 128
children, Confucius on, 164–65
China, and idea of Confucius, 2
Chinese language, study of, 12
Chu (state), 46, 86, 105, 107, 108, 109–10,
    125, 140, 145, 214
Chunshen, Lord, 214–15
Cixi, Empress Dowager, 218
Classic of Documents, 152, 211, 222
Classic of Rites, 173–74
clothing
    mourning rituals and, 186
    rites connected with, 175–76
common gentlemen (*shi*), 13–14, 24, 77
companions of Confucius. *See* disciples of
    Confucius
Confucius
    birth of, 24–25
    China and idea of, 2
    conundrums in stories of life of, 28–31
    daughter of, 25, 40
    death of, 184–85
    eulogy by ruler of the state of Lu, 188
    marriage of, 25, 40
    mourning period for, 185–88
    parents of, 24–25, 99, 182

    son of, 25, 40, 141, 149–50
    sources on life of, 3–6. *See also Analects*,
      disciples of Confucius, Lu (state),
      minister of crime in Lu, teaching
Confucius Institutes, 12
Confucius Mansion, 11
Confucius Temple, 11, 218, 221, 222
Confucius Tomb, 11, 222
counselors. *See also* hereditary counselors
    Confucius' admiration of, 14–15,
      57–58, 68
    Confucius as, 6
    Confucius' desire for position as, in the
      state of Wei, 91–95
    Duke of Zhou as, 14–15, 46, 48
    Jiwuzi as, 50–51
    Shusun Bao as, 51–53
    state of Wei and, 89
    Zhaozi as, 53–54, 61–62, 89
    Zijiazi as, 59–61, 62, 68, 89
court doctors, 93–94
Cultural Revolution, 10–11

Dao and Daoists, 75, 140
death
    Confucius on, 80, 180–82
    rites connected with funerals and
      mourning, 178–80, 182–84
Deng Xi, 157–58, 160
dictates of decorum (*li*), 54, 56
Dilu Zifang, 88*n*
Ding, Duke, 27, 31, 36, 76, 123
Ding Jiang, 97–98
disciples of Confucius, 63–84
    Analects on, 64–65, 105, 140
    Confucius' death and mourning period
      and, 186
    Confucius' return to the state of Lu
      and, 130
    Confucius' travels and, 63–64, 82,
      83–84, 206
    dialogues with, 18–20, 130
    early career of Confucius in Lu and, 26
    Gongxi Hua as, 126–27, 139, 162
    range of men as, 15
    Ran Qiu as, 82–83, 84, 119, 126–28,
      133, 139, 162, 216
    reasons for joining Confucius as, 84
    Shaozheng Mao and, 159–60
    schools founded by, after Confucius'
      death, 192
    Sima Qian on, 6
    spiritual heir of Confucius and, 192
    Yan Hui as, 17, 19, 71, 72–76, 78, 80, 82,
      83, 84, 106, 108, 109, 141, 183, 222

You Ruo as, 186, 192
Zaiwo as, 64–69, 82, 84
Zeng Dian as, 139–40
Zengzi as, 170, 183, 186, 193
Zhonggong as, 83, 84, 168
Zigong as, 15–17, 19, 64–65, 69–72,
    80, 82, 84, 89, 107, 109–10, 119,
    144, 159, 160, 161–62, 168–69,
    181, 183–84, 186–88, 191, 197
Zilu as, 15, 17, 19, 26, 31, 68–69,
    76–82, 84, 104, 106, 107–08, 127,
    139, 140, 141, 162, 175
Zixia as, 133–38, 186
Zizhang as, 130–34, 142, 166, 186, 216
disciples of Mencius, 199–200
doctors, 93–94
Dong Zhongshu, 145–46
dress, rites connected with, 175–76
Du Xie, 53, 54, 166

Eastern Zhou, 3, 45–46
eating, rites connected with, 172–75
education. *See also* learning; teaching
    Confucius on, 144, 149
enfeoffment system in Zhou dynasty, 13,
    43, 49–50, 125

Fan Chi, 121–22, 123
Fan Li, 63–64
fathers
    Confucius on, 199
    Mencius on duties of, 199–201
    rites of sons for, 164–66
fengjian enfeoffment system, 13, 43,
    49–50, 125
"Fishhawk" (poem, *Book of Odes*), 151–52
followers of Confucius. *See* disciples of
    Confucius
food, rites connected with, 172–75
friends, Confucius on, 150
funerals
    of Confucius, 184–86
    of counselor Shusun Bao in the state of
        Lu, 54–55
    dictates of decorum (*li*) on, 54
    of disciple Yan Hui, 76
    grave objects and, 185–86
    rites connected with, 178–79

gentlemen
    Confucius on, 150–51
    renren (humane man), 68, 69
    rites connected with clothing and
        dressing and, 175–76
    shi (common gentlemen), 13–14, 24, 77

Gongshan Furao (Gongshan Buniu), 30,
    31–32, 35–36, 161
Gongsun Long, 161
Gongwen family, 98
Gongxi Chi, 184–86. *See also* Gongxi Hua
Gongxi Hua
    Confucius on, 162
    as a disciple, 126–27, 139, 162
government
    Confucius on moral way in, 42, 46, 89
    Confucius on qualifications of men for,
        57
    Confucius on rites and, 149, 151
    Confucius' vision of, 46–47
    Duke of Zhou and, 46–48
    hereditary counselors in, 41–42
    dictates of decorum (*li*) and, 54, 56
grave objects, 185–86
Guan Zhong, 15
Guan Zhoufu, 121
guoren (a man of the city), 77–78

Han dynasty, 104
Hanfeizi, 112
Heaven, Confucius on, 106–07
hereditary counselors. *See also* counselors
    government and, 41–42, 88–89
    Three Families in state of Lu and,
        48–49
    Zichan in the state of Zheng as, 56–57
Hou family, 58, 59
Hua family, 99, 100
Huan Tui, 10, 101–02
Hui Shi, 161
humane man (*renren*), 68, 69
human nature
    Confucius on, 131–32, 163, 196, 197
    Mencius on, 196–97, 217

Jie Yu, 113–14
Jihuanzi, 23, 24, 27, 34–35, 39, 40, 41, 123
Jikangzi, 121, 122, 127, 130, 147, 178
Jin (state), 46, 89, 125
Jing, Duke, 87
jing (respect), 169
Jipingzi, 58–59, 60, 61
Jisun family
    Chen Heng and succession crisis in the
        state of Qi and, 129
    Confucius on, 50, 124–25
    creation of Three Families in state of
        Lu and, 49
    Jipingzi as head of, 58–59, 60
    Jiwuzi as counselor and, 50–51, 58
    land tax in the state of Lu and, 124–26

Jisun family *(cont.)*
  Ran Qiu and, 82, 83, 84, 121–22, 124–26, 128
  Three Families and internal strife in state of Lu and, 29–30, 31, 32, 33, 34, 36
Jiwuzi, 50–51, 54–55, 58
Jixia Academy, 211
journey of Confucius, 85–118
  Analects on, 85, 86, 87, 90, 91, 101, 221
  disciples and, 63–64, 82, 83–84, 206
  four states visited in, 86
  Sima Qian on, 85–86
  sources of information on, 85–87
  in the state of Cai, 105–09
  in the state of Chen, 100, 105–09, 113
  in the state of Song, 99–102
  in the state of Wei, 89–100
  Yang Hu and, 102–04
  Zhuangzi on, 86–87, 101
justice, Xunzi on, 211–12

Kangshu, 87–88
Kang Youwei, 20
kingship. *See also* rulers
  in Zhou dynasty, 42–45
Kong family, as Confucius' ancestors, 24, 25, 99
Kong family, in state of Wei, 81–82
Kong Yu, 119–21
Kuang (town in the state of Zheng), 102–05
Kuang Zhang, 200–201

Lai (city), in Lu (state), 36, 37, 38
land tax in the state of Lu, 124–26
language, Confucius' interest in, 12
learning. *See also* education; teaching
  Confucius and, 144, 147
  Zixia's description of, 135, 136
li (dictates of decorum, rites), 54, 56, 66–67, 148, 149–50, 163–64, 172–91
Lin Biao, 11
Ling, Duke, 89, 90, 91, 94, 95, 100
Liu Baonan, 65–66
Lu (state)
  Analects on musicians of, 140–41
  brotherly relationship between state of Wei and, 87–88
  Confucius as minister of crime in, 23, 24, 26, 27, 28, 30, 31, 36, 44, 155–57, 159, 194, 209
  Confucius' death and, 188

Confucius' departure from, 26–28, 196
Confucius' reputation as a teacher and, 143
Confucius' return to, 121, 123–24, 143
creation of Three Families in, 48–49
hereditary counselors in, 41–42, 88–89
Jiwuzi as counselor in, 50–51
land tax in, 124–26
origin of, 46
political situation in, during Confucius' lifetime, 57–62
Qi (state) as adversary of, 27, 36–39, 46, 121–22
Shusun Bao as counselor in, 51–53
Spring and Autumn Annals as chronicle of, 4
Three Families and internal strife in, 29–36
Yang Hu and, 103

man of the city (*guoren*), 77–78
man of the field (*yeren*), 77–78, 79
Mao Tse-tung, 11
meals, rites connected with, 172–75, 180
meat, rites connected with, 173, 174–75
Mencius, 9, 73, 113
  on Confucius' achievement, 154
  Confucius compared with, 206
  on Confucius' death and mourning period, 186–87
  Confucius on village goody men and, 155
  on Confucius' stay in the state of Wei, 91–92, 93–95, 101
  Confucius' teachings adopted by, 196–97
  critics of, 208
  on departure of Confucius from Lu, 26–27, 28, 100
  disciples of, 199–200
  on human nature, 196–97, 217
  knowledge of Confucius gained by, 193–95
  on prigs, 201–02
  rulers and, 205–08, 216–17
  Song dynasty thinkers and, 217–18
  as source for life of Confucius, 7
  teachings of, 194–206
  on transmission of Confucian values, 192–93
  Xunzi on, 208–10
  Zisi (Confucius' grandson) and, 193–94, 208, 216
Mencius' temple, Shandong province, 219

Mengsun family
  Chen Heng and succession crisis in the
    state of Qi and, 129
  creation of Three Families in state of
    Lu and, 49
  Jipingzi as head of the Jisun family
    and, 60
  Three Families and internal strife in
    state of Lu and, 30, 35
Mian, 142
minister of crime in Lu, Confucius as, 23,
    24, 26, 27, 28, 30, 31, 36, 44,
    155–57, 159, 194, 209
Mr. Lü's Spring and Autumn Annals, 112,
    118
Mi Zixia, 94
Mo Di, 203–05
moral achievement, and humane man
    (*renren*), 68, 69
moral way
  Confucius on the heart and, 146–47
  conversation between Yan Hui and
    Confucius on, 75–76
  in government, 42, 46, 89
mourning
  rites connected with, 179–80, 182–84
  Zaiwo in conversation with Confucius
    on, 66–67
Mu, King, 44–45
music
  Confucius as a teacher and, 163, 164
  Confucius on, 148, 149, 150–54
musicians of the state of Lu, 140–41, 154

Nan Kuai, 33–34
Nanzi, 90–91, 94
Ning Wuzi, 104–05
Niu, 53–54

Odes. See Book of Odes

parents
  Confucius on, 198, 199
  Mencius on duties of, 199–201
  rites for, 164–66
Ping, King, 45–46
poetry. *See Book of Odes*
politics, 41–62
  advice of Duke of Zhou on, 47–48
  Confucius on hereditary counselors
    and, 14–15, 57–58, 41–42
  dictates of decorum (*li*) and, 54, 56
  early Zhou dynasty and, 42–46
  fengjian enfeoffment system and, 43,
    49–50, 125

  Jiwuzi as counselor and, 50–51
  Shusun Bao as counselor and, 51–56
  vision of government held by
    Confucius and, 46–47
  Zhaozi as counselor and, 53–54, 61–62
  Zichan as hereditary counselor and,
    56–57
  Zijiazi as counselor and, 59–61, 62
power
  Mencius on, 210–11
  Xunzi on, 210
purification rites, 179

Qi (state), 140
  authority of sovereign in, 45
  Chen Heng and succession crisis in,
    128
  Confucius on, 88
  Confucius' travels in, 86–87, 152, 196
  Duke Zhao escape from the state of
    Lu to, 60–62
  grudge against Confucius in, 39–40
  Lu (state) as adversary of, 27, 36–39,
    121–22
  Mencius in, 206–07
  Ran Qiu in war against, 121–22
  Shusun Bao in, 52–54
Qin (state), 46, 125, 140, 213–14
Qing dynasty, 218
Qu Boyu, 93
Qufu (county), 9, 11–12, 221

Ran Qiu
  on Confucius, 122
  Confucius on, 83, 162
  Confucius' return to the state of Lu
    and, 121–22, 123
  as a disciple, 82–83, 84, 119, 126–28,
    133, 139, 162, 216
  Jisun family in Lu and, 82, 83, 84,
    121–22, 124–26, 128, 143
  Zilu and, 82, 83
reciprocity (*shu*), 168–69
ren (benevolence), 19–20, 21, 167–70
renren (humane man), 68, 69
respect (*jing*), 169
rites (*li*), 172–91
  clothing and dress and, 175–76
  Confucius as a teacher and, 148, 149,
    163–64
  Confucius on, 149–50
  Confucius on basic guidelines in,
    176–80
  Confucius on benevolence and,
    167–68

rites *(cont.)*
  Confucius on sons and parents and,
    164–66
  food and, 172–75
  Zaiwo in conversation with Confucius
    on, 66–67
  Zigong as expert on, 123
rulers. *See also* kingship
  authority of, 145–46
  Mencius and, 205–08, 216–17
  rites connected with, 177–78
  Xunzi and, 212–13

Shandong (province), 9–10, 219
Shang dynasty, 42, 149, 211
shao (ancient music), 152–53
Shaozheng Mao, 155–56, 159–61, 162
She district in the state of Chu, 86,
    110–11, 113
shi (common gentlemen), 13–14, 24, 77
shu (reciprocity), 168–69
Shu-liang He, 24–25
Shun, Emperor, 73, 152, 153, 192–93,
    217
  Mencius on, 197–200, 202, 205
Shu Qi, 107
Shusun Bao, 50, 51–56, 58
Shusun family
  Chen Heng and succession crisis in the
    state of Qi and, 129
  creation of Three Families in state of
    Lu and, 49
  Duke Zhao and, 60, 61
  internal strife in state of Lu and,
    29–30, 39
  Jipingzi as head of the Jisun family
    and, 60
  Jiwuzi as counselor to the Jisun family
    and, 50–51
  Shusun Bao as head of, 52–53
Sichuan, 157
Sima Qian
  on adversarial relations between states
    of Lu and Qi, 38
  on birth of Confucius, 25
  on Confucius and the crisis in Chen or
    Cai, 107–10
  Confucius' comments about women
    recorded by, 96–97, 99
  Confucius' travels recorded in, 85–86,
    90–91, 92, 100–101, 103, 104–05
  on departure of Confucius from Lu,
    27–28
  on Duke Ling of the state of Wei, 96,
    100

Qin campaign against Zhao soldiers
    reported in, 213–14
  on Ran Qiu and land tax in the state of
    Lu, 126
  on Ran Qiu in war on the state of Qi,
    122
  on Shaozheng Mao, 155–56
  as source for life of Confucius, 5–6,
    221
  on threat to Confucius in Kuang, 103,
    104–05
  on Zilu meeting Confucius, 78
  on Zhou dynasty, 45–46
Song (state), 24, 95, 145
  Confucius' travels in, 86, 99–102, 105
Song dynasty, 20, 217–19
sons
  Confucius on, 199
  Mencius on duties of, 199–201
  rites for parents and, 164–66
sources for life of Confucius, 3–6
Spring and Autumn Annals
  land tax in the state of Lu described in,
    125
  ruler's authority and, 145
  as source for life of Confucius, 4, 29
  Three Families and internal strife in
    state of Lu recorded in, 29, 33
Spring and Autumn period
  common gentlemen (*shi*) in, 24
  strong women in, 97–98
  yeren (a man of the field) and *guoren* (a
    man of the city) categories in,
    77–78

"Talking about Public Spirit" (Cheng
    Yaotian), 111–12
Tang, King, 192–93
Tan Sitong, 20
teaching, 142–71. *See also* education;
    learning
  categories of instruction by Confucius,
    148–49
  Confucius on teachers and teaching,
    143–44, 147
  Confucius' reputation as a teacher, 13,
    143
  Confucius' withdrawal from life and,
    138
  Yan Hui as a student, 144–45, 148
  Zilu as a student, 148
Three Families
  internal strife in state of Lu and, 29–36
  Jiwuzi as counselor and, 50–51
  land tax in the state of Lu and, 125

Zaiwo's advice to Duke Ai about,
  65–66
Zigong as expert on rites and, 123
see also Jisun family; Mengsun family;
  Shusun family
travels of Confucius. *See* journey of
  Confucius

Upright Gong, 110–12

wanderings of Confucius. *See* journey of
  Confucius
Wang Sunjia, 94
Wang Yangming, 140
Wan Zhang, 194, 198
Warring States, 7, 213–14
Wei, ruler of, 137
Wei (state, Spring and Autumn period),
  62*n*
  brotherly relationship between state of
    Lu and, 87–88
  Confucius on ruler of, 89
  Confucius' travels in, 86, 87, 89–100,
    119
  exile of ruler from, 62
  meeting between Duke Ling and
    Confucius in, 95–96
  Zilu's death in, 81–82, 175
Wen, King, 42, 46, 103, 144, 162, 193,
  211, 217
Wey (state), 62*n*
women, Confucius on, 96–99
Wu, King, 14, 42, 46, 144, 153, 162, 202,
  209, 211, 217
Wu (state), 105, 123

Xia dynasty, 149, 184
Xiagu valley, 36–39, 87
Xuan, King, 206–07
Xunzi
  on Confucius and Shaozheng Mao,
    156–57, 159, 161
  on Confucius and the crisis in Chen or
    Cai, 105–06
  Confucius' career compared with,
    215–16
  on Mencius, 208–10
  rulers and, 212–13
  Song dynasty thinkers and, 218–19
  as source for life of Confucius, 7
  Warring States and, 213–14

Yan family, 24–25
Yang Hu, 34, 74, 87–88, 102–04
Yang Zhu, 203–04

Yan Hui
  Analects on, 73–74
  Confucius on, 72–73, 74–75, 78, 83
  conversation about benevolence
    between Confucius and, 167–68,
    169
  conversation about governing between
    Confucius and, 149, 151
  death and funeral of, 76, 141, 183, 186
  as a disciple, 15, 17, 19, 26, 71, 72–76,
    80, 84, 106, 108, 109, 159, 222
  as a student, 144–45, 148
  Three Families and internal strife in
    state of Lu and, 32–35, 36, 39
  Zhuangzi on, 75–76, 106–07, 109,
    221
Yan Ke, 103
Yao, Emperor, 192, 217
yeren (a man of the field), 77–78, 79
You Ruo
  as a disciple, 186, 192
  as a spiritual heir to Confucius, 192
Yu, Emperor, 202, 203, 205, 217

Zaiwo
  advice to Duke Ai about the Three
    Families, 65–66
  Analects on, 64–65
  conversation between Confucius and,
    66–69
  as a disciple, 64–69, 82, 84
Zan family, 58, 59
Zeng Dian, as a disciple, 139–40
Zengzi
  Confucius' mourning period and, 186
  as a disciple, 170, 183, 193
Zhao, Duke, 58–62, 68
Zhao (state), 213–14
Zhaozi, 53–54, 61–62, 89
Zheng (state)
  Confucius on music of, 148, 151–52
  Confucius on Zichan of, 56–57
  Confucius' travels in, 102–05
  execution of Deng Xi in, 157–58
Zhonggong, as a disciple, 83, 84, 168
Zhou, Duke of
  admiration of Confucius for, 14–15,
    46, 48
  advice to son given by, 47–48
  Emperor Shun and, 202, 203
  fengjian enfeoffment system and, 43,
    125
  state of Lu and, 87–88
  vision of government of, 46–48, 217
  Xunzi and, 208–09, 210

Zhou dynasty
 Confucius on rites of, 149
 fengjian enfeoffment system in, 13, 43,
  49–50, 125
 funeral rites in, 184
 kingship in, 42–45
 life of Confucius and sources on, 2–3
 reforms in, 45–46
Zhou Ren, 54
Zhuangzi
 on Confucius' travels, 86–87, 100, 101,
  106, 114
 on Duke Ling in the state of Wei, 95
 on Qu Boyu and Confucius, 93
 on Yan Hui as a disciple, 75–76,
  106–07, 109, 221
Zhu Xi, 19–20
Zichan, 15, 56–57, 157–58
Zifan, 146
Zigao, 82
Zigong
 Analects on, 64–65
 Confucius' death and mourning period
  and, 184, 186–88
 Confucius' description of, 69–71
 Confucius on burial rites and, 183–84
 Confucius on counselors and, 57
 Confucius on death and, 181
 Confucius on reciprocity (*shu*) and,
  168–69
 as a disciple, 15–17, 19, 26, 64–65,
  69–72, 80, 82, 84, 89, 107, 109–10,
  119, 136, 144, 159, 160, 161–62,
  191, 197
 discussion of *Odes* with, 72, 136, 138
 return to the state of Lu by, 119,
  122–23, 143
Zijiazi, 59–61, 62, 68, 89, 166
Zilu
 Analects on, 80
 Confucius in the state of Wei and,
  90–91, 94, 104
 Confucius on, 31, 79, 83, 106, 127, 162
 Confucius' travels and, 114–16, 117
 death of, 81–82, 141, 175, 186
 departure of Confucius from Lu and,
  27–28
 as a disciple, 15, 17, 19, 26, 31, 68–69,
  76–82, 84, 104, 106, 107–08, 127,
  139, 140, 162

as a student, 148
Three Families and internal strife in
  state of Lu and, 29–30, 31, 32
 as a *yeren* (a man of the field), 77
Zisi (Confucius' grandson), 193–94, 208,
  216
Zixia
 Analects on, 136
 Confucius' mourning period and, 186
 Confucius on, 134
 as a disciple, 133–38
 discussion of *Odes* with, 137–38
 You Ruo as spiritual heir of Confucius
  and, 192
Ziyou, 186, 192
Zizhang
 Confucius' mourning period and, 186
 Confucius on, 134
 as a disciple, 130–34, 142, 146–47, 166,
  216
 You Ruo as spiritual heir of Confucius
  and, 192
 Zixia and, 133–35
Zou district, in the state of Lu, 193, 219
Zuo Commentary (Zuo zhuan)
 on adversarial relations between states
  of Lu and Qi, 38, 39, 121–22
 on Chen Heng and succession crisis in
  the state of Qi, 128
 on Confucius in the state of Chen, 105
 on Confucius' return to the state of Lu,
  121
 on death of the disciple Zilu, 81
 on Duke Ai and the Three Families, 66
 on execution of Deng Xi in the state of
  Zheng, 157
 Huan Tui described in, 101
 on Jiwuzi as counselor in the state of
  Lu, 50–51
 land tax in the state of Lu described in,
  125–26
 on Ran Qiu in war on state of Qi, 122
 remarks by Confucius in, 52
 on rulers and counselors, 62
 on She, a district in the state of Chu,
  110
 on Shusun Bao as counselor in the
  state of Lu, 52, 53
 as source for life of Confucius, 3, 4–5
 on Yang Hu, 34, 87–88, 103

About the Author

ANNPING CHIN studied mathematics at Michigan State University and received her PhD in Chinese Thought from Columbia University. She was on the faculty at Wesleyan University and is currently teaching in the History Department at Yale University. She is the author of three previous books: *Children of China: Voices from Recent Years, Tai Chen on Mencius,* and *Four Sisters of Hofei.* She has also coauthored, with Jonathan Spence, *The Chinese Century: A Photographic History of the Last Hundred Years.* Her fields of study include Confucianism, Taoism, and the Chinese intellectual tradition.